Masterly... full of good jokes... the best work of history this year.
AN Wilson, Book of the Year, *Evening Standard*

The outstanding history book of the year... A perceptive work of
radiant scholarship. Brilliantly evokes the thrilling and often
dangerous role of poetry in the court of Henry VIII. Wyatt's life
as courtier, spy, lover and diplomat was extraordinary enough. What
makes Shulman's work such a joy is the revelatory urgency with
which she engages with language.
Lisa Hilton, *Independent*

Really exciting: a literary thriller... I'm already dreading finishing it.
Rachel Cooke, *Independent*, Best Summer Reads

Beautifully intelligent and lucid... Shulman does a wonderful job of
showing how Wyatt is one of those poets (one of the best types
of poet) whose work conceals enormous complexity and strong
countercurrents of thought and feeling underneath an apparently
plain and transparent surface.
John Lanchester, Book of the Year, *New Statesman*

In this poised, lucid, often arresting and frequently witty biography,
Nicola Shulman strides confidently where academics fear to tread...
Depicting Henry's court as a world of terror and uncertainty,
she shows how lyric poetry with its dangerously subversive
possibilities became in Wyatt's hands an ideal medium for
saying what could never be said.
John Guy, *Sunday Times*; Book of the Year, *Glasgow Herald*

Nicola Shulman pulls off the tricky task of moving between the
edgy life and the wonderfully elusive writing of Henry VIII's greatest poet, without reducing the poems to mere biographical ciphers.
Jonathan Bate, *Sunday Telegraph*, Book of the Year

A clever biography, captivating as
charming as an historic
Times Sat Review, Best Su

GRAVEN
with
DIAMONDS

GRAVEN

with

DIAMONDS

NICOLA SHULMAN

First published in 2011 by
Short Books
3A Exmouth House, Pine Street, EC1R 0JH
10 9 8 7 6 5 4 3 2 1

This paperback edition published 2012

ISBN 978-1-780720-88-3

Printed in Great Britain by CPI Group (UK) Ltd, CR0 4YY
Cover design: *The*BookDesigners

To Janet Gough

I knew I had slypper riches, nat nayled with a sixe penny nayl.

Thomas Wyatt, *The Quyete of Mynde*

Then Peter knelt beside her and found his button. You
remember she had put it on a chain that she wore round
her neck.

'See', he said, 'the arrow struck against this. It is the kiss
I gave her. It has saved her life.'

'I remember kisses,' Slightly interposed quickly, 'let me
see it. Aye, that's a kiss.'

J.M. Barrie, *Peter Pan and Wendy*

AUTHOR'S NOTE

Because this book is intended as an introduction,
most spellings have been modernised for the sake of
intelligibility. Early modern spelling has been retained in
places where I thought that changing the spelling would
spoil the sense or erase the emphasis. It is quite easy to
understand if read aloud. Wyatt's lyrics also benefit
from being read aloud, if convenient.

The Wyatt lyric canon is fraught with problems of
attribution. I have tried to select examples where the
attribution to Wyatt is most secure.

PROLOGUE

Time that is intolerant[1]
Of the brave and innocent,
And indifferent in a week
To a beautiful physique,

Worships language and forgives
Everyone by whom it lives;
Pardons cowardice, conceit,
Lays its honours at their feet.

Time that with this strange excuse
Pardoned Kipling and his views,
And will pardon Paul Claudel,
Pardons him for writing well.

W.H. Auden wrote these verses to commemorate the events of January 1939, the month that W.B. Yeats departed life and Auden, England and her coming wars. He later took them out on grounds of tact; but he left in the famous parting shot that liberated poets from their political responsibilities. 'Poetry makes nothing happen,' he wrote; meaning, it is not the business of poets to be right, or brave, or just, or useful. What poets should do, is write well.

These words, and the ones above, kept recurring all the time

---

[1] W.H. Auden, 'In Memory of W.B. Yeats', in *Another Time* (Faber & Faber, 1940).

I was making this book about Sir Thomas Wyatt. It was partly because there are just comparisons to be made between Auden and Wyatt. The pair of them are the lyric poets who bookend the period of England's political greatness; both are poets of unreciprocated feeling, of frenetic inertia, and of fear. But I think the main reason why these particular lines kept coming back to me was that Wyatt's posthumous career refutes them on every count.

It isn't hard to refute Auden's claims for language. Anyone surveying the literary scene of half a millennium or so ago will of course find the intervening prospect strewn with the husks of writers whose gifts have not, in fact, survived, contrary to the expectation of their peers: the 14th-century lyricist 'Richard', for instance, the undisputed literary star of the baronial hall:

> Richard, root of reason right,[2]
> In poetry and rune and rhyme,
> Of gentle maidens you can write
> The finest verses of our time!
> As gentle-tempered as a knight,
> A scholar versed in mysteries,
> In every house his fame is bright

No longer. Now no one knows who 'Richard' was, or which of the surviving lyrics he wrote, if any. Time has never had a soft spot for language. In our own reading lifetimes especially, it has turned on language as if with the dedicated aim of proving Auden wrong. Writing styles that seemed to us supple and exact only 20, 30 years ago begin to coarsen and sag; they even develop the very same look of faintly shameful grotesquerie that human beauty assumes in decay. No need for names; we can all think of examples closer to home than a semi-obscure courtier poet like Sir Thomas Wyatt the Elder. But the case of Wyatt has a

---

[2] Harley Lyrics, no. 74, in Brian Stone, *Medieval English Verse* (Penguin 1964).

special relevance. For time has forgiven him on both of Auden's counts – that is, for being dead, and for being frail – despite an almost universal consensus that he can't write. Down the centuries whenever his name is spoken, there has been someone to say that language, far from living in him eternally, was dead in him to begin with. Even his first promoter, the Earl of Surrey, thought his work 'unparfited' (unperfected). By Shakespeare's time he was politely acknowledged as a pioneer[3] but commonly held as a joke; his badness was rediscovered in the 18th century and again in the 19th when his first proper editor, George Nott, found him an unoriginal thinker, clumsy translator and a harsh versifier. Few disagreed, but by the middle of the twentieth century he had somehow, in defiance of this, become established in the English literature canon and a fixture on the university syllabus; while continuing to disappoint those scholars who elected to study him. 'Can we doubt,' asked his editor, H.A. Mason, in 1959, 'that if we had all the songs sung at court between Chaucer and Wyatt we should be able to shew that every word and phrase used by Wyatt was a commonplace? ... There is not the slightest trace of poetic activity.'[4] Likewise, C.S. Lewis defended him with the barely discernible commendation: 'When he is bad he is flat or even null. And when he is good he is hardly one of the irresistible poets.' Thirty years later, when I was an undergraduate, some eminent professors thought him too bad to teach.

And yet, he has triumphed. Behind Wyatt's reluctant champions other voices emerged to admire the 'plainness' of his style. Poets in particular got his point. Historicist critics meanwhile, looking at the past from the end of their terrible century, began to realise that Wyatt, like Mandelstam or Akhmatova, was a poet writing under tyranny, who might yield insights into

[3] By George Puttenham, whose *The Arte of English Poesie* (1589) was an early attempt to describe the state and history of English poetry.
[4] H.A. Mason, *Humanism and Poetry in the Early Tudor Period* (Routledge & Kegan Paul, 1959).

life under the Tudor Stalin. And so he has survived in the universities – where extensive new editions of Wyatt's diplomatic letters, his political, religious and secular poetry are now in preparation – and out of them, where his love lyrics continue to be read, collected, anthologised, quoted and printed in new selections. He has survived, as C.S. Lewis says 'in the only sense that really matters: his works are used as their author meant them to be used'. And here is the really crucial word for any discussion of Wyatt and his works: *used*. Wyatt intended his poems for use. Five hundred years later we still use them. Though it is not approved for serious readers to seek their own experience in literature, self-recognition is what most people want out of love poetry; in Wyatt they find it directly. When we read for the first time such lines as

The stars be hid that led me to this pain,

or

They flee from me that sometime did me seek,

or

I am of them that farthest cometh behind[5]

we are conscious of a thrill of acquisition. Here is something we can use.

All lyric poetry aims at the impersonal expression of some intense experience, but few achieve it so purely as Wyatt. There is a difference in intention, for example, between two simple lover's 'plaints' separated by 100 years:

---

[5] Unless otherwise indicated, all Wyatt's poems quoted here are from R.A. Rebholz (ed.), *Thomas Wyatt: The Complete Poems* (Penguin, 1978). These three lines are from poems numbered in Rebholz as, respectively, XIX, XI, and LXXX.

Go, lovely rose –
Tell her that wastes her time and me
That now she knows
When I resemble her to thee
How sweet and fair she seems to be.

[Edmund Waller]

and:

To wish and want and not obtain
To seek and sue ease of my pain
Since all that ever I do is vain
What may it avail me.[6]

[Thomas Wyatt]

Neither of them got the girl. But if we take the Waller, we have to imagine we are him, with his girl and his rose and his framework of 17th-century manners. While we can appreciate the sentiment, we are obliged to take it within its context. No such impediments prevent the Wyatt from delivering its shot of self-recognition: he hands us a howl of frustration to use on anyone we like. It's the difference between a book token and a ten-pound note.

This, as we shall see, is the strength of Wyatt's lyrics; but it is one of the problems with him as a biographical subject. Another is the availability of source material, which is very scarce until 1536 and then comparatively abundant in the years of his diplomatic work. There is nothing remarkable about this: diplomats sent letters, courtiers didn't. Henry VIII's court, where Thomas Wyatt spent most of life, was not a place of paper transactions. Business was done lip to ear and face to face. Petitioners, waiting for days to place a word with the right person, delivered their message by mouth. The most important man at court, Sir

---

[6] Wyatt, CVII, in Rebholz, op. cit.

Henry Norris, died without leaving a single letter. The exception to this paperless existence is the lyric poetry of the inner court, much of it written by Sir Thomas Wyatt. It's almost all that remains of the private life of the court.

For all of these reasons, the present book is not intended as a life of Thomas Wyatt but as a life of his lyric poetry. Unlike most books on his love lyrics, it is not concerned with how he wrote – his metrics – or what he wrote – the complex canon of his verse. This is a book about the uses of Wyatt's love poetry: *why* he wrote. He wrote at a time when poetry made things happen. Not just Wyatt's poetry – though that too – but all the poetry, ancient and modern, which the early Tudor court admired, wherein the attitudes and activities which are the central concern of this book were distilled and which, for the sake of concision, I will sometimes call 'poetry'. At Henry's court, Sir Thomas Wyatt and his poems were the hub and centre of this; and if we run the story of Wyatt's life and times behind his lyrics, they – these apparently slight, unaddressed, undated, unadorned songs – will show us that they had more uses than we might imagine. Not all of their uses are evident to us now. Some of them would have been hidden even to Wyatt, at the outset. When Wyatt began to write poems he could not have guessed into what strange service they would be pressed by the changing times. To see their changing purpose is the purpose of this book.

CHAPTER ONE

The story of Thomas Wyatt begins, appropriately enough, at a place which is not what it seems: the battlefield of Bosworth Field, where the rebel Henry Tudor challenged the last Plantagenet king, Richard III. Recent scholarship has discovered that this battle was neither what we thought it was, nor where: Richard and Henry's captains fought with bullets at a place a mile or more away from the site where tourists come to dream of plumed and lancéd warriors at its newly redundant visitor centre.

But for Richard, the outcome was the same: he ended the day as a corpse, strapped, like a sack, over the back of a horse, 'nought being left about him so much as would cover his privy member'. He had feared as much. He had lately lost his son and heir, and along with him the certainty of God's support for his kingship. The night before the battle he was visited with premonitions of doom.

Henry Tudor, his upstart adversary, had spent the eve of the battle in a more resourceful frame of mind. He had done something then to demonstrate the peculiar genius for creative self-legitimising that would come to characterise his line. Though only an earl with a scant trickle of royal blood in him, he sent a letter signing himself 'the King', thus pre-dating the start of his reign to the day before his insurrection. By this simple manoeuvre, he transformed treason to sovereign loyalty. It meant that the next day, King Richard's general, Sir William Stanley, could change sides in the middle of the battle with no loss of allegiance to a crown that was on Richard's head at the time. It meant that the Duke of Norfolk, loyal to Richard, could be attainted for treason, with his titles and lands removed; and his family, the Howards, plunged into ignominy until the Tudor or his heirs saw fit to restore them.

Good luck for the Stanleys, bad luck for the Howards, neither of whom felt any particular personal loyalty to the individual they had backed. After decades of civil war during which they had had to rally behind a succession of insecure and transient monarchs, they had learned that loyalty was a transferable asset and what mattered was not the incumbent but the legitimacy of monarchy itself. Norfolk's son, Thomas Howard, spoke for many change-sickened subjects when he explained his family's position to the new king, Henry VII: '[Richard] was my crowned king, and if the parliamentary authority of England set the crown on a stock, I will fight for that stock. As I fought then for him, I will fight for you.'

There were among this crowd of waverers some who had taken another view, and one of them was a Kentish gentleman of dim northern origins, called Henry Wyatt. This Wyatt, so the family chronicle tells us, supported Henry Tudor during bad times. Under the Yorkist king Edward IV and his brother, Richard III, there had been an active policy of bringing the civil wars to an end by killing any Lancastrian with a claim to the throne. Young Henry Tudor's title, though notoriously weak, was not beneath that kind of notice. He fled to France with his uncle and a small band of fellow exiles, leaving his English supporters behind to do what they thought best in the circumstances. Henry Wyatt, who must have been a person of some substance even then, was noticed, arrested and put in prison by Richard III.

King Richard tried to talk him round: 'Wyatt, why art thou such a fool? Thou servest for moonshine in the water. Thy master is a beggarly fugitive. Forsake him and become mine. I can reward thee, and swear unto thee I will.' 'Sir,' was Wyatt's answer, 'If I had first chosen you for my master, thus faithful would I have been to you, if you should have needed it; but the Earl [of Richmond, Henry Tudor], poor and unhappy though he be, is my master, and no discouragement or allurement shall ever drive or draw me from him.'[1]

This passage appears in some Wyatt family papers compiled by a descendant, partly published in the 19th century by the antiquarian John Bruce, and sharing a tendency to emphasise devotion and blamelessness as typical Wyatt characteristics. The earliest anecdote concerns Sir Henry, harshly imprisoned for his fidelity, as we have seen, and only saved from starving because a passing cat took pity on him and agreed to supply him with pigeons. This is rather hard to believe, even for stout admirers of cats, and casts the shadow of doubt upon the other dramatic assertion in the story, that Sir Henry's captors tortured him with a horse-barnacle. A barnacle was a farrier's tool, a hinged implement a bit like a sharply serrated nutcracker, used to subdue horses. An open barnacle would be positioned where the horses' muzzle is soft and loose, then pinched shut and twisted. It would be used in much the same way on a man. It sounds unlikely, but there are a number of reasons to believe it true.

First of all, the Wyatts made a virtue of this ordeal, alluding to it wherever possible as a symbol of their pioneering loyalty to the Tudors. Henry Wyatt commissioned some 'carpets' – that is, tapestries, for public display – 'in which the figure of the barnacles is eminently conspicuous' says Bruce, adding that the tapestries were still in the family possession in 1735. His son Thomas added a commemorative barnacle to his coat of arms in early 1537: a sensitive moment, as we shall see. And there is another reason. Holbein's portrait of Wyatt, now in the Louvre, shows him with a curiously weak, almost lifeless musculature in

[1] John Bruce, 'Unpublished Anecdotes of Sir Thomas Wyatt the Poet', *Gentleman's Magazine* (September 1850).

the lower half of his face. The cheeks hang from his bones like cloths from a rail, most unlike the firmly modelled cheeks and lips of Holbein's other sitters. The lower lip flops open to show the sole survivor of a row of herbivorous teeth. He is not the only old, cold man Holbein painted, but he's the only one who has chosen to put his broken teeth on display. In fact, he is the only one of all Holbein's sitters, both in England and elsewhere, to show his teeth at all.

A barnacle

When Henry Tudor became King Henry VII, he took Wyatt on in the accountancy department. We can assume that he was a very, very good accountant, for history has singled out this king for his genius at thrift, and the choosing of brilliant men to serve him: as G.R. Elton remarked, 'not even Elizabeth surrounded herself with a brighter galaxy of first-rate ministers than did her grandfather.' Henry had inherited an empty treasury, and now supplied it with a system of creative taxation that turned all connections, all relations, all arrangements with his subjects into financial transactions. He began by divesting those 'traitors' who had fought for King Richard at Bosworth Field of their wealth and lands, and continued in the same vein, taking

Sir Henry Wyatt (*Hans Holbein the Younger*)

fees for favours and fines for wrongdoing , with special emphasis on trimming the great nobles of lands and of men who might
be persuaded to fight for an ancient name against the Tudor
upstart. The fines for retaining were particularly sharp.[2]

A small, private gentleman with no ambitions that his monarch didn't share could prosper under this arrangement, particularly if he was clever with money; and Henry Wyatt prospered
amazingly. An early grant of lands commends his 'services
in England and beyond seas'. This may mean that he served
Henry Tudor on business in Scotland, where Wyatt seems to

[2] retaining: maintaining liveried men, other than household servants, in one's own
service without royal permission.

have undergone another period of imprisonment, or in exile in Brittany; in either case it meant he was one of a tiny, exclusive set of men whom the king trusted. Once in the king's employment, he acquired lands, grants and positions with admirable rapidity. He was a justice of the peace, was placed on various commissions of audit and investigation, and in 1504 he was made a member of the king's council. He was appointed keeper of the jewel house in the third year of the reign, then controller of the mint, keeper of the change, essayer of the king's money and coinage: positions connected with the collection, valuation, allocation and transportation of the king's swelling revenues. The gatekeeper of the king's coffers was someone everyone wanted to know, and Henry Wyatt farmed his influence well. He became extremely rich and formed a series of useful alliances in town and at court, not least amongst a group of important Kentish families including the Guildfords, the Cobhams and the Boleyns. These were more splendid men than Wyatt, with grander antecedents and more refined, honorific positions at court. The fact that they had properties in Kent was in itself an indication of current favour, since Kent was a turbulent region, sensitively located between London and continental Europe, and lands and offices here were only granted to the most demonstrably loyal of the king's servants.

Henry Wyatt's cultivation of this group was part of a long, careful programme of aspiration and adherence that would not yield its full rewards until the next reign. It included the purchase, in 1497, of Allington Castle in Kent. This was a lovely moated building of ancient foundation, and still exists in an altered version. Its silver-white battlements are set at water-level, low in a piece of land like a tipped bowl, with wooded hills round one side and round the other, the Medway River that runs into the Thames and thence, conveniently, to Richmond Palace, Henry VII's favourite residence. It was like living on a good branch line.

Wyatt improved it. It was difficult to consolidate lands around Allington because they tended to be parcelled into small plots under several ownerships, but Wyatt addressed the problem with a demonstration of the fiscal creativity that endeared him to two Tudor kings: he extended credit to his poorer neighbours, then foreclosed on them, obliging them to sell.[3] He also brought the house up to the requisite spec. for high-level entertaining. In went fashionable large windows and new fireplaces (to replace the lost heat), a new kitchen, and a lady's bower for the wife he married at the age of 42: one Anne Skinner, of Reigate in Surrey. In 1503, the first of their three children was born. This was Thomas, a blond and blue-eyed child who appeared equipped with every quality that an ambitious, first-generation father hopes to see in his son and heir. He was clever, quick-witted, fluent, studious, tall, graceful and athletic: good-looking enough to play himself on network

Allington Castle, Kent, as it is today

[3] I am greatly indebted to Dr Stephen Gunn for this point.

television – the very boy, in short, to go for a courtier and complete Henry Wyatt's programme of advancement. The younger son, Henry, remained in the country and seems to have come to so little that the case for him having existed at all rests largely on the steps his father took to exclude him from his estates.[4] Henry Wyatt was now one of the largest landowners in Kent, and he wanted his oldest son to have everything.

*　　*　　*　　*

It was once settled among historians that the principal difference between the court of Henry VIII, where Thomas Wyatt grew up, and that of Henry VII, where Henry VIII himself grew up, was that the father's court was frugal and the son's magnificent. As far as historiography is concerned, however, we live in an age of demolition. Historians of the last 50 years have bent themselves to plucking out useful boundary lines, denouncing historical platitudes and bundling off any anecdote, no matter how ancient, amusing and illustrative, that can't account for itself on paper. The earliest Tudor period has attracted much notice of this sort, with the result that the long-held view of Henry VII as a man of cheerless parsimony, hosing down the firewood in the grates in Richmond Palace with his account book tucked underneath his arm, has made way for a new account of Henry VII as master of a splendid court, a patron of arts, builder of palaces, leader of the hunt, putter-on of jousts and revels, feaster of foreign ambassadors robed in coats of cloth-of-gold. But the element of exuberance, the keynote of his son's establishment, is missing: most of this was a calculated display of magnificence to support the legitimacy of a kingship resting principally on the king's own assertion of the fact. The allegiance of the men who had listed to his side in 1485 was

---

[4] The Allington estate was subject to the Kentish law of gavelkind, whereby land was divided equally among all the owner's sons. Henry Wyatt changed this so that the estate was bequeathed under the English system of primogeniture.

by no means secure, and foreign countries would hesitate to treat with a shifting nest of squabbling barons. He wished to be treated like a king, so he must look like one, and do what kings did. Accordingly, he set aside time for 'crown-wearing' sessions, occasions where subjects could nourish conviction in his kinghood by viewing him seated silently on a throne in his robes and crown.

One of the things that kings did in the late 15th century was participate in the craze for chivalry. Chivalry was not new, but had been recently revived in the most splendid court of the late medieval period, that of the dukes of Burgundy, and had found an enthusiastic uptake in all the courts of Europe. Although England was often a dog-leg on the itinerary of European culture, it was not in this case. Arthur's court, of course, had been in England, and this gave the English, situated though they were on the edge of the known world, a natural stake in the matter. Indeed, the main discernable aim of English letters in the century preceding the Tudors was to reclaim the Arthurian legends from the French, who had made a whole literature around them, with a programme of translation and adaptation of the French texts.

One can scarcely overstate the degree of influence that chivalric notions exerted over the princely class of late 15th and early 16th-century Europe. In the education of rulers, chivalry formed the third leg of a princely tripos, the other two being religion and those ideas of Renaissance humanism that would in time supplant both the others, but which, in its initial stages, chivalry could incorporate and, with a surprising show of suppleness, adapt to its own ends. The princes of the early 16th century believed themselves the pattern of chivalric virtue, and none more so than Henry VIII.

The school of chivalry offered an extensive curriculum of social organisation, moral observance, personal conduct, of martial combat and sexual relations, expressed through a variety of disciplines including art, literature and a vigorous programme of outdoor games. These last had been devised as training exercises for knights in real combat, but by the accession of Henry VII, wars were already fought with longbows and – as the finds at Bosworth Field confirm – gunpowder, and captained by professionals, and by the following reign, the realities of warfare had drifted far from the joust and the tourney. Specialist jousting armour was now developed solely for tournament use, far too heavy for proper fighting but perfect for breaking lances upon without harming the occupant of the suit. Nor was the knight himself what he used to be, as the early Tudors found it useful to expand the range of people entitled to bear arms. In other words, there was a conscious element of atavism at work in the tournament, operating to extract status from ancient and reputable activities and confer it on the not-so-ancient and reputable participants of the Tudor games. So when we think of plumed and armoured Henrician knights charging each other in the lists, fluttering with favours and larded with French mottos, we may see back to Crecy and Poitiers, but with a small adjustment of perspective we can see forward, as well, to the sporting excesses of Edwardian England, when beer magnates blackened the skies with gamebirds for the king, or even to the corporate junkets of today when city traders, kitted out as Edwardian gentlemen with tweed knickerbockers and walnut-stocked shotguns, shoot pheasants they rent by the day. To a man on the make like Henry Wyatt, a particularly appealing feature of Allington Castle would have been its authentic tiltyard, reputedly the oldest in England.

Yet it would be quite wrong to suppose that the players thought they were participants in a romantic revival of a dead cause, for the purposes of window-dressing a legally dubious regime. On the contrary, they were in deadly earnest and regarded themselves as inheritors of a sacred charge. The three great princes, Henry VIII, Francis I of France and Charles V of Spain, all thought themselves the embodiment of chivalric virtue. All excelled at pageant sports, and the last two offered, more than once, to replace their warring armies with their own persons and solve their territorial disputes by hand-to-hand combat, king on king – though somehow these challenges always came at the wrong moment and were never taken up.

And yet – another qualification – this was a time of immense change, when medieval values mingled with those of the in-pouring Renaissance humanism in varying degrees of emulsification – and so attitudes to chivalric ideals were neither static nor consistent. There were people who believed in them deeply and thought to find in them a model for a virtuous life; there were those who thought they were puerile nonsense; and there were those – perhaps the majority – who shifted their views as occasion demanded.

For a very clear instance of the latter position we must jump forward to 1536, when Thomas Howard, the 3rd Duke of Norfolk, was sent by Henry VIII to put down a dangerous rebellion in the north of England. Finding himself outnumbered and perceiving the need to buy time, he made promises to the rebels on his honour as a nobleman, knowing their susceptibility to this appeal (one of their complaints was that the king took advice from men of lowly origin like his chief minister, Thomas Cromwell) and also knowing that he had already written to the king begging him to 'take in good part [i.e. ignore] whatsoever promises I shall make unto the rebels... for surely I shall observe no part thereof for any respect of that other might call mine honour distained.'[5] In other words, he exploited the belief in a chivalric code of honour in order to do something that violated every principle of that code. The interesting thing about this, however, is his own moral verdict on the matter: 'none oath or promise made for policy to serve you, mine only

[5] distain: defile, sully

Thomas Howard, the 3rd Duke of Norfolk
(*Hans Holbein the Younger*)

master and sovereign, can distain me.'

To the modern reader this remark seems disingenuous, or cynical, or at the very least nervously optimistic. But we must allow for the possibility that he really believed it. The point that concerns us here is, how very hard it is to judge. Sincerity is hard to read across 500 years. It is often a question of tone. Time hates tone even more than it hates language, and, as Philip Larkin noted, quickly washes it away. Historians of early Tudor England often accuse one another of mistaking the tone and missing the point, but it is no wonder if they do, when the people who were alive at the time commonly, as we shall see, mistook one another's meaning, took jokes for earnest and figures of speech for facts. These misinterpretations – the consequence of rapid change in language and the structure of society – would one day feed the wit of Shakespeare, but before that they were used for more sinister purposes, as convictions could be secured on a light remark, or a joke taken the wrong way. It is impossible, then and now, to know if a misunderstanding was genuine or deliberate. There was a lot of room for the disingenuous.

This is the essential background to the practice of love and production of love poetry that concerns us here; for these were open to misconstructions of precisely the same kind, and for the same reasons.

The poems are the remains of a peculiarly specialised and ultimately mysterious activity called 'courtly love'. Courtly love was the domestic arm of chivalry and, like all chivalric practices, subject to erosions of sincerity in the years between the 12th century – when people were in earnest to some degree – and the late 16th, when it descended into ornamental pastiche. But what exactly was in earnest and what was in game is, again, hard to determine. Literary critics, like historians, cannot agree on matters of sincerity.

Chaucer is a good case in point. Critics know that Chaucer made jokes, both about love and about poetry, in the 14th century. In *The Canterbury Tales*, where a group of pilgrims including Chaucer compete to tell the best story on their journey to Canterbury, there is a very good joke about poetry. Chaucer, the narrator, gives himself a dreadful bit of chivalric doggerel called *The Tale of Sir Thopas* to tell. This poem is so dire that it offends the literary sensibilities of a Southwark publican, the referee of the contest, who cuts Chaucer off in mid-rhyme –

Chaucer, poet to the most exquisitely refined court England had ever known – and makes him tell his tale in prose.

> *'Namoore of this, for Goddes dignitee,'*
> *Quod our Hooste…*
> *'By God', quod he, 'for pleynly, at a word,*
> *Thy drasty[6] rymyng is nat worth a toord![7]*
> *Thou doost noght else but despendest[8] tym*
> *Sire, at O word, thou shalt no lenger rhyme'[9]*

Everyone agrees that this is an excellent, sophisticated, many-layered joke. Chaucer's courtly audience would have been particularly amused by it, as people are when flattered, because it pays an implicit compliment to their powers of discrimination: to get it, you need to know the difference between good verse and doggerel, as well as knowing who Chaucer is.

But what about this, also by Chaucer:

> *Nas never pyk walwed in galauntyne[10]*
> *As I in love am walwed and ywounde*
> *For which ful ofte I of myself devyne*
> *That I am trewe Tristam the secounde.*

(No pike was ever doused so deep in sauce as I am doused and embroiled in love, and so I often think of myself as a veritable second Tristam.)

Is this a joke? Was it a parody, aimed at the posturings of courtly lovers' rhetoric? Was it also supposed to be a litmus for

---

[6] drasty: crappy, worthless.
[7] toord: turd.
[8] despendest: waste.
[9] Geoffrey Chaucer, *The Tale of Sir Thopas*, in Larry Benson (ed.) *The Riverside Chaucer* (Houghton Mifflin, 1987).
[10] Chaucer, *To Rosamounde*, in Benson, op. cit.

readerly sophistication? Not everyone thinks so: C.S. Lewis, that great 20th century investigator into medieval literature, thought it was an earnest but unsuccessful shot at a novel simile, and that anyone who thought its humour intentional was hopelessly divorced from the medieval cast of mind. C.S. Lewis's sense of humour is arguably his own weak point. There is only one joke in the Narnia books.[11] But it is also possible that even a poet as confident and witty, so irreverent of institutions, so astute in his observation of character and handling of verbal nuance, as Chaucer, could hit a duff note.

If he did, it was a sign of things to come: for the next 150 years, poetry in England declined astonishingly. Poets did not just cease to be good, they almost ceased to be poets at all: they couldn't scan, or write two lines together in the same metre; all they could do was rhyme.

Academics have pondered the great mystery of this deterioration. The years of civil war, the instability of court life under constantly changing kings, the decimation of the great baronial houses as their menfolk died for York or Lancaster have all been held accountable. One ingenious theorist proposed that changes in pronunciation over this time – especially the loss of the pronounced terminal 'e' in Chaucerian English – rendered Chaucer's metre inaudible to the poets of the following generations, causing confusion when they tried to imitate him. Some, like Lewis, concluded that people simply forgot how to do poetry and 'that the causes of this barbarism are unknown'. At any rate, the years of civil war did nothing for England's verse, and the poets of Henry VIII's formative years were the most dismal of all her history.

[11] It is on page 119 of *The Silver Chair*, in the Collins hardback edition (1990).

CHAPTER TWO

The seventh Henry was not especially interested in English poetry. Much of his life had been spent in France and, if the contents of his library are any guide, his tastes inclined to the romances in that language that would greatly influence his second son: stories of Lancelot, Arthur, Tristan, allegorical tales of knights purified by war and passion. As king, he saw no necessity to divert any funds into supporting a court poet, preferring to invest in a state-of-the-art games-and-gambling complex at Richmond Palace, with facilities for jousting, bowling, tennis and archery, on all of which he bet profusely. But there were nevertheless individuals who took it upon themselves to bring poetry to this court, and chief among them was the poet Stephen Hawes, one of Henry VII's grooms of the chamber, and a man whom it is very hard to dislike although his chef-d'oeuvre, *The Pastime of Pleasure*, may be the most boring poem ever written.

The Pastime is an extensive allegorical work on the theme of courtly love, in imitation of the best French models such as Guillaume de Lorris' *The Roman de la Rose*, one of the most successful books of the Middle Ages. It begins in the familiar way when a young man personifying Graunde Amoure (True Gallantry) falls asleep, and has a feature-length vision. Fame comes to him and tells him of a beautiful lady, la Bell Pucell, living in the Castle Perilous. To meet her, he has to pass through a series of trials, and undergo instruction from the various allegorical figures who bar his way. In the classical French allegories of Hawes's models, these are personified aspects of the hero's moral drama, such as Chastity, Covetise (envy), Honte (pride), and so on. But Hawes was an inveterate educationalist and, impressively, saw underused didactic potential in the form. In a move without precedent or followers, Hawes sends Graunde Amoure to a sort of allegorical crammer, staffed by such ladies as Dame Rhetorique, Dame Geometrie, Lady Logic and Lady Arithmetique 'in a golden weed', where he is put through a stiff course in the seven sciences. Here he is in conversation with Lady Grammar:

> *'Madame', quod I, 'for as much as there be*[1]
> *Eight partes of speeche, I would know right fain*
> *What a noun substantive is in his degree*
> *And wherefore it is called certain?'*
> *To whom she answer'd right gentlie*
> *Saying always that a noun substantive*
> *Might stand withoute helpe of an adjective*

One feels for Hawes. He was a young man, though he doesn't write like one, and he was trying to do something difficult, laudable and kind, that is, to instruct and entertain at the same time, putting his lesson into the sweet coating of a romance. There is an endearing uncertainty about him: he thinks he may not be equal to his self-appointed task, and often seems alarmed by his own audacity in even attempting such a long and ambitious piece of writing. He meant it as a pleasing and popular work. Sad for him, then, that when his poem is mentioned in print, which is rarely, the writer never fails to say that it is entirely unreadable, only to be enterprised by the dauntless medievalist in the line of his professional duties.

A more cheerful corollary to this is that when viewed in

---

[1] Stephen Hawes, *The Pastime of Pleasure*, ed. W.E. Mead (Early English Text Society, 1928).

this way, purely as a research tool, *The Pastime* shows us how skill in reading, as well as in writing, had declined in the 15th century. Although his core readership was the court, Hawes expects very little from it in the way of readerly erudition, and evidently considered the task of bringing literary polish to the first Tudor court as something of an uphill struggle. He wonders if anyone will be able to read such a demanding text. As well as doubting his readers' proficiency in geometry, rhetoric, logic and the rest, he fears they may not even know how to read an allegorical poem, and has to explain that they are not to take it literally: 'poets do write' he says, '...in a mysty cloud/ Of covert likenesse/And underneath the truth doth so shroude.' The first printed edition included helpful woodcuts.

The Pastime of Pleasure is dedicated to King Henry VII, who is unlikely to have read it, being a busy man with tastes that ran anyway to French literature, and to his second and sole remaining son, Henry, who almost certainly did. We do know that Henry VIII, as he became, was exceptionally clever and read prodigiously in his youth. The details of his education are dark, however, because he was a younger son, brought up at Eltham with his sisters, the other secondary figures in the great Tudor enterprise, away from the attentions of recording scribes. Then, when his older brother, Arthur, died, he became inexpressibly precious. According to the Spanish ambassador, he was kept under close supervision in a room accessible only through his father's own chamber, and so repressed that 'he rarely spoke in public except to answer a question from his father.' So there is a lot to be guessed about his early life, but it is certain he spent his time reading and it is assumed that his education followed the model of his elder brother's (history, grammar, rhetoric, poetry, all from the best Latin authors) with certain modifications. One historical source has proposed that he was destined originally for a career in the church and if this were so it would explain his command of, and later proprietorial attitude towards, doctrinal theology. He could quote the Old Testament verbatim (in Latin – there was no bible in English at this date). He read deeply into the biblical commentaries of learned scholastic divines such as Saint Jerome, who explained scriptural and sacramental mysteries, and acted as filters for the terrifying glare of revealed truth that blazed from the gospels. All his life he loved theological inquiry. He could always impress onlookers with the range and penetration of his mind.

Obviously, a primer like Hawes's *Pastime of Pleasure* would fill no academic purpose in a case like this, but would have a place among the mass of chivalric literature read for improvement and pleasure, much of which remains among Henry's surviving books. And in that company it would stand out for two reasons: for its unique association of courtly love with a humanistic education, and for its unusual denouement, in marriage. The classic courtly liaison of the 12th- and 13th-century tales has nothing to do with marriage. It is an adulterous relationship, often (but not always) chaste and usually between a young man and a married lady of high rank. Indeed, the whole courtly concept evolved as a way of negotiating social realities in a fortified castle, where the necessary presence of squadrons of young fighting men, plus the likelihood of an absent seigneur, could place the lady of the castle in an awkward situation. But by the end of the 15th century the lord was descending from his castle into the peaceful, mercantile life of the towns, and poets of the age of cloth, like Hawes, began to change the endings. Graunde Amoure married la Bell Pucell, and with that a dangerous thing happened: love and marriage took a step closer.

This of course affected no one's marital obligations, nor did it reflect a softened attitude to marriage as a financial contract; but it did reflect a change in attitudes to love. And if one can judge from their subsequent histories, its lesson resonated in the expectations of the royal children growing up at Eltham: Mary, Margaret and Henry Tudor, all of whom thought they should marry for love, and did.[2]

Did the young Henry read it? One cannot know exactly what people read, unless they specifically refer to it, or by some fluke of evidence such as marginalia written in their hand. Ownership of books proves little, as books came into a prince's possession for numerous reasons, few of them to do with personal taste; as we shall see. Everything in Henry's later life suggests he was greatly addicted to chivalric romance and had a special liking for poetry. He wrote poetry himself and heard it for pleasure. *The Pastime* was reprinted several times in Henry's reign and its author, surviving into it, continued to delight the court with his poetical skills, which included the ability to recite the entire works of Chaucer from memory. Moreover, and most importantly, Henry's first tutor was John Skelton, who thought enough of the English language and its poets to boast of being one himself, nominating himself as 'England's Catullus, her Homer'.

Support for this view was not abundant at the time, though a verse penned by the Dutch humanist scholar Erasmus Desideratus appears to concur:

The debt that ancient Greece
To Homer owed, to Vergil Mantua,
That debt to Skelton owes Britannia
For he from Latium all the muses led
And taught them to speak English words instead.

But this judgement must be qualified by the fact that Erasmus, like all civilised Europeans, wouldn't have dreamed of speaking English words himself. In fact, we learn from this more about Skelton's priorities than his poetry. Erasmus may have spoken no English, but his fluency in flattery meant he would never pitch a compliment in the wrong place. Someone had let him

[2] Margaret, first to Archibald Douglas, Earl of Angus, then to Henry Stewart; and Mary to Charles Brandon.

know that – though Skelton also wrote in Latin – he prized his *English* works more highly.

Why such a great man as Erasmus – at that time an international superstar and the cynosure of intellectual Europe – should have bothered to compliment a dim English cleric will emerge from the context of the verses. These pleasing lines were the result of the meeting between Erasmus and the children of Henry VII.[3] Erasmus had been staying with Lord Mountjoy, an English humanist and pupil of his, and Mountjoy had decided to take him round to nearby Eltham Palace, where the nine-year-old prince Henry and his sisters were installed.

The meeting has become famous for Henry's display of precocious scholarship – he presented Erasmus with a piece of writing he had made, greatly embarrassing his guest, who had come empty-handed, and prompting him to the hasty production of an answering encomium, including the plug for Skelton – but it is also illustrative as a meeting between old and new ways of thinking. If the party were depicted in allegorical form, the figure of Skelton would bear a scrolling label reading 'scholasticism' and the two younger visitors would bear one reading 'humanism'. All would be carrying books, for Skelton's scholasticism and Mountjoy's humanism were both ideologies of the book and both revered the works of antiquity; but they operated in very different ways. Baldly put, Skelton believed that old texts and deep matters could be best understood through studying the commentaries of wise men, accumulated over centuries; Erasmus and Mountjoy respected these mediations as much as a picture conservator respects crude overpainting and yellow varnish on some fresh, delicate panel. For them, the truth was present in the actual words of an original text; everything on top of that was just obstruction and error. To get at it they scraped off the commentaries, they stripped the medievalised Latin so far back that the Greek it derived from began to appear, and then

---

[3] Excepting Prince Arthur, the heir to the throne.

they took off the Latin; and at last the Greek originals were exposed to the scholar's intimate investigations.

In a very short time, the humanists would turn their liberating attentions to the Bible, and then thousands of people would die in flames, but at this moment they were more interested in a classical reading list and a good Latin style, and there was nothing about them to alarm an orthodox monarch seeking instruction. On the contrary: a humanist education was fast becoming the indispensible ornament of the Renaissance prince. When Henry became heir to the English throne, this Lord Mountjoy swiftly replaced Skelton as Henry's tutor, and Skelton, poet, withdrew to a benefice in the village of Diss in Norfolk, to work on his recent invention: a verse form for the short line, known to diligent poetry students as 'Skeltonics'. The official description for his contribution to English metre is 'short, irregular lines (usually of two stresses, though often rising to three or more), linked together by alliteration, parallelism and rhyme-run', but this does no justice to the defiant and inventive crankiness of the form, which seems, at this time when everyone was reverently copying old models and seeking the endorsement of the ancient and decorous, to have found itself in the chaos of the farmyard and the pump. Skeltonic verse gives the impression of having been composed in the sound props department of a radio play about medieval village life – the hammering of bells and nails, clanging of buckets, squawking of chickens, the clattering of shod hooves slipping on the cobbles at a barking dog or flapping bit of rag. Here, for example, he describes the physical charms of the village alewife, Elinor Rumming:

A man would have pity[4]
To see how she is gummed,
Fingered and thumbed,

[4] John Skelton, 'Elinor Rumming', in Philip Henderson (ed.), *The Complete Poems of John Skelton* (Dent & Sons, 1931).

Gently jointed,
Greased and anointed
Up to the knuckles;
The bones (of) her huckels
Like as they were with buckels
Togeder made fast.
Her youth is far past!

There is vigour and realism here, but Skelton had to wait until the 20th century to find admirers – such as Auden – for those qualities. In his own time, no one thought well of him.[5] When Henry acceded in 1509, Skelton, now unexpectedly the old tutor not merely of dukes but of kings, waited to be called to some suitably elevated and confidential post at court. It was not an unreasonable expectation. Kings could do much for their teachers, and did; Charles V gave his old tutor a papacy. But no call came for Skelton, so he copied out his *Speculum Principis* – the book of homiletic advice he had written for Henry in boyhood – in his own hand, and sent it reproachfully to the king, along with a prose complaint where he debated the causes of his present obscurity, wondering if the king or the gods had decreed it, and finding for the latter. It was headed 'Skelton Laureate, once royal tutor, in mute soliloquy with himself, as a man wholly given over to oblivion, or like one struck dead through the heart'. Henry continued to ignore him, but at last relented. Skelton was offered a post as 'poet' to the court, and there he went, armed with letters patent and primed with the Skeltonic line, ideal for prosecuting personal quarrels and for inspiring in other poets a sense of their own elegance.

---

[5] Though it is now thought that Cardinal Wolsey may have encouraged some of his satires on the quiet. Nor have all 20th century readers admired him: a Professor Burdan, writing in the 1920s, worried that 'descriptions written with such gusto show a familiarity with disreputable resorts unexplained in a scholar and an enjoyment of them undesirable in a churchman'.

*It longeth not to **my** science or cunning*
For Philip the Sparrow the Dirige *to sing*[6] [emphasis mine]

wrote the poet Alexander Barclay, with more hauteur than metrical skill.

Meanwhile, joy was unconfined among the humanists. The young king, only 19 years old, so good-looking, so ebullient, so rich, was a scholar! He had a natural aptitude for learning and this was joined to an even more exceptional interest in the progress of scholarship itself, or so it seemed. One delighted English humanist, Richard Pace, declared that his monarch 'far surpasses in distinction all other princes in learning as well as power. He is so well disposed to all *eruditi* that he hears nothing more willingly than conversations about scholars and books'. Lord Mountjoy wrote to Erasmus in the same vein. Guess what Henry had said to him the other day? 'I wish I was more learned.' And Mountjoy had replied, 'But learning is not what we expect of a king, merely that he should encourage scholars.' The king returned, 'Of course. For without them we could scarcely exist.' 'What better remark could be made by any?' asked Mountjoy.

These passages have often been quoted as proof of Henry's intellectual precocity, but what they demonstrate equally well is the solipsism and self-interest of the writers. Both see Henry's scholarship entirely from their own point of view and think what academics have always thought when a rich and powerful man takes an interest in their field: that it is the summit of his ambitions to fund their research. Mountjoy was not listening to what Henry actually said: 'I wish *I* was more learned.' If he had done, he would have noticed that his pupil's egotism was not the kind to be satisfied with patronage. Though not at all interested in the details of state business, when it came to pursuits of glory, Henry wanted to be doing: to lead his own armies, to

---

[6] Skelton wrote an elegy to a dead sparrow, called 'Philip Sparrow'.

star in his own pageants, to debate his own laws, write his own manifestos and generally be in the direct line for any praise. Mountjoy was one of many to underestimate and misunderstand this aspect of the king's personality, and it is easy to see where the confusion arose, because at first Henry's egotistic narcissism manifested itself as a passionate urge for orthodoxy: he would excel by conforming; he would be right because he went by the book. In time things would go the other way, and the king's desire to be right would become the doctrine to which men and laws would conform; but for now he was remarkable for fidelity. Clerics noted his devoutness, soldiers his martial spirit, courtiers his courtliness, scholars his scholarship, and all heard in his wonderful, exuberant enthusiasm a resounding confirmation of how right they all were.

He was a model husband.

Henry VIII (*Joos van Cleve*)

CHAPTER THREE

Prince Arthur died in 1502, and seven years later his brother, Henry, married the dead boy's widow, the Spanish princess Catherine of Aragon. The substitution of the younger brother for the older was somewhat irregular and difficult to arrange, and had required not only a dispensation from the pope but a final decision from her father-in-law, always on the look-out for advantage, that she was still useful to his plans. For a long time Catherine had waited, unconsulted and suddenly poor, while her father, Ferdinand of Aragon, squabbled with her father-in-law over who was to pay for what, and negotiators ambled from court to court. Henry VII turned against the idea and died in that opinion, but his son wanted the marriage, and, after a momentary hesitation over the legitimacy of marriage to a brother's widow, he did marry her, on June 11, 1509, a few days before his official coronation.

Catherine of Aragon was a pretty girl, according to the portrait by Michael Sittow, with fine auburn hair, a smoothly oval face with an incipient frown, and a little pointed chin like a lemon. Her six years' seniority to her husband left her still barely 24. Henry's enthusiasm for her was unquestionable, and lent a notably uxorious flavour to the round of pleasures that now constituted life at the new court. He was forever breaking into her chambers with a group of merry men 'disguised' in preposterous costumes of many cloths:

in mantels of cloth of silver, and lined with blew velvet,

the silver was pounsed in letters, so that the velvet might be sene through... this straunge apparel pleased every person, and especially the Quene, and thus four lordes and foure ladies came into the Quene's chamber with great light of torches, and daunced a great season, and then put off their visors, and then they were well knowen, and the queen hartely thanked the king's grace... and kissed him.

Catherine of Aragon (*Michael Sittow*)

At the joust, she was his lady – or at least, he was her lord – a subtle but important difference, tethering the forms of courtly love to the obligations of the marital state. After the joust, Catherine (or someone representing her) sang a song that began:

My sovereign lord for my poor sake[1]
Six courses at the ring did make
Of which four times he did it take
Wherefore my heart I him bequest
And of all other for to love best
My Sovereign Lord.

and continued

So many virtues given of grace
There is none on-live that have;
Behold his favour and his face
His personage most godliest!
A vengeance on them that loveth not best
My Sovereign Lord.

One notes that this lyric is a celebration of Henry and his manifold virility, including the sexual prowess hinted at in his ring-penetrating activities. When Henry sang back in his own poetry, he also warmed to this theme of himself:

Though sum saith that youth ruleth me[2]
I trust in age to tarry;
God and my right and my duty,
From them shall I never vary:
Though some say that youth ruleth me.

I pray you all that aged be
How well did you your youth carry?
I think some was of each degree;
Therein a wager lay dare I:
Though some say that youth ruleth me.

---

[1] Carol, found in what Professor John Stevens calls the 'Henry VIII MS' in his study of early modern lyrics, *Music and Poetry in The Tudor Court*(Methuen, 1961). Spelling modernised.
[2] Henry VIII MS, in Stevens, op. cit. Spelling modernised.

Pastimes of youth sometime among
None can say but necessary;
I hurt no man, I do no wrong
I love true where I did marry:
Though some say that youth ruleth me.

Then soon discuss that hence we must
Pray we to God and Saint Mary
That all amend; and here an end,
Thus sayth the King, the eighth Harry:
Though some say (etc).

This is a very characteristic production. Disapproval from an older generation of counsellors for his choice of young, irreverent 'minions' as friends had moved Henry to this litany of self-justification, but we can see that beneath the surface jocularity of the song, these are the sentiments of a self-righteous, slightly bullying nature wounded in his self-regard. He especially resents the idea that his youthful indulgences might be mistaken for vices, when they are really ornaments. Have his critics forgotten his virtues (first verse)? Perhaps they are so old they have forgotten their own youth (second verse). Enjoyment is an essential part of youth, everyone says so, and besides, his pleasures are harmless (third verse). And finally (fourth verse): do you know who I am?

The profession of matrimonial love in the third verse is highly illuminating in view of what was to come. Kings in the 16th century could love and be married, but few of them sought to combine these two states. But this writer evidently considers marital love a moral virtue and thinks well of himself for having achieved it. *I love true where I did marry*. He intended a credo of fidelity, but in fact he had devised the motto of the serial monogamist.

Both these poems were found in a handsome manuscript

collection of songs and lyrics that is thought, because it contains Henry's own compositions and because of where it was discovered, to have been used for court amusements in the earlier part of Henry's reign. As a representation of the king's taste in these things, it is interesting for containing songs of reciprocal and decorous – one might almost say romantic – love, in contrast with a similar collection from the previous reign, where the ladies conform to patterns of cruelty and duplicitousness. It was found in the Kentish house of Sir Henry Guildford, who, as master of the revels and then comptroller of the household in Henry's court, was in charge of organising parties, pageants, banquets and the like. These posts had grown considerably since the accession of young Henry VIII. Although his father had entertained splendidly, there was an air of purpose to those proceedings, and his sumptuousness in public display was at odds with the natural restraint of his personal expenditure: he loved hunting, for example, but he kept such a modest stable that he had to call in horses and harness, as an exceptional provision, to convey Catherine of Aragon to her first marriage.

Things were very different after 1509, for Henry's ordinary domestic entertainments were hardly less grandiose than the diplomatic spectaculars of the previous reign, and more heartfelt. Released onto the throne of England and allowed to do what he liked, he stepped into what his biographer, Scarisbrick, calls 'a world of lavish allegory, mythology and romance'. It was the job of Guildford and his like, as party planners, to make this metaphorical world a physical reality, using wood, cloth, canvas and cheap theatrical labour. Carpenters and painters built enchanted castles outside and made magical forests grow inside 'with rocks, hylles and dales'. Or they might drag a galleon 'in ful sayle' into the park where the king, riding by with his companions, could happen upon it by accident and then, after a manful exchange with its 'captain' (who 'sayed he was a mariner and was come from many a strange port, and

[48]

had come hither to see if any dedes of armes were to be done in the countrey, of the which he might make report in other countries'), follow the ship – which now, impressively, took off overland with all guns firing – into the tiltyard.

There was work too for mythological personnel, now deployed through the royal landscapes to act out Henry's dreams of Albion. On May morning 1515 – a festival day in the Romance calendar, liberally observed since Henry's accession – he and the queen rode out to Shooter's Hill to 'fetch the May', that is, to cut sprigs of the new-leaved May-tree[3], and bring them back in their hats as a tribute to the new season. As they were cantering by the way, whom should they meet but Robin Hood, and 200 of his merry men? After a salvo of novelty whistling arrows, Robin invited the royal party to breakfast 'in the grene wode, and to se how the outlawes lyve. The kyng demaunded of the queen and her

Sir Henry Guildford (*Hans Holbein the Younger*)

---

[3] common hawthorn, *Crataegus monogyna.*

ladyes, if they durst adventure to go into the wood with so many outlawes.' The queen, of course, who was properly brought up as a Spanish princess and knew that her role was to be a little afraid of such manifestations, and then, invariably, astonished when it all turned out to be a masquerade, said that if it pleased the king, she would venture. And the comptroller had so organised it that Robin Hood's living quarters were arranged as a perfect sylvan replica of the royal chambers, all in boughs and flowers, with the same tripartite structure of outer hall, great chamber and inner chamber: the whole fantasy perfectly devised to make the legendary past flow into the political present and anoint Henry's monarchy with English myth. It was a conceit of genius, and the crowning moment came with the breakfast. '"Sir," said Robin (Hood), "outlawes breakfastes is venison, and therefore you must be content with such fare as we use."' Historically, venison was the meat of kings, available only to those nobles with extensive deer parks or – as Guildford's production makes clear – to poachers.

This kind of carry-on was not to everybody's taste. The humanists deplored its childishness and saw, rightly, that such a mingling of politics and fantasy would pollute their hard-sourced historical truths. If Erasmus had his way, princes would not be allowed to read 'Arthurs and Lancelots' which 'smacke of tyrannie and are moreover rude, foolish and anile'.[4] Thomas More went further, criticising all manner of princely gorgeousness, including jewellery, wars fought for Glory, and fine clothes.

These were opinions unlikely to catch on among the sovereign class of the time. Strictures against clothing were particularly antipathetic in a country where every transaction was oiled with lanolin. The sheep of an island kingdom, un-like those of mainland Europe, did not have to make lunch for

---

[4] rude: unlearned; anile: old-womanish, imbecile. More, Cromwell and all contemporary polemicists employed misogynistic invective.

passing armies, and this, combined with the weather and a series of unpopular acts of land enclosure, ensured that English flocks were as plentiful as the clouds in the English sky. They supplied northern Europe with cloth and London with a teeming mercantile population of drapers, mercers, tailors and weavers, and foreign merchants who came with goods and new ideas from other countries.

Henry himself made a cult of cloth, as his predecessors had of furs, and everything he valued was covered in it. Books wore brilliant velvet jackets, harness came sleeved in satin and velvet. His court had no geographical location, but consisted of a group of men (and ladies, when a queen was in place) riding from one large, cold, unfurnished palace to another. Ahead of them went trains of wagons loaded with what it took to create a suitable court setting. Pictures and mirrors could never survive that journey on medieval roads, but cloth and plate – the other ornamental staple of the regime – could. The great gold-thread narrative tapestry sequences from Henry's immense collection, hanging edge to edge and tier upon tier, filled the temporary halls with warmth and glitter; and, because textile is better than painting at representing cloth itself, the heroic figures in the tapestries mirrored and approved the figures milling below, in their slashed satins and damasks and sarcanets and brocades. The king was always a mountain of cloth, even as a young, fit man, and the accumulated dazzle of his gold and silver stuffs showed, by the sumptuary laws, that he was indeed the king.

More's censure of glorious warfare fell on equally poor ground. To put it simply, Henry VIII believed that invading France was what English kings did. His own views took inspiration not from any humanist text but in the unreconstructed call to arms of Caxton's preface to *The Ordre of Chivalry*, one of the first books to come off the English printing presses:

Oh ye knights of England, where is the custom and usage of noble chivalry that was used in those days [of Arthur]? What do ye now but go to the bagnios and play at dice?... leave this... and read the noble volumes of the holy grail, of Launcelot, of Galahad, of Tristram, of Perseofrest, of Percival, of Gawain... read Froissart. And also behold that noble king, Harry the fifth, and the captains under him.

Henry had read all these; he had beheld his namesake, Harry, the conqueror of France; he intended to copy him. The Venetian ambassador, Andrea Badoer, reported that on the very day Henry VIII succeeded his father, he swore to wage war on France.[5]

There was support for this attitude both at court and in the wider country. Hortatory biographies of Henry V appeared around the time of Henry's first advance against the French, in 1513, led by himself: a campaign radiant with *sprezzatura*, and so popular that no subject grudged the extra taxation to pay for it or greatly minded that it resulted in the gain of a single French citadel, Tournai. All the fabulous people went: the Earl of Surrey 'could scantly speak' with indignation at being left behind to fight a far more important, but dingy, war against the Scots.

Henry's victory at Tournai was to have surprisingly extensive consequences, but they would not be measurable in territory and didn't really begin until 1518, when the new, young French king, Francis I, sent an embassy of French noblemen and 'freshe younge gallantes' to negotiate its redemption. They came bringing a thrilling rabble of French 'rascals and peddlers, and juellers' with 'hats and capes and divers merchandise unaccustomed', to sell to the curious English; and left behind a number of elegant hostages from the French court, who carried

[5] Charles Grey-Deloison, 'Anglo-French relations and the Treaties of 1527', in David Starkey (ed.), *Henry VIII: A European Court in England* (Collins, 1991).

in their diplomatic bags the seeds of an envious, competitive Francomania that took root in the king, and flourished.

History has found Francis I a rather silly king, but Henry saw him quite another way, aspiring to his accomplished frivolity, his large culture, his easy virtuosity in everything to do with manners, taste and display. Perhaps he saw in him some element of custom, or pedigree, that he lacked. At any rate, the letters of Henry's reign are scattered with attentive diplomatic descriptions of how, precisely, Francis conducted his leisure – how he hunted and dressed, who attended him, what the ladies did, how his palaces looked – which have the air of being earnestly solicited from the English side for Henry to study and compare with his own proceedings. It always appeased the English king to hear himself likened to Francis. As late as 1542,

Francis I (*Jean Clouet*)

ambassadors would ease diplomatic negotiations by dilating on this topic: how they both delighted 'in hunting, in hawking, in building, in apparel, in stones, in jewels, and of like affection to one another'. Such remarks were intended for Henry: Francis would have had no reciprocal interest, or even belief, in English culture. He was interested only in Italy.

In England though, in 1518, the French hostages were the toast of the season, and the following year some selected English courtiers made a reciprocal visit to the French court. The young courtiers on this prototype French exchange got to 'ride disguised through Paris, throwinge egges' and fell into such frenchified habits that when they got back it was complained that 'They were all Frenche, in eatyng, drynkyng and apparel, yea, and in French vices and bragges,[6] so that all the estates of Englande were by them laughed at.' The French language, which had been banned at court, now began to be fashionable. Opportunities arose for enterprising French-speakers to set themselves up as language teachers. In 1521, the same year that Henry and Francis met in Calais for the competitive chivalric triathlon of tournament sports, dress and bowing known as 'the Field of the Cloth of Gold', Alexander Barclay published his *Introductory to Speak and Write French* with an appendix of the latest French dances at the back.

The publication found favour at court, to the evident annoyance of rival Francophone John Palsgrave, chaplain to Henry, schoolmaster to the Royal family, all-round martinet and a man whose general tone exemplifies the tendency of early Tudor prose writers to seem in a permanent bad mood. Palsgrave's own book, *L'Esclarcissment de la langue Francoyse*, came out garlanded with self-recommendations and, in the prefatory dedication to the king, a warning to the unwary. This concerned 'a boke, that goeth about in this realme, intitled The Introductory to writte or pronounce French, compiled by Alexander

---

[6] bragge: boastfulness, arrogance.

Barclay, in which 'k' is moche used, and many other thynges afirmed, contrary to my sayings in this boke'. The present author has read this book 'at length'; his opinion of it will be all too apparent in his own book, so he will not mention it here, but (mentioning it straight away), the learner should be aware of a dark coincidence: 'that I have sene an olde boke written in parchment in maner of all things lyke to his introductory: which, by conjecture, was not unwritten these 300 years. I wot not if he happened to fortune upon such a book.'

Palsgrave had, for a teacher, an exceptionally retentive attitude to the flow of knowledge. So worried was he that some other French teacher might profit from the *Esclarcissment*, that he forbade his publisher to sell it to anyone with a didactic air about him; with the result that it is now a very rare book. There is evidence that French teachers were in fact in short supply. In 1527, when 900 noblemen accompanied Cardinal Wolsey on his diplomatic mission to France, most were monoglot and had to be briefed on the hazard of Frenchmen talking to them 'in the French tongue as though ye understood every word they spake'. Wolsey's solution was robust: 'If they speak to you in the French tongue, speak you to them in the English tongue; for if you understand not them, they shall no more understand you.'[7]

Some people recognised the purchase of foreign languages from the earliest days of the reign. Among them were that cluster of prominent courtiers in Kent who steadily gained in influence through the early years of the new century and included Henry Wyatt. Wyatt was a man of bustle and dispatch, and popular, and he prospered even more under the second Tudor than the first. Though his son and rebellious grandson[8] are better known to us, neither did nearly as well, by the lights of their own time, as this thrusting bureaucrat, three different kinds of

---

[7] George Cavendish, *The Life and Death of Cardinal Wolsey*, ed. R.S. Sylvester (Early English Text Society, 1958)
[8] Sir Thomas Wyatt the Younger headed an unsuccessful rebellion against Queen Mary I in 1553-4.

knight under Henry VIII and occupant of some of the most important posts in government finance. In 1521 'Sir Harry' became master, or keeper, of the king's jewels – a position evidently worth having, as it is the one Thomas Cromwell chose to display in his portrait by Holbein – and in 1524 he got the top post of treasurer of the chamber, the revenue department that funded everything from tips to travel and the provisioning of armies. This post would decline in importance as the reign wore on, but under Sir Henry it was still the principal source of disbursements. From this eminence he could see into every aspect of court life, and he kitted out his son with French and Latin in the knowledge that a man would go far with languages. He had before him an excellent example of just such a man, in the form of his Kentish neighbour and fellow courtier, the ambitious Sir Thomas Boleyn.

Boleyn spoke the best French in the English court – a slight and ornamental accomplishment, as it seems today, but one that set in train events with seismic repercussions. Because of it he was sent as an ambassador to Margaret of Austria, and got on so well with her that she offered to take his younger daughter, Anne, as one of her *filles d'honneur*. Such opportunities do not come twice: Margaret was regent of the Netherlands in the minority of her nephew, Charles of Burgundy, and her court was, according to Anne's biographer, Eric Ives, 'Europe's premier finishing school'. Anne would go at 13 and be educated alongside European royalty; she would learn perfect French and acquire her courtly manners at the fount of that Burgundian ceremonial to which all other courts aspired. The resulting French fluency – a rarity, as we have seen, in English noblemen, let alone their undereducated sisters – recommended her to the English controllers of ceremonies. She and her sister, Mary, would go as ladies in the train of Henry's sister, also Mary, whose marriage in 1515 to the elderly King Louis XII of France was an early symptom of the erratic warming trend that now prevailed in Anglo-French relations. Louis died almost at once, and Mary returned to England scandalously, as the wife of Charles Brandon, the courtier sent over to deal with the diplomatic fallout of her widowhood. The whole enterprise was over in under a year.

The Boleyn sisters stayed behind, as ladies to the new queen, Claude, wife to the new king, Francis. Mary had a brief vogue as Francis's mistress, but Anne put her bilingualism to work elsewhere, and made herself an indispensable figure at any occasion involving English visitors. She learned the machinery of the French court, and it may be here, as an interpreter, that she acquired her exceptional ability to negotiate court politics.

How much of this her father, Thomas Boleyn, foresaw or expected cannot be known. Most likely she had begun to outstrip anything his ambition had devised. We do know, however, that he liked to promote the notion that his daughters, with their English birth and French manners, had become embodiments of the Anglo-French cultural exchange. He alluded to this with the commission of two boats, the *Mary Boleyn* and the *Anne Boleyn*, which appear on the records in the 1520s, plying the route between Dover and Calais. Certainly, too, he saw his daughters' foreign education as a form of exotic bounty, with which to barter for position at the English court: with this French polish they could enter the household of Catherine of Aragon. But Catherine was herself the embodiment of the Spanish-English alliance. She had noted with unease the waxing of French influence, and its pull on Cardinal Wolsey's foreign policy. France and Spain had been at war; an English alliance with France would probably mean war with Spain. At the Field of the Cloth of Gold, where to be young and to be French was very heaven, she showed the first signs of that obduracy for which she is chiefly remembered, by appearing in full Spanish costume, stiff with reproachful pomegranates.[9]

[9] The pomegranate of Granada was Catherine's heraldic badge.

It need hardly be said that Catherine of Aragon would never have considered the daughters of an English knight, no matter how frenchified, as any kind of Trojan horse from France. Before Mary Boleyn became her husband's mistress, she may well have welcomed Mary and, later, Anne, to court for their ornamental value. She was not then such a stick as she later became. She had been happy to entertain the French hostages in 1518, when it was evident that they had the king in tow. Now 33, and the mother of many miscarriages and a daughter, she realised her husband was more likely to seek her company if her household was well stocked with entertainments and comely young women such as the Boleyn sisters.

Anne was a prize from the start. When she returned to England in about 1521, there was, according to her biographer Eric Ives, 'no one to touch her' at the English court. She had a magnetism far beyond her modest beauty. She could dance and sing and, to judge from what remains of her reported conversation, banter with a fearless attack that must have made her exciting to be around. In her, recklessness and stratagem coexisted, linked by a formidable intelligence. She was a magnet for stories and court gossip, and her wit was so remarkable that even her most dedicated detractors have given her credit for it. And furthermore, as a French observer remarked, 'no one would ever have taken her to be English by her manners, but a native-born Frenchwoman.'[10] With this, she was propelled at once onto the A-list at court entertainments. In the revels of Shrove Tuesday 1522, when Henry was host to Emperor Charles V of Spain, his wife's nephew, she was one of only eight ladies to take part in the crowning entertainment, the 'Assault on the Chateau Vert'.[11]

The emperor's visit was the most splendid diplomatic extravaganza of Henry's splendid reign, and was among the last

[10] Lancelot De Carles, French diplomat, quoted in Eric Ives, *The Life and Death of Anne Boleyn* (Blackwell, 2004).

fitful upflarings of Anglo-Spanish concord for a while. Much depended on it: for Catherine of Aragon, a strengthening of the Spanish accord and a marriage with her nephew for her daughter, Mary; for Henry, an ally in his new French wars, who would cede him France in the event of a successful outcome; for Cardinal Wolsey, the promise of Charles's support at the next papal election. The presence, therefore, on the 'Chateau Vert's' green tinfoil battlements of Anne Boleyn, so soon after her arrival and alongside such as Mary Brandon, lately Queen of France, shows she was already one of the heaviest guns in Henry's courtly artillery.

All hands were to the tiller for this event: Charles had trimmed his retinue from 2044 to 'the very smallest possible number of servitors',[12] calculated as 1000, including six surgeons, three furriers, nine master cooks and a personal fruiterer; but this still meant that every available house and stable in London was requisitioned for the visitors, and substantial pressure placed on those with conveniently situated houses, to vacate them and put out their best 'stuff of household' for the guests. Armies of grocers, vintners, chandlers, butchers, poulterers and fishmongers toiled to provision the guests with the gargantuan daily rations specified in advance by the imperial party. The task of Sir Henry Wyatt (whose meticulous accounts must form the basis of the surviving chronicle) would test his command of his books. In addition to paying for everything, he had to find appropriate lodgings with 'discreet folk' for the emperor's train, and furnish each chamber with such specimens of plate from the king's jewel house as would accurately reflect each guest's rank and position. Here and

---

[11] In essence, a glorified food fight. Allegorically attired ladies and gentlemen hurled sweets at one another over the battlements of a substantial model castle, built for the occasion and equipped with an interior staircase and space for a troupe of minstrels in addition to the eight defending ladies. Edward Hall, *The Triumphamt reign of King Henry VIII*, ed. Charles Whibley (T.C. and E.C. Jack, 1904).
[12] This account of the event is taken from *The Visit of the Emperor Charles V to England, A.D. 1522. The Rutland Papers*, ed. W. Jerdan (1842).

elsewhere, he was expected to make the king's wealth conspicuous. In the banqueting house, the dressers reached almost to the ceilings, and on their shelves great hosts of plate and goldsmith's work rose up, like the ranks of the angelic orders, in shining crowded tiers above the heads of the participating dignitaries.

By now, Sir Henry had his son, Thomas, to help him. The earliest appearances of Thomas Wyatt in the records show that he began life as an accountant. Time would show that he was most unsuited to a career in accountancy; but in a client society considerations of aptitude did not register at entry level. The challenge was to get your protégé in wherever you could; after, he could rise to notice. Young Wyatt soon proved to have other uses.

CHAPTER FOUR

Thomas Wyatt was a clever young man with the good fortune to begin life under the direction of an ambitious father. It is likely that Wyatt sent him for a spell to the newly founded St John's College in Cambridge University,[1] the forcing ground, though no one in that second decade of the century knew it, for almost all the principal actors in the English Reformation. Then, having secured him a place in the treasury, as 'clerk of the jewel house', Sir Henry eased him out into the world as a courier for treasury funds.

Young Thomas must have attracted notice as a good negotiator among roads and people, because in 1526, when he was 23, Sir Thomas Cheney chose to take him on a diplomatic mission to the French court. He sent him back to Wolsey with messages and the commendation that young Wyatt 'hath as much wit to mark and remember everything he seeth as any young man hath in England'. Not only could he retain and relate diplomatic information – a very important skill at this period in Henry's reign, when ambassadors still trusted their messengers to deliver the bulk of their messages by mouth – but he had a noticing eye and a mind to grasp those elusive details of French court life and appurtenances that the king, with his competitive interest in such matters, wanted to know. He would be able to tell Wolsey, said Cheney, about 'a part of the commodities belonging to this house, and the names and

---

[1] The Thomas Wyatt whose name appears in the St John's records is usually thought to be him, but this is not corroborated anywhere else.

characteristics of characters at the French court'.

Thomas Wyatt knew about courtly matters because he was already a prominent and successful young courtier.

What does that mean? The term 'courtier' is capacious, and covered men of widely disparate gifts, offices and assets, rather like 'banker' today. The court was just a name for a place where the king was, and a courtier, in the largest sense, was just a person with a place in his peripatetic household. Because the king 'removed' around 30 times a year, the court would swell and shrink according to such factors as the size of the house he moved to, his mood, the festivities of the season and the determination of his household officials to repulse the many human appurtenances who invariably swarmed up, looking to be fed or advanced, when the king's party arrived. The inner court – of which Wyatt was a member – contained about 100 people who were entitled to an official lodging, but even among these a great variety of status obtained, measurable in actual distance from the person of the king. At the top were the gentlemen of the privy chamber, who kept Henry company in his own private apartment, some of them sleeping at the foot of his bed. Beyond this small core of the ultra-elite, the remaining courtiers extended in complex patterns of precedence calculated by a combination of social rank, favour and official position, and converted by the household officers into the materials of life. Precedence governed where courtiers could go, what they could wear, what games they could play, what they could eat, how warm they could be, where they could stand. A courtier always knew where he stood, just from where he was standing; also from the 'diet' or daily ration he or she collected from the various dispensaries of the household. Here, as elsewhere, the king's favour trumped all other considerations. In July 1522, the king's secretariat directed the lord steward of the household to improve the diet of one 'right dere and welbeloved Lady Lucy', so she would receive provisions as follows:

Every morning 'at breakfast, one chine of beef, one cheat loaf[2] and one manchet,[3] and a gallon of ale; after noon, a manchet and half a gallon of ale; at dinner, a piece of beef, a stroke[4] of roaste and a rewarde,[5] a cast[6] of cheat bread, and a gallon of ale; at supper, a mess of porrage, a piece of mutton and a reward, a cast of cheat bread and a gallon of ale and half a gallon of wine at our cellar bar.' Every morning 'at our woodyard' four tall 'shyds'[7] and two faggots; 'at our chandlery bar', in winter, every night, 'one pricket[8] and four sizes[9] of wax', with eight candles, white lights and one torch; 'at our pitcherhouse' weekly, six white cups; and 'at every time of our removing one whole cart for the carriage of her stuff'.[10]

A courtier's success, then, was precisely measurable. Wyatt had evidently given satisfaction because at the age of 21 he was one of the 15 'esquires of the court', men of 'name and arms' who issued a challenge to Henry at the Christmas Joust at Greenwich. The participants on both sides of this joust had won their place in it through graft and patronage. They were a group of thrusters, many of whom would achieve success – or notoriety – later in the reign; and Sir Henry Wyatt had so arranged it that Thomas was now related to most of them. At 15, he had married him to Elizabeth Brooke, the daughter of an important Kentish neighbour, Thomas, Lord Cobham. It was a wretched marriage, but it placed him well.

On this occasion, Christmas 1524, the games were centred

---

[2] cheat loaf: wheat bread of the second quality, made with flour more coarsely ground than that of 'manchet'.
[3] best bread, made with finest-ground white flour.
[4] stroke: a slice, or cut.
[5] reward: an extra portion.
[6] cast: a quantity (not now known) of loaves of bread or of beer. Lady Lucy was probably not expected to consume all this herself, but to distribute some of it to her own hangers-on.
[7] This word is lost to us. Presumably, a quantity of firewood.
[8] pricket: spiked candle-stick.
[9] size: a small cylindrical candle.
[10] Lady Lucy's diets, July 16, 1522, *Letters and Papers*, ed. J.S. Brewer, J. Gairdner and R.H. Brodie [LP] vol. 3, ii, 2391.

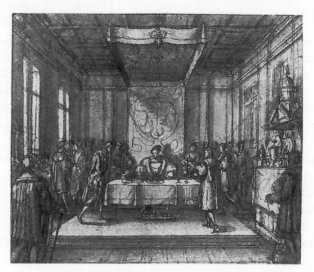

Henry VIII dining in his privy chamber
(*Follower of Hans Holbein the Younger*)

around a tremendous castle set up in the tiltyard, 'square every way twentye foote and fiftie foote on heigh, very stronge and of great timber, well fastened with yron': the *Chasteau Blanche*. The special defensive features of this castle, which will be familiar to any watcher of Japanese game shows, were the 'great rolles (rollers)' set at all points of entrance, that 'turned as sone as they were touched', and the 15-foot ditches on its north and south sides.

The episode of the *Chasteau Blanche* is worth pausing for, not just because Wyatt was in it, but because it shows the role of courtly pageantry in generating occupation. We have seen that chivalric games were devised as the simulacrum of war, but in the early 16th century, when wars were expensive and often unpopular, and diplomatic solutions were starting to encroach on military prerogatives, chivalry was just as useful to fill the new and potentially dangerous *longueurs* of peacetime.

Hence Henry VII's expenditure on leisure facilities at Richmond Palace, and hence the saga of the *Chasteau Blanche*.

The castle in question occupied the entire court for weeks, absorbing much manly potency in puzzling over tactics and arrangements. Proceedings advanced at a glacial pace, with ritual dragging at every step. First there was the theatre of the challenge, when a herald appeared with a specially painted placard, to issue a physical and – unusually – intellectual challenge to the king. The Wyatt team (captained by Lord Leonard Grey) would defend the castle against all comers; the king's team were to go away and devise whatever 'engines' they could, not counting proper weapons, to assault it. Any prisoners taken could ransom themselves with yards of satin. After this came the formal answer. Then the king must recruit for his side, and special apparel of suitable symbolic complexity must be designed, commissioned, cut, sewn and embroidered for all concerned; then the castle itself – presumably already constructed – lumbered into view and everyone inspected it, some claiming, says the chronicler Hall, that it was so impregnable 'it could not be wonne by sport, but by ernest.' The sight of it stimulated Henry, whose great love for mechanical curiosities was equalled by his interest in military fortifications, into the frenzied production of designs for 'engines' to assail it; but, annoyingly, the English carpenters were 'so dull that thei understode not his entent, and wrought al thing contrary'. So there was a further delay, filled with the usual jousting and tilting, while everybody wondered how to proceed; until at last 'after long debate', Sir Francis Bryan, a courtier of whom we will hear more, proposed a combination of artillery that might be both effective and non-lethal, and the assault could go ahead. The whole tourney was made to last until February 8. It was a great success. 'There was never battaile of pleasure,' concluded Hall, 'better fought then [sic] this was.' And afterwards, in the evenings, the warriors repaired to the queen's chamber for what was called, honestly enough, 'pastime'.

Pastime was another kind of recreation. The word was used for formal court entertainments, like the masque that was held on this occasion, or the plays and musical performances put on by professional players under William Cornishe, master of the king's chapel. But it is also the term for a more mysterious activity: a series of diversions and amusements played on the theme of courtly love, in which the players were not professionals but the members of the inmost court, and which – as has already been said – might be described as the indoor, or feminised, division of chivalric games. Any attempts to describe it must proceed gropingly. The players were few and the rules were not written down. All that is left of it now is the poems, themselves counters in this game, many of them written by Thomas Wyatt. He was the supreme master of this genre. If we are to understand his genius, then we have to try and understand the area of his operations and the materials of his craft.

The place to look is in the poems themselves.

*   *   *   *

The intention here is not to add to the immense volume of writings on courtly love poetry, but to take from those writings the least that is necessary to analyse the attitudes and expectations behind the lyrics. But even before that, there must be a word to explain how the poems circulated. The most important single fact about Wyatt's lyric poems is this: they were written by hand and circulated among a tiny group of Wyatt's intimate friends. The total audience, even for lyrics that featured in performance, would rarely have exceeded 100 key courtiers. In many cases the readership was much smaller. None of the lyrics was printed in Wyatt's lifetime. They were intended for a closed, incestuous coterie consisting of the most precocious and sophisticated men and women of the court. They were not primarily a 'literary' form, nor – and this is a critical point – did anyone consider them a suitable conveyance for serious ideas. Wyatt thought enough of his lyric poems, and of himself as the author of them, to copy a selection of them into his own book.[11] Admiring contemporaries also made collections of his lyrics, as we will see, and some may have studied them as models of the fashionable form. But most of their readers would never have encountered them in a book, or felt the inducement to read them at a single sitting. Most of the lyrics started life on a single folded piece of paper tucked purposefully into Wyatt's doublet, so it could be passed slyly to a friend as he was waiting in the crowded presence chamber, or left somewhere a girl would find it. It might make its public debut on the programme of pastime amusements for the inner court. But it could also be borrowed, circulated and copied, quoted in part or whole, a line or two murmured into someone's ear while dancing, or gambling, or walking in the palace grounds, to make them laugh or blush.

A Wyatt poem might come into being after a bad night:

What means this when I lie alone?[12]
I toss, I turn, I sigh, I groan.
My bed me seems as hard as stone
 What means this?

I sigh, I plain continually.
The clothes that on my bed do lie
Always methinks they lie awry
 What means this?

In slumbers oft for fear I quake.
For heat and cold I burn and shake.

[11] Wyatt's own MS, containing poems written and corrected in his own hand, is known as the 'Egerton MS'.
[12] Wyatt, CIII, in Rebholz, op. cit.

For lack of sleep my head doth ache
 What means this?

A mornings then when I do rise
I turn unto my wonted guise,
All day after muse and devise.
 What means this?

And if perchance by me there pass
She unto whom I sue for grace,
The cold blood forsaketh my face.
 What means this?

But if I sit near her by
With loud voice my heart doth cry
And yet my mouth is numb and dry
 What means this?

What it principally means is that people like Wyatt had nothing very pressing to do in the long days at court. Only a man with nothing much on could spend 'all day after muse and devise' working up his poem, hoping that a girl would pass by. Nothing makes poetry happen.

Poetry, on the other hand, was the catalyst for plenty of happening things. Love was newly fashionable. In the previous reign, English continence in matters of love had greatly impressed a visiting Italian: 'he had never noticed anyone, either at court or amongst the lower orders, to be in love' he said, '... either the English were the most discreet lovers in the world, or they were incapable of love'. But now, in the 1520s, the young and chic of Henry's court were all at it, tossing and pining on their pallets for love, or saying they did in lyric poetry. Stephen Hawes had seen this coming in the last reign, and warned of lowered standards and dumbing-down among the young, who

Fain no fables pleasaunt and covert
But spend their time in vainful vanitie
Making ballades of fervent amitie.

Why did they? What did they themselves hope would happen as a result? Here we come to the primary social purpose of courtly love lyrics: they and all the activity they generated were a way of dealing with sexual frustrations at court. In emulation of Francis I's practices, attractive women were more and more visible at Henry's court, and yet no more sexually available to the many young men in attendance than they had been before. Women were aloof, and men continually supplicated for favours that must not, under the rules of the system, ever come. The lyric operated in the gap between hope and expectation.

I have sought long with steadfastness[13]
To have had some ease of my great smart
But naught availeth faithfulness
To grave within your stony heart.

... But of your goodness all your mind
Is that I should complain in vain.
This is the favour that I find
Ye list to hear how I can plain.

As we see here, the lyric had to express the urgency and the hopelessness of the supplicant's case at the same time. This is because the courtly love convention is built on a central contradiction: the amorous relation between a courtly lady and a suitor is an adulterous one, and yet the lady must be chaste. Hence the lyrics are like those grammatical constructions that ask a question anticipating the answer 'no'. Don't you?

[13] Wyatt, CX, in Rebholz, op. cit.

Won't you? Can't you?

No.

In this way, they allowed a game of love to be played without compromising the valuable chastity of the female players.

> *To wish and want and not obtain*
> *To seek and sue ease of my pain*
> *Since all that ever I do is vain*
> *What may it avail me?*

Within the confines of her acknowledged chastity, the courtly lady could be cruel or kind to her suitor. As his social superior, she might be able to grant him the favours of patronage, but in courtly ideology these benefits were subsidiary to those benefits she could bring him through the practice of her virtues. Her chastity would teach restraint and fidelity and encourage him to valorous deeds. Moreover, because the medieval mind was shaped for allegory, and would effortlessly see through the things of this world to the higher reality behind them, when the virtues of this lady were celebrated in a lyric they gave, like a window, onto those parallel virtues of the female saints, particularly the blessed virgin; and her physical description – the eyes like glass, the jewelled breast, the twined gold of her hair – was meant to evoke the saintly effigies, often made of gold and precious stones, that were placed in every church. Everyone knew this: when Shakespeare wrote his sonnet mocking the unreal women of poetic convention,

> *My mistress' eyes are nothing like the Sun.*[14]
> *If hairs be wires black wires grow on her head*

he was showing his post-Reformation origins; but he was also

---

[14] William Shakespeare, Sonnet 130, Colin Burrow (ed.), *The Oxford Shakespeare: The Complete Sonnets and Poems* (OUP, 2002).

being deliberately obtuse. If, on the other hand, the lady was represented as cruel and fickle – as she generally was in misogynistic medieval Europe – she gave, as it were, onto a number of disagreeable female personages from classical and biblical texts, but particularly onto Fortuna, the changeable goddess of fortune who was held to blame for every upset in the Middle Ages and kept medieval man in a permanent state of nervous tension:

> *Each man me telleth I change most my device,*[15]
> *And on my faith me think it good reason*
> *To change purpose like after the season.*
> *For in every case to keep still one guise*
> *Is meet for them that would be taken wise;*
> *And I am not of such manner condition*
> *But treated after a diverse fashion,*
> *And thereupon my diverseness doth rise*

In either case, she was chaste. On the occasions when poets wrote about erotic fulfilment, they sealed the encounter in a bubble of somnolence, using the medieval convention of the dream-vision. Few poems like this survive in English, but here is the gist of one which Wyatt might have known, as it is in the so-called 'Henry VIII MS' with connections to Henry's court entertainments:

> *In a goodly night as in my bed I lay,*[16]
> *Pleasantly sleeping this dream I had:*
> *To me there came a creature brighter than the day,*
> *Which comforted my spirits that were afore full sad...*

---

[15] Wyatt, XXX, in Rebholz, op. cit.
[16] Sharon L. Jansen and Kathleen H. Jordan (eds.), *The Welles Anthology*, Medieval & Renaissance Texts and Studies, vol. 75 (New York, 1991). Spelling modernised, my punctuation.

Then when she saw that I lay so still
Full softly she drew unto my bed's side.
She bade me show her what was my will,
And my request it should not be denied
With that she kissed me…

I prayed her heartily that she would come to bed.
She said she was content to do me pleasure.
I know not whether I was alive or dead
So glad I was to have that goodly treasure.
I kissed her, I bassed[17] her out of all measure,
The more I kissed her, the more her beauty shone.
To serve her, to please her that time I did me deavour,[18]
But when I awoke, there was but I alone.

Lovemaking ensues in 'goodly sports all night', but then the final verse comes whisking in, like matron, to restore order. Pop goes the dream-bubble. The satisfied lover is revealed as a foolish and still frustrated boy, 'with no thing but my pillow in my arms'. Everyone laughs, partly from relief; and though we may not admire this poet, we can see he has acknowledged the possibility of full sexual consummation, while upholding the taboo against it. When Wyatt came to address this problem, he would find more ingenious ways to do the same.

Opportunities for ingenuity arose from the fact that an early 16th-century lyric was more than the words that were written in it. It had a life as a material object as well. To us now, a poem means the same whether we read it on a computer screen or in a newspaper or a book of poetry; but to the ladies and gentlemen of the early Tudor court, a poem on a piece of paper was also a material thing, like a flower or a handkerchief, or a jewel. Like them it could cluster with multiple symbolic meanings and,

---

[17] bassed: kissed.
[18] deavour: endeavour

perhaps more importantly, you could change its emphasis by doing things to it. The writer, or suitor (they were not the same; Wyatt's poems were requisitioned by less talented members of the court) could eke out its significance by leaving it in a particular place, or folding it in a certain way, or tying it with a particular knot, and so on; and the recipient had another set of responses. If there was ever a precise key for this activity it is lost, so we are spared the tedium of a table of correspondences. What we do have is poems that show how the interplay between material and sentimental transaction was entirely delightful to the participants in this game.

Here is Wyatt punning on a poem that he gave to a girl, and came back torn:

> *Sufficed not, madam, that you did tear*[19]
> *My woeful heart, but thus also to rent*
> *The weeping paper that to you I sent*
> *Whereof each letter was written with a tear?*

Tear/tear! The pun as well is woeful, but typical. Fastidious scholars have recoiled before the general enthusiasm for this sort of thing, some thinking it kinder to Wyatt's reputation to ignore it altogether. But the poems weren't written for them; they were meant for people who thought it brilliantly apposite and inventive; and unless we can put ourselves into that punning state of mind where the literal and the metaphorical, the trivial and the serious, the painful and the comical, the base and the sublime can co-exist and interpenetrate as equals, we will slide straight off the surface of these apparently bald and blank little offerings. We will certainly miss the point of a lyric like this:

> *Help me to seek for I lost it there;*[20]
> *And if that ye have found it, ye that be here,*

[19] Wyatt, CXXV, in Rebholz, op. cit.
[20] Wyatt, V, in Rebholz, op. cit.

And seek to convey it secretly
Handle it soft and treat it tenderly
Or else it will plain[21] and then appair[22].
But rather restore it mannerly
Since that I do ask it thus honestly,
For to lose it it sitteth me too near.
Help me to seek.

Alas, and is there no remedy
But have I thus lost it wilfully?
Iwis it was a thing all too dear
To be bestowed and wist not where:
It was mine heart! I pray you heartily
Help me to seek.

This looks like a very slight riddle, written with Wyatt's customary disdain for metrical smoothness and able, if tortured, to yield a single scholarly footnote: 'to describe falling in love as the heart leaving the body was a commonplace of medieval love poetry'. But what if 'mine heart' is also an actual object, a heart-shaped envelope made of cloth with a balloon, or squeaking thing inside? Now the poem comes to life. Under that construction, the otherwise mystifying lines 'Handle it soft and treat it tenderly/Or else it will plain and then appair', make sudden sense: if you are rough with it, it will pop or squeal, and go flat.

Now we see what this is: the instructions for a kind of game of hide-and-seek, still tantalisingly occult, but a game nonetheless. 'Ye that be here' are a group of players trying to 'convey it (the heart) secretly' from one place to another. Was the heart hidden in the room, or on someone's person? Was it part of a dance or a word game, or did everyone run around trying

[21] plain: complain.
[22] appair: be damaged, with a sense of shrinking.

to find it? In any case, we have pressed a spring and a hidden window opens onto a world of fun and games, where the young people of the court are equipped with these inflated hearts, and use them in the language of the pastime. We will now have a very different response to a song beginning sadly,

> Comfort thyself, my woeful heart,[23]
> Or shortly on thyself thee wreak,
> For length redoubleth deadly smart.
> Why sighs thou, heart, and wilt not break?
>
> To waste in sighs were piteous death.
> Alas, I find thee faint and weak.
> Enforce thyself to lose thy breath.
> Why sighs thou then and will not break?

and concluding

> Then in her sight, to move her heart
> Seek on thyself thyself to wreak
> That she may know thou sufferd'st smart.
> Sigh there thy last and therewith break.

when we picture Wyatt declaiming it to a circle of laughing partygoers, while holding up a bladdered heart and giving it comical squeezes. Alas, I find thee faint and weak! (*squeak*). Then – to extrapolate from the last verse – he would pop it at the end, giving the signal for the game to move on to the next player ('in her sight, to move *her* heart'). And it casts a new light on a tiny Holbein drawing where a young couple in elegant dress are shown with a cup and a large heart.

When we consider these poems as performances we must

---

[23] Wyatt, CXII, in Rebholz, op. cit.

come to the question of musical settings, which has exercised scholars for years. Was Wyatt a musician? Were his 'songs' *songs*? C.S. Lewis certainly thought so. 'We are having a little music after supper' was the way he saw it. For him this exonerated the verses from their plainness, for 'richness and deliciousness would be supplied by the air and the lute'. But Professor John Stevens, whose book on the subject[24] is still definitive, could find no evidence for the lyrics as musical entertainments, nor for Wyatt as a man with a lute. If these are songs, he said, why are there no contemporary musical settings for any of them? The earliest English lute music dates from 1540, long after most of these songs were written, and at this date (the years 1524-37) there are no instrumental tutors or books to learn from. Descriptions of courtiers accompanying themselves on the lute come later, from the reigns of Henry's children.[25] If Wyatt had

A Courtly Couple (*Hans Holbein the Younger*)

---

[24] Stevens, op. cit.

[25] Notable exceptions to this include Anne Boleyn, an accomplished musician on the harp, lute and rebec (*Memoirs of Viscount Chateaubriand*, quoted in Agnes Strickland, *Lives of the English Queens* – reprint, ed., 1972) and Henry VIII himself, whom even Prof. Stevens will allow as a proper troubadour courtier.

musical skill, how come John Leland, his eulogist, left it out of a list of Wyatt's attributes that stretched to include a ring he happened to own and the vigour of his beard? Wyatt may have been 'taught to sing a little and strum upon the lute as a courtly skill, but this is the most that can be offered for him and there is not evidence even of this'. If he sang at all, he simply pressed old tunes into service; but the possibility must be faced that all the references to lutes, singing and so on may be pure literary convention. In fact – to add to Stevens – if one had to assign a purpose to the presence of lutes in Wyatt's verse, it wouldn't be anything to do with music. Lutes in Wyatt are generally used to denote freedom of opinion. Here, a lute with broken strings means not 'disharmony', as the art historians have it, but enforced silence.

> *Blame not my lute for he must sound*[26]
> *Of this or that as liketh me.*
> *For lack of wit the lute is bound*
> *To give such tunes as pleaseth me.*
> *Though my songs be somewhat strange*
> *And speak such words as touch thy change*
> *Blame not my lute...*

> *... My lute and strings may not deny*
> *But as I strike they must obey.*
> *Break not them then so wrongfully*
> *But wreak thyself some wiser way.*
> *And though the songs which I indite*[27]
> *Do quit thy change with rightful spite*
> *Blame not my lute.*

> *Spite asketh spite and changing change*

[26] Wyatt, XCIV, in Rebholz, op. cit. For the sake of compression I have omitted the second and penultimate verses.
[27] indite: compose.

And falsed faith must needs be known.
The faults so great, the case so strange
Of right it must abroad be blown.
Then since that by thine own desert
My songs do tell how true thou art
  Blame not my lute...

Farewell, unknown, for though thou break
My strings in spite with great disdain
Yet have I found out for thy sake
Strings for to string my lute again.
And if perchance this foolish rhyme
Do make thee blush at any time
  Blame not my lute.

The point here is not that he has a lute, but that he won't be silenced. Of course, the declaration of candour is an illusion: with characteristic slipperiness he has revealed nothing of this 'case so strange' except the intent to speak of it.

This is a marvellous poem. It shows Wyatt at his most twinkling and playful. We can think of him holding the paper above his head and reading it out while a girl tries to snatch it away. And at the same time, there is real menace in it. Secrecy was the prerequisite of the courtly love relation, and in Wyatt's time the integration of women into the court made it a place where people were sometimes really in love, as well as pretending to be. For them, the games of courtly love were a perfect camouflage for real, illicit love, and a threat of disclosure put a gust of fear into them.

Take heed betime lest ye be spied.[28]
Your loving eyes you cannot hide.
At last the truth will sure be tried.

---

[28] Wyatt, CXVIII, in Rebholz, op. cit.

Detail of *The Ambassadors*, showing the lute with broken strings (*Hans Holbein the Younger*)

Therefore take heed!

For some there be of crafty kind,
Though you show no part of your mind,
Surely their eyes ye cannot blind.
Therefore take heed!

For in like case theirselves hath been
And thought right sure none had them seen.
But it was not as they did ween.[29]
Therefore take heed!

Although they be of diverse schools
And well can use all crafty tools,
At length they prove themselves but fools.

---

[29] ween: think, suppose.

Therefore take heed!

The queen's chamber, where the ladies were, was a small place in every sense. Everyone knew which of the young men who visited was suitor to whom, and what had been said among them. If a poem like this was read out,

> *Perdie, I said it not[30a]*
> *Nor never thought to do*
> *As well as I, ye wot*
> *I have no power thereto*

Everyone knew exactly who 'I' and 'ye' were, and what was the thing that had (or had not) been said.

It was the business of the young women to keep the atmosphere light by encouraging the (formal) attentions of more than one suitor; hence the persistent accusations of feminine inconstancy in these lyrics, which actually confirmed that nothing improper was going on. But sometimes the game became reality, endangering female virtue and careful marital strategies. A young woman in that situation who found Wyatt's 'lute' poem in her pew at mass, or tucked among her things, might feel like she'd got a dead fish in the mail. But the semi-public context of the pastime pulls its teeth: it becomes a tease, not a threat.

The manner of delivery changed the meaning. Their role in the games of the pastime removed the payload of sex or menace from poems with an otherwise dangerous intent. In a culture where dalliance and chastity clash by night, a ludic environment made things safer:

> *She sat and sewed that hath done me the wrong[30b]*
> *Whereof I plain and have done many a day,*
> *And whilst she heard my plaint in piteous song*

[30a] Wyatt, LXXVII; [30b] Wyatt XLI – in Rebholz, op. cit.

Wished my heart the sampler as it lay.
The blind master whom I have served so long,
Grudging to hear that he did hear her say,
Made her own weapon do her finger bleed
To feel if pricking were so good indeed.

If this is representative snapshot of sexual relations at court, it shows how important it was to restrict visiting hours and invigilate forgatherings of men and women. There is motiveless spite on the one side and vindictive rape-fantasy on the other. The tart young woman sticks her needle in repeatedly, wishing her sewing was her suitor's heart; in revenge, Love ('the blind master') shows her what 'pricking' feels like and lets Wyatt relish the prospect of the pricker pricked. The current of sexual frustration running under all these poems has carried its toxic burden of malice and distrust a bit too close to the surface. Luckily for everyone's reputation, a gelded reading was available in the context of the pastime. If Wyatt's pierced heart can be *either* his tender feelings *or* a heart-shaped cloth (a proper object for a needle), then we have two different sorts of poem in one: one of them is venomous and predatory, the other a joke. If the heart is a dummy, the poem fires a blank.

*   *   *   *

To conclude: in the world of these lyrics 'my heart' could be a real thing and 'my lute' a figure of speech. Abstraction and reality are intermingled. It is perhaps becoming clear that much of the fun of these poems, both in conception and execution, lay in the way they were hung on a double hinge, and could open onto very different prospects. They are like those puzzle-pictures produced in the 19th century, with unstable or animorphic images that change without moving, according to the viewer's focus. Is it an urn, or a pair of lovers? Is a courtly lyric a polite trifle or a red-raw exposure of the heart?

The company in the queen's chamber loved puns and riddles and they must have loved Wyatt, because he could really write this kind of poem. He swung on the gate, opening and closing. Today we require mutiny in art. Our highest and laziest term of praise is to call a thing subversive, and this has become the *sine qua non* of seriousness in art; to the extent that we impose it as a standard upon those artists of the past who had no conscious subversive tendencies at all, and whose own artistic impulse was to imitate their betters. So it might be hard for us to admire a mind that worked so beautifully upon a convention, as Wyatt's did, not subverting it but expanding it, bringing it on, showing us capabilities that it barely knew it had, and certainly not in English.

Wyatt's mind would naturally have had the allegorising tendency of his time, but he combined this with other less commonplace gifts that seem inherent in his character and were perfectly suited to bring out the best in the courtly convention. At a time when most writing was an exercise in dilation, he had a talent for compression that squeezed the small, abstract vocabulary of the courtly lyric till it bulged with implications. He was ironic at a time when sarcasm was the common instrument of wit. In a Wyatt poem, for example, the elements of the dream-vision (in which a man dreams of an amorously obliging lady) are ironically recast to produce a woman asleep, dreaming of the hurt she can do her lover. Nor was it lost on him that he, the writer of love poems, was doomed to repeated misfortune in the lover's month of May, and he underlined the point by setting it to a sonnet, as we shall see.

He was predisposed to think paradoxically, and take things hard. In his hands, the so-called 'Petrarchan contraries', the 'pleasant pain' and 'freezing heat' of Italian love poetry, swell up into titanic, irreconcilable forces that trap and pin the speaking persona, and stop him from doing anything to help himself. The predicament typically described by a Wyatt poem is one of paralysis:

> They flee from me that sometime did me seek[31]
> With naked foot stalking in my chamber.
> I have seen them gentle, tame, and meek
> That now are wild and do not remember
> That some time they put themself in danger
> To take bread at my hand; and now they range
> Busily seeking with a continual change.
>
> Thanked be fortune it hath been otherwise
> Twenty times better, but once in special
> In thin array after a pleasant guise,
> When her loose gown from her shoulders did fall
> And she me caught in her arms long and small,
> Therewithal sweetly did me kiss,
> And softly said, 'Dear heart, how like you this?'
>
> It was no dream: I lay broad waking.
> But all is turned thorough my gentleness
> Into a strange fashion of forsaking.
> And I have leave to go of her goodness
> And she also to use new-fangleness.
> But since that I so kindly am served
> I would fain know what she hath deserved.

Everyone notices the extreme passivity of Wyatt in this, his great anthology piece. People come and go, he just lies there. All this activity of quest and betrayal surges over him like rising and ebbing tides. He follows with his eyes. And while the poem has a trance-like quality, there is no suggestion of repose; he is more like one of those victims of botched anaesthesia who wake up

---

[31] Wyatt, LXXX, in Rebholz, op. cit.

under surgery, unable to move or signal their sentience while the surgeon continues to carve.

Wyatt wrote brilliantly about being stuck, and often seems to enjoy the opportunities for wit that a world of paralysing contradictions could bring, while deploring the predicament itself. He knew it brought out the best in him: 'I am of them whom plaint doth well content,'[32] he said, rather wittily. It inspired him to some of the most complete expressions of frustration ever written, like this characteristic lyric where paralysis grips the poem itself:

Such hap as I am happed in[33]
Hath never man of truth, I ween.
At me Fortune list to begin
To shew that never hath been seen –
A new kind of unhappiness.
And I cannot the thing I mean
Myself express.

Myself express my deadly pain,
That can I well if that might serve.
But why I have not help again,
That know I not unless I sterve[34]
For hunger still amidst my food –
So granted is that I deserve
To do me good.

To do me good what may prevail?
For I deserve and not desire
And still of cold I me bewail
And raked am in burning fire.
For though I have – such is my lot –

[32] Wyatt, LXXVI, in Rebholz, op. cit.
[33] Wyatt, LXXXVII, in Rebholz, op. cit.
[34] sterve: starve

> *In hand to help that I require,*
> *It helpeth not.*

There's no progress here, especially not for the reader. Each successive verse promises an explanation that never comes, because we are sent, for clarification, back to something we already don't understand, except as a pregnant indication of something unclear. The poem can't get anywhere and nor can we. I doubt there is anything so baffling in English letters between this and the 'explanatory prefaces', as those masterpieces of obfuscation are known, of Henry James's novels, which employ a similar technique. And perhaps for the same reason: it's not *supposed* to be informative. It's a poem about a secret.

> *And I cannot the thing I mean*
> *Myself express*

Only the knowledge of what 'hap', exactly, it is that Wyatt has fallen into can press its spring. People – some people – would know what that was; the rest wouldn't and would have, like us, to tap and knock at it in endless bafflement. And here we come to the other most salient characteristic of courtly lyrics: they were occasional poems, animated by circumstance. An epigram was a comment on the day's news, like a pocket cartoon, 'written on the wall', says Puttenham, or scratched on a stairwell, or slid into a gentlemanly hand to make a point about his particular concerns. When we think of a courtly lyric we must imagine it as a thing with latent energy, that lit up when the right social circuitry was connected. Reading them now, printed in books and solemnised with footnotes and prefaces, we are looking at something inert. Moreover – and it is good to remember this when thinking of the uses of these poems – when circumstances changed, they could animate the same poem in a different way. A poem after supper isn't like a cigar: it is not consumed. It can be brought out again for a different occasion, or a different set of participants, and made to reflect some other impossible love, or even some 'hap' that is nothing to do with love. So, to say a Wyatt poem is 'about' this or that occasion (even when we can say such a thing), is to miss the point of these lyrics, which was to adapt. A single lyric could be 'about' one thing and then another. As was said earlier, the way to bring them back to life is not to try to 'match' each lyric to an occasion, but to play the story of Wyatt's life behind them and see how often they change, as Wyatt would put it, their devise. And why.

*   *   *   *

Wyatt raised the stakes of the courtly game by writing poetry that sounded like he meant it. Poet-as-lover and lover-as-poet melt into one; a poet can mean it or not mean it, a recipient can take the suit as earnest or game, with the result that the sincerity of the verse itself becomes a central theme.

> *Madam, withouten many words*[35a]
> *Once I am sure you will or no.*
> *And if ye will then leave your bourds*[35b]
> *And use your wit and shew it so*

What do you say, yes or no? What do you mean by your words? *Show me how to take it.* There is something peremptory and exasperated in the tone, which is not quite that of a humble suitor. We have the impression that Wyatt, though always drawing his language from the certificated store of courtly utterances (*Madam*, withouten many words), has nevertheless made from those dry materials a scaffold to shin up and point his finger in her face. He gives a plausible impression of thwarted entitle-

---

[35a] Wyatt, XCVI, in Rebholz, op.cit. [35b] bourds: mockery, jokes.

ment, a position quite far removed from the traditional courtly posture of prostration in the mud.

One way of looking at this is as a reflection of social developments. Henry wanted ladies to fill his court, and this ambition assorted well with that of his servants to place their wives and daughters there. But after the years of civil war, not many of these were baronial magnates with the blood of royal dukedoms mingled in their veins, and their daughters were no grander than they. So, among Henry's queens' ladies there were Margarets and Besses and Annes who were well within the marital (as well as the physical) reach of some of the young men in Henry's train; though that choice was not theirs to make. Out of this dangerous situation came a poetry in which the possibility of getting lucky is ever-present, and often took the view that a suitor denied was to some extent a suitor *deprived* of his reasonable deserts. This idea never crossed Petrarch's mind. In Wyatt's lyrics, however, one finds plenty of joking and nudging about ladies who have succumbed out of frame, riddles about virgins who aren't, a depressingly cantankerous offering about an 'Old Mule' whom no one wants to ride any more (sometimes thought to be a hate-poem about Anne Boleyn)[36] and even a sonnet about a wet dream. All this implies licence: yet historians have awarded Henry's court low marks for harlotry in comparison with its European peers. It has been said that gluttony, not lust, was the vice of early Tudor choice. Henry himself had taken only two known mistresses[37] by the age of 30, and had managed to father a single illegitimate child: which was one fewer than Cardinal Wolsey and the same number as the papal nuncio who was sent to try his divorce. Against this, one might place the doubt expressed by the Spanish ambassador, in 1536: whether Jane Seymour, 'being an Englishwoman and having been long at court... would not hold it a sin to be

[36] Rebholz, VII, op. cit.
[37] They were Elizabeth Blount, mother of Henry's illegitimate son, Henry Fitzroy, Duke of Richmond, and Mary Boleyn, Anne's sister.

still a maid.' But foreign ambassadors often said such things about rival courts, in a similar spirit of mutual insult to the one that attributes foreign origins to venereal disease. And besides, by then Anne Boleyn had reigned and died, and it had become important for political and religious reasons to maintain the dogma of her whoredom and the licentiousness of her court, where Jane had been a lady-in-waiting.

As for Wyatt, his case is complicated, and obscured by the fact that none of his poems are dated. Even if we allow some of them to refer to actual love affairs, either his own or others', it is impossible (with a few notable exceptions) to extract from them the details of specific court amours. We do know that he repudiated his wife, Elizabeth Brooke, on grounds of her adultery in about 1525 or 1526. There was no divorce, but lasting bitterness for Wyatt. We know that he did not live a life of restraint thereafter. In 1542, the Spanish ambassador referred to him having loved 'two ladies'[38] since his wife; probably there were more intrigues than that. He allowed as much in a court of law, saying, 'I grant I do not profess chastity, but yet I use not abomination.' It seems likely that his status as a married, but single, man, made him something of a moral outsider in the sexual politics of the court. We know he took a serious mistress, Elizabeth Darrell, in about 1536 or 1537, and that she lived with him and bore him a child. And we know that he was associated with Anne Boleyn before her marriage, and that at the time of her condemnation for adultery, he was one of the men arrested in connection with her crimes.

[38] I am grateful to Dr Susan Brigden for this point.

CHAPTER FIVE

Was Thomas Wyatt Anne Boleyn's lover? This question has exercised both Wyatt and Boleyn scholars to the point of exhaustion. Once it was assumed that almost all Wyatt's lyrics were written to, for or about Anne; the twentieth century brought that number down to a handful, and modern scholars are, frankly, bored with the whole debate. The current entry for Wyatt in the *Oxford Dictionary of National Biography* concludes: 'Neither Wyatt's imprisonment nor his poetry indicates that he was a lover of Anne Boleyn.' This exasperation is understandable – the 'I' of Wyatt's lyrics is carefully devised to conceal identity and must not be assumed to mean himself – but severe. There is a small group of poems that Wyatt's editors have accepted as connected to Anne, and in the context of other evidence for the relationship, which we will look at now, they bring a fitful luminosity to bear on the question.

*   *   *   *

The story most often rehearsed in connection with Anne and Wyatt is the one, ponderously set down by Wyatt's grandson, George,[1] relating how Wyatt made overtures to Anne when she arrived at court from France, and incurred the jealousy of the king. In this story Wyatt, 'coming to behold the sudden

---

[1] George Wyatt, in 'The Life of Anne Boleigne', in S. W. Singer (ed.), *The Life of Cardinal Wolsey* (1825).

appearance of this new beauty' in their midst, and enraptured by her 'witty and graceful speech' even more than by her appearance, made his advances, but she kept her distance from him as a married man. She did not altogether scorn him, however, having noticed 'the general favour and good-will she perceived all men to bear him, which might the (sic) rather occasion others to turn their looks to that which a man of his worth was brought to gaze at in her, as indeed there after happened'.

Anne Boleyn (*artist unknown*)

One day, continues our narrator, when Wyatt was talking to Anne 'as she was earnest at work, in sporting wise [he] caught from her a certain small jewel hanging by a lace out of her pocket, which he thrust into his bosom.' But he was not her only suitor, for the king, meanwhile, whom no one knew to be in serious pursuit, had secretly determined to 'win her by treaty of marriage, and in this talk took from her a ring, and that ware upon his little finger; and yet with all this such a secrecy was carried, and on her part so wisely, as none or very few esteemed this other than an ordinary course of dalliance.'

Some days later, they are all out playing bowls – Henry's brother-in-law the Duke of Suffolk, Sir Francis Bryan, Wyatt ('the Knight') and the king, watched by assorted ladies. The king claims the winning cast. Wyatt demurs, as it doesn't look like a win to him. 'And yet still [the king] pointing with his finger whereon he ware her ring, replied often it was his, and especially to the Knight he said, "Wyat I tell thee it is mine," smiling upon him withal.' Wyatt takes the hint but misjudges the situation: after a characteristically prudent pause to assess the king's mood as 'bent to pleasure', he plumps for a bit of badinage: 'The Knight replied, "and if it may like your Majestie to give me leave to measure it, I hope it will be mine." And withal took from his neck the lace whereat hung the tablet, and therewith stooped to measure the cast, which the king espying knew, and had seen her wear, and therewithal sporn'd[2] away the bowl, and said, "It may be so, but then I am deceived."'

This is a pleasant story. One imagines a man in a doublet a short way off with his ankle on his knee, strumming a little background lute music. George Wyatt took it down in Elizabeth's reign from Anne Gainsford, one of Anne's ladies-in-waiting, who would by then have been a very old woman. We can see that her memory isn't perfect: the foreshortening of time has erased the four years or so between Anne's first arrival at court in 1522 and the king's campaign to court her. She was all the same an eye witness, and a number of interesting and credible things show up in her recollection. We see courtly love acting as camouflage for real love (everyone thought the king's ring was 'in the ordinary course of dalliance'), and that

[2] sporn: kick away in disdain, spurn.

Anne Boleyn is remembered as quite an operator, calculating the value of each courtier's attentions and keeping a strategic silence while she reeled in the king.

It is not an idle story, however: it's a working story with a serious purpose. After she died, Anne Boleyn vanished as a person, and her reputation became a cipher for the excellence or evil of the reformed church which she had championed in life. This little story is a weapon in the battle against the forces of recusant Catholicism in the later 16th century. Its author, George Wyatt, was the son of Wyatt's only son, also Sir Thomas, who was executed under Catholic Queen Mary as a rebel and a traitor. Much of George's life was spent in trying to make the Wyatt family acceptable to her (Protestant) successor, Queen Elizabeth, and his book, the *Life of Anne Boleigne* was part of that campaign. It was neither well done nor widely read, but it was a countersqueak, at any rate, to the blasts of Catholic propaganda which had always blamed Anne Boleyn for the English Reformation and attacked the new Church by impugning her personal morals. It was done at the suggestion of Elizabeth's Archbishop of Canterbury.

Scurrilous rumours about Anne continued to circulate. Those that had surfaced in Mary's reign were invigorated in that of Elizabeth by the recusant Nicholas Sanders, whose book on the subject, *De Origine ac Progressu Schismaticis Anglicani Liber* (*A Book Concerning the Rise and Growth of the Anglican Schism*, published in Cologne in 1585) went into many editions and was smuggled into Protestant England. In 1683 a French translation appeared. The thought that this book could jump, like some mutating influenza, into the non-Latin reading population so alarmed Gilbert Burnet, the then Bishop of Salisbury, that he was driven to attempt the first fully documented history in our language – his *History of the Reformation* – for the sole purpose of exposing Sanders's calumnies. Enlisting the help of the Master of the Rolls, he dug out the old documents and brought the might of their proofs down upon Sanders, refuting him line by line and statement by statement in 123 points of fact.

Point number four was this: 'when she came over into England, Sir Thomas Wiat was admitted to base privies with her, and offered to the king and his council, that he himself should with his own eyes see it'. This explains the community of interest between George Wyatt and Elizabeth's archbishop: Wyatt wanted to clear his grandfather from accusations involving the present queen's mother, and the archbishop wanted to protect the Protestant Church, still in its vulnerable infancy under Elizabeth.

The original source for this story was not Sanders, who embellished it, but another Catholic propagandist (confusingly, also called Nicholas), Nicholas Harpsfield, whose manuscript, supposedly produced in Mary's reign, was hidden in the house of one Cartar, a Catholic printer, and began to circulate after Cartar was hanged in 1584. Harpsfield had it from a merchant from Lucca called Antony Bonvisi. Nobody knows who Bonvisi had it from. He was much around London from the 1520s and well connected with the court, though far from neutral on the subject of Anne, being a close and dear friend of both Thomas More and Bishop Fisher, the senior martyrs of the king's divorce.

Harpsfield's story tells how Wyatt approached the king in private to warn him off Anne Boleyn, saying:

Sir, I am credibly informed that your grace intended to take to your wife the lady Anne Bulleyn, wherein I beseech your grace to be well advised what you do, for she is not meet to be coupled with your grace, her conversation[3] hath been so loose and base; which thing I know not so much by hear-say as by my own experience as one that

[3] fornication.

have had my carnal pleasure with her.[4]

Harpsfield reports that the king was 'something astonied' to hear this, and so he might be. However, Henry recovers himself enough to thank Wyatt as an 'honest man', and tells him to keep quiet and sends him away.

The story became more elaborate when Sanders retold it, and less becoming to Wyatt: in this version, Wyatt realises the king is planning to marry Anne and, cravenly fearing 'that his own life might be imperilled' if the truth of his affair with her gets out, goes to the king's council and tells the entire assembly 'that he had sinned with Anne, not imagining that the king would ever make her his wife'. The council pass this information to the king, who frankly disbelieves it. Sanders continues the story:

Thomas Wyatt was very angry when he heard that the king would not believe him, and so he said to some members of the council that he would put it in the king's power to see with his own eyes the truth of the story, if he would consent to test it, for Anne Boleyn was passionately in love with Wyatt. Charles Brandon the Duke of Suffolk repeated the words of Wyatt to the king, who answered that he had no wish to see anything of the kind – Wyatt was a bold villain, not to be trusted... The king told everything to Anne Boleyn, who shunned Wyatt; and that avoidance of him saved his life, for he too might have suffered death with the others when Anne's incest and adultery were detected.[5]

Not everyone has disbelieved this story. Until very recently people were prepared to believe the worst of Anne's character,

[4] Nicholas Harpsfield, *A Treatise on the Pretended Divorce between Henry VIII and Catherine of Aragon*, ed. N. Pocock (1878).
[5] Nicholas Sanders, *Rise and Growth of the Anglican Schism* (1877).

and, in the absence of conclusive evidence either way, may do again. Wyatt's editor and biographer, Kenneth Muir, concluded that this smoke proceeded from an actual fire of some sort; so did G.W. Bernard as recently as last year. But Eric Ives, Anne's most comprehensive biographer, disagrees: 'the very notion that Henry would overlook Anne's sleeping with Wyatt at the same time as she was holding him at arms' length is ludicrous.'[6] George Wyatt[7] and Bishop Burnet had both reached the same conclusion before him: evidently finding no documents relating to this incident, Burnet reasonably argued the unlikelihood 'that a king could pursue a design for seven years together, of marrying a woman of so scandalous a life, and so disagreeable a person; and that [Henry] who was always in the other extreme of jealousy, did never try out these reports, and would not so much as see what Wiat informed?'

Despite Burnet's mighty refutation, the story refused to lie down. It appears in its most spectacular form in the undated Spanish document, known as the *Cronica del Rey Enrico*, said in the next century to have been found 'amongst the papers left in the house of a Spanish merchant in London by a Valencian lawyer, or man of letters, who had gone to England with Queen Catherine of Aragon'. The *Cronica* was much copied (in Spanish) at the time of its first appearance, but Burnet does not seem to have known about it. When it was published in English in the 19th century, the editor (writing for the Catholic cause) presented it, yet again, as triumphant proof of everything that Catholics had suspected and Protestants denied about Anne's conduct for 350 years.

As a documentary resource, the *Cronica* has a strange relationship with the fastidious historians of our own time. Generally held as unreliable, it nevertheless turns up here and

---

[6] Ives, *The Life and Death of Anne Boleyn*, op. cit.
[7] George Wyatt, 'The Defence of the Sir Thomas Wyatts', in *The Papers of George Wyatt*, ed. D.M. Loades, Royal Historical Society, Camden Fourth Series (1968). Loades suggests this essay is not the work of George Wyatt himself but of a kinsman, working with his sources.

there in even the most scrupulously documented histories, when there is no other support to be had. The trouble with it is its intensely relaxed attitude to historical facts. The author was said to be a Spanish lawyer or 'man of letters', but he is most unlikely to have been either of these as he is quite illiterate, dates nothing, gets almost everything utterly wrong (he puts the king's fourth and fifth wives in the wrong order; gets the wrong date for the reign's greatest crisis, the northern uprising of 1536) and seems not to know the difference between a credible anecdote and a saucy episode from *The Decameron* with the names changed: as we will see. He may have been a Spanish merchant. Whoever he was, he was a witness to events in Henry's reign, and he did somehow have access to detailed information about Thomas Wyatt, in particular, that he could have obtained only through personal contacts. He was friendly with the nephew of Thomas Cromwell, the king's chief minister from 1534, and possibly with Wyatt's son, also Thomas; his account of Wyatt's close relations with Cromwell are accurate. It is now thought that his word on specific events, such as the execution of Anne Boleyn (at which he claimed to be the only foreigner present), is not as worthless as formerly supposed.

The *Cronica del Rey*'s version of the Wyatt story has a different premise from the others. It begins much later than the others, with Wyatt in prison, as he indeed was, at the time of Anne's fall in May 1536. Anne's 'paramours' have been executed and she is awaiting execution in another part of the Tower. Fearing for himself, Wyatt writes to his sovereign to remind him of their conversation before the king's second marriage. Henry may recall, writes Wyatt, that he had asked Wyatt's opinion about his proposed marriage to Anne, and Wyatt had counselled against. Then, the king refused to ask for details and banished him for two years. Wyatt now wants to tell him in writing the reasons for his advice 'which I could not tell you then by word of mouth'. They are as follows:

It happened that one day when the lady Anne's father and mother were in the court eight miles from Greenwich, where, as everybody knows, they had taken up residence, that night I took horse and went there. I arrived when Anne Boleyn was in bed, and went up to her chamber. When she saw me she said: 'Lord! Master Wyatt, what are you doing here at such a late hour?' I replied: 'Lady, this heart of mine, which is so tormented, has been yours for so long that for love of you it has brought me here into your presence, thinking to receive consolation from the one who for so long has caused it such suffering.' And I went up to her as she lay in bed and kissed her, and she lay still and said nothing. I touched her breasts, and she lay still, and even when I took liberties lower down she likewise said nothing.[8]

Understandably encouraged by this reception, Wyatt starts to undress, but just then they are interrupted by a commotion overhead. Anne gets up and vanishes up a secret staircase behind her bed, not to return for an hour, and when she does return 'she would not let me approach her'. Pursuing this mystery in his mind, Wyatt remembers a story about an Italian gentleman in a similar situation, who followed the lady upstairs only to find her being pleasured by a groom. This, he concludes, was evidently his own case. 'And I tell your Majesty that within a week I had my way with her, and if your Majesty… had permitted me to speak, I should have told you what I now write.'

This is such nonsense that one hardly knows where to begin. The only remotely plausible new element is that of Wyatt's writing some kind of letter to the king from prison, which, as will appear, he may well have. Otherwise, it is of interest mainly to show what lubricious stories circulated about Anne in the aftermath of her death, and how the Catholic apologists were

<hr>

[8] *Chronicle of King Henry VIII of England*, ed. M.A.S. Hume, (1889).

happy to suspend every faculty of reason – even centuries later – to think the worst of her. However, as with the other versions, it does prompt the question, where did these stories come from? And, *why Sir Thomas Wyatt*? If the sole purpose of the stories was to discredit Anne, there were at the time of their writing perfectly good dead men – no fewer than five 'lovers' executed along with her, with their guilt apparently proven – to furnish a made-up tale. If someone was needed with a proven interest in Anne before her marriage, then the young Henry Percy, son of the Earl of Northumberland, would have done better, as he was known at court to have wanted to marry her, and died soon after her execution. There has been some suggestion that the stories were a kind of Henrician 'aetiologue' invented to explain the otherwise inexplicable, in this case, why Wyatt should have escaped the fate of the other men arrested along with him in 1536. But again, his situation wasn't quite unique. There was one other man in a similar case. So we need to ask where else the story could have originated.

There is in fact one document that relates to this incident, a letter of 1530 from the Spanish ambassador, Eustace Chapuys, to his master Charles V.

> It is now a long time since the Duke of Suffolk has been at court. Some say he has been exiled for some time owing to his having denounced to the king a criminal connection of the lady [i.e. Anne] with a gentleman of the court on such suspicion. This time the gentleman had been sent away at the request of the lady herself, who feigned to be very angry with him, and it was the king who had to intercede for his return.

That's the English translation. We can see shared elements in this and Sanders's story (see p94): the Duke of Suffolk as the whistle-blower, the resulting coldness of Anne towards Wyatt.

But the French of the original document reads slightly differently; here,

> ...[Suffolk] revealed to the King that the lady had been discovered in the act[9] with a gentleman of the court, who had *already once been banished under suspicion, and this last time* we saw him exiled from the court at the request of the lady.

When Wyatt's and Anne's biographers have looked at this matter, trying to establish if the unnamed gentleman could be Wyatt, some have mentioned that Wyatt cleared out of England at extremely short notice in January 1527, and some that he went to Calais for two years in 1528, but they have tended to elide these into a single exeat. The ambassador, however, clearly alludes to two separate occasions. This lends support to the Wyatt identification. When one adds to this Wyatt's own disclosure (in 1541) that the Duke of Suffolk hated him and had always tried to make trouble for him,[10] and the well-known animosity of Suffolk's wife (the king's sister) to Anne, we begin to see it as a distinct possibility that the Sanders story began here.

Now we must turn to the poems, always with the caveat that they are poems and not legal documents. Of the handful of Wyatt's poems that relate directly to Anne Boleyn, only three or four are informative and none are dated. Some refer to actual events, but that only gives an earliest date of composition: despite Wyatt's present tense and the seeming freshness of his feelings, we can't assume he wrote his poems punctually, like diary entries, though he may have.

An epigram of Wyatt's is thought to allude to the autumn of

---

[9] Spanish Calendar, May 10, 1530. The French original has '*trouvé au delict avec un gentilhomme de court, qui desia en avoit autrefois est chassé par suspicion, est ceste dernier foys lon la voit aussy vuyde a instance de ladite dame*'.

[10] Thomas Wyatt, 'Defence', in Kenneth Muir (ed.), *The Life and Letters of Sir Thomas Wyatt* (Liverpool, 1953).

1532, when Henry VIII and Anne Boleyn, soon to be his wife, made an official visit to Francis I at Calais. It implies that Wyatt was a servitor in Anne's train. That would be perfectly possible even if he were still out of favour with Anne, as her attendants were not a matter of personal preference, and Wyatt's experience of Calais would recommend him for a place. But it seems he was restored to her good graces, as a letter of the following year describes him as one 'whom she loves very much'.

If so, the feeling wasn't mutual.

> *Sometime I fled the fire that me brent*[11]
> *By sea, by land, by water, and by wind,*
> *And now I follow the coals that be quent*[12]
> *From Dover to Calais, against my mind.*
> *Lo, how desire is both sprung and spent!*
> *And he may see that whilom was so blind*
> *And all his labour now he laugh to scorn,*
> *Meshed in the briers that erst was all to-torn.*

This will reward attention. The first quatrain presents one of those intercrossings of flight and pursuit that Wyatt loved, hinging on his sense of gloomy irony. It manages to say a lot. Once he was in love and had to flee – for whatever reason – the 'fire' resulting from this love. Now he is no longer in love with this person (hence, the quenched coals); but such is his luck that now, when he doesn't love her, he has to follow her to Calais. A typical Wyattian predicament.

In view of the historical situation, there is no reason to think this is not Anne; indeed, it is hard to know what other woman would oblige him to follow her to Calais, especially considering the subordinate connotation of the word 'follow' (as in foot-follower). We will understand the poem better if we take the

[11] Wyatt, LV, in Rebholz, op. cit. (brent: burned)
[12] quent: quenched

whole of the fourth line, 'From Dover to Calais, against my mind' as applying to everything that precedes it: that is, in *both* cases he had to go to Calais, and in *neither* case did he want to go there – once because he loved Anne Boleyn and now, paradoxically, because he doesn't. If we accept this reading (as stronger, and more typical of the poet's latinesque compression) then it does follow the narrative of Chapuys' letter: Wyatt had cleared off to Calais in 1528 to get away from Anne Boleyn, whom he still then loved.

The next quatrain expands on the matter: he marvels at his change of heart and, not very gallantly, at his present clearsightedness. The interesting line is the last one: 'meshed in the briers that erst was all to-torn.' Wyatt sees himself as one whom briars once tore apart, but now 'meshed' (enclosed, netted, intertwined) among them. The same briars that tore him now trap him and keep him safe, if, perhaps, compromised. The movement mirrors that of the first quatrain, from fleeing to following, from wildness to docility, from danger to an ignoble safety, and the line conveys the same impression, of exchanging one unsatisfactory state for another. The line acquires a more specific biographical significance if the 'briars' are the emblematic thorns of the Tudor rose, once sharpened against him, now sheltering (and a Tudor courtier wouldn't have far to strain for this conceit, since everything in his view was clambered with roses) – for that would indicate that an angry king, as well as Anne, had had a role in Wyatt's departure for Calais.

If this poem is a treatment of the emotional and political dangers of Wyatt's involvement with Anne, it nevertheless has nothing explicit to say about the nature of that involvement. Does any? There is another poem – a sonnet written in the after years of Anne – that may. It begins with a catalogue of the usual amorous symptoms – sudden paleness, sighing, dawdling one minute, hurrying the next, and wondering if they could be signs of love. If they are, he is in love again. And with whom?

> *If thou ask whom, sure since I did refrain*[13]
> *Brunet that set my wealth*[14] *in such a roar,*
> *Th'unfeigned cheer of Phyllis hath the place*
> *That Brunet had. She hath and ever shall.*
> *She from myself now hath me in her grace.*

The key to this poem is the identity of the women. 'Phyllis' – meaning country girl – here is almost certainly Elizabeth Darrell, daughter of Sir Edward Darrell of Littlecote, Wilts, who became Wyatt's mistress in about 1537, bore him a son, lived in his house, and became a permanent part of his establishment. She was blonde-haired, as we know from other poems, and appears in instructive contrast to the troublemaking 'Brunet' of Wyatt's past. 'Brunet' is Anne Boleyn. There can be very little doubt about this, because Wyatt originally wrote:

> *If thou ask whom, sure since I did refrain*
> **Her that did set our country in a roar,**

Then he thought better of it and amended the line in his own handwriting. In place of the too-explicit reference he put one word 'Brunet' – just enough to invoke Anne, but only to those people at court who knew both that Wyatt was the author of this poem *and* that he had once pursued Anne Boleyn.

If Brunet was Anne, what can we learn from this transfer of affection? Not much, if we think that Wyatt's 'love' for Anne Boleyn here is merely the service of a courtier due to a great lady. There are a number of reasons to think it isn't. To begin with, the poet clearly nominates this 'Phyllis' as the first woman he has loved since he 'refrained' – a word, by the way, with pow-

---

[13] Wyatt, XXVIII, in Rebholz, op. cit.
[14] wealth: not pecuniary but meaning 'my state, my wellbeing'.

erful connotations of backing off – Anne Boleyn. Anne's past tense, and the impudent tone he takes mean she must be dead, dating the poem to sometime after May 1536 – at least ten years after Wyatt's first interest in Anne, which pre-dated, as we will remember, that of the king. This means that in spite of his reputation for promiscuity, he has reached back ten years to find an experience of comparable intensity.

One could argue that this is a function of Anne's high position, which would make her the pattern mistress for every courtier and the natural comparison of resort for one wanting to express a high-flown love and pass a compliment at the same time. But Anne's death and disgrace take away any motive of that sort. Secondly, the poet is at pains to emphasise two things: the difference between the two women – the one who makes him happy and the one who didn't – and the sameness of his feelings. This is what drives the poem. Dealing with the differences, Wyatt does something very witty and subtle, and only possible if your readers are your cronies and know all the people involved: he makes the reader supply half the information. He sets up a system of opposites by calling one woman 'Brunet' and relying on his readers to know (as they would) that his current mistress is blonde. Then he calls his new mistress 'Phyllis' (country girl), and leaves the reader, accordingly, to supply the opposing quality in Anne: that she was a creature of high urbanity and sophistication, as she was. So when he speaks of Phyllis's 'unfeigned cheer' he manages to communicate, without saying so, that there was something contrived and disingenuous about Anne: the very same quality Anne Gainsford remembered all those years later, talking to George Wyatt about Henry and the game of bowls. Coming to similarities, he is simple and emphatic. Now:

Phyllis hath the place
That Brunet had. She hath and ever shall.

It is the same place. And what place is that, exactly? This is our question. Wyatt goes into detail:

> *She from myself now hath me in her grace.*
> *She hath in hand my wit, my will and all.*

Phyllis's place – the place that Brunet had – is that of one who fully condescends to take him, and holds his wit and his 'will' in her hand. What does that mean? Among other things, that she is his mistress. Wyatt loved to invest words with as many meanings as possible and with this one, 'will', his considerable range includes something near the top of the 'carnal desire' spectrum, perhaps the inhabitant of his codpiece. Shakespeare certainly used the word for male and female sexual organs, so the definition has often been thought to originate with him; but Shakespeare has the credit for many words and usages that pre-date him. If words were patent inventions, like light bulbs or telephones, there would be a crowd of angry petitioners at the offices of the *OED*, demanding recognition for ancestral innovators. The conjunction of Wyatt's 'will' and his mistress's hand deliberately invites a salacious construction; nor would a poet of this date find anything inept or boorish about letting a bawdy pun obtrude on a solemn protestation. The present author's conjecture is that Wyatt – neither cloth-eared nor naïve – was fully conscious of the implication, and also of what, by extension, it suggested about his relations with 'Brunet' – so much so that later, when he was in trouble, he changed the line and buried the connection.

All conclusions drawn from these equivocal, ambiguous lyrics must be at best conjectural. All they can do is lend their suggestiveness to a story that, taken in all, shows the Anne/Wyatt connection as, at the very least, much warmer and more dangerous to Wyatt than the courtly exchange of trinkets of Anne Gainsford's account. The one thing, however, that we must remember when considering the evidence of the poems, is that Wyatt was never clumsy or approximate with language. He didn't bung in words as makeweights; he used them with exquisite consideration for everything they could achieve for him, in all their potential meanings. He prided himself on his verbal discrimination. It would be what he reached for to save his own life, and his most notable diplomatic achievement was to come about through the careful deployment of a single word. But those things came later. Now we must pick up the chronological thread where we began, at the time around 1526 or 1527, when Wyatt was a married but unattached young man and Anne Boleyn a new beauty at court.

*   *   *   *

It will have been noticed that there is uncertainty surrounding the dates in this narrative of Henry, Wyatt and Anne. That is because there is no scholarly consensus about the chronology of the king and Anne's affair. The issue was purposely obscured at the time by the requirements of his divorce suit. It was crucial to the success of this enterprise that his involvement with Anne be seen to post-date his decision to divorce his wife, which he announced to her in the summer of 1527. Protestant historians have emphasised this order of events, while Catholics have tended to incriminate Anne in the decision. Even in our own secular times, titans of Boleyn scholarship stand opposed. David Starkey, for example, has Henry in pursuit of Anne since the *Chasteau Blanche* of January 1525, and committed to marriage with Anne by the new year of 1526/7. (In this narrative, desire for the Boleyn marriage was the driving force of the divorce.) Eric Ives, on the other hand, prefers the summer of 1527 for the date of this fateful decision – a date also often suggested for the composition of the most famous of Wyatt's 'Anne' poems, and the last to be discussed in this chapter.

One reason for dating this poem (which we will read in a moment) to 1527 was its distinctive form. It was a sonnet. Sonnets were Italian, goes the argument, and Wyatt, famously the first Englishman to write one, went to Italy for the first time in 1527. From here he 'brought back' Italian poetry – that is, he began to study and experiment with Italian metrical forms such as the eight-line *strambotto* and *terza rima*, as well as the Petrarchan sonnet which will always be associated with his name. He also acquired a taste for Petrarch's ingenious ambiguities and dense allusions – a feature of Italian poetry that could be applied even in forms of non-Italian origin.

It may be due to England's later successes in global exploration that Wyatt's poetic discoveries in Italy ('bringing back Italian poetry') have attained an expeditionary flourish: as though he had flushed the sonnet into a bison-trap and displayed it in the Crystal Palace to crowds of apprehensive ticket-holders, draped in the Union Jack. There's even a rival narrative about Chaucer beating him to it, reminiscent of Burton and Speke.

In fact, 16th-century Europeans could acquire Italian literature without the need to mount an expedition. It is possible that Wyatt, with his connections, had seen collections of Petrarch's *rime* and Serafino d'Aquilano's *strambotti* before he went to Italy – perhaps in Paris, where their innovations had already enraptured all the court poets. Nevertheless, it remained an elevated and rarefied taste throughout Henry's reign, and was evidently hard to supply. In 1530 we find an English diplomat badgering Thomas Cromwell to lend him his volume of Petrarch and 'make me a good Italian'. So Wyatt may really have drawn England's first sonnets out of a book he got in Italy: Vellutello's edition of Petrarch. It was the most popular edition of the 16th century and published in 1525 in Venice – the ultimate destination of Wyatt's first important diplomatic mission.

Wyatt's departure in January 1527 may, as we have discussed, have been precipitated by friction between himself and the king over Anne Boleyn– the same circumstances, so it is thought, to germinate his most famous sonnet:

> Whoso list to hunt, I know where is an hind,[15]
> But as for me, helas, I may no more.
> The vain travail hath wearied me so sore,
> I am of them that farthest cometh behind.
> Yet may I by no means my wearied mind
> Draw from the deer, but as she fleeth afore
> Fainting I follow. I leave off therefore
> Sithens in a net I seek to hold the wind.
> Who list her hunt, I put him out of doubt,
> As well as I may spend his time in vain.
> And graven with diamonds in letters plain
> There is written her fair neck round about:
> Noli me tangere for Caesar's I am
> And wild for to hold though I seem tame.

There is a Petrarchan sonnet behind this,[16] but so unlike that the most cursory comparison with Wyatt's 'translation' shows up his preoccupations as though under infra-red. Petrarch's sonnet opens when a mystical white, golden-horned deer materialises at the confluence of two rivers. The vision inspires the poet to 'leave every task' and follow her in reverent solitude, as one might follow Christ. The deer reveals to him her collar on which is written, in topazes and diamonds – the emblems of chastity and steadfastness – 'noli me tangere (touch me not: the words of the risen Christ to Mary Magdalene when she saw him by his empty grave and reached for him). It has pleased my Caesar (i.e. God) to make me free.'

The poet follows her until he falls into the river and the

---

[15] Wyatt, XI, in Rebholz, op. cit.
[16] 'Una candida cerva sopra l'erba', in Robert M. Durling (ed.), Petrarch's Lyric Poems, (Harvard University Press, 1979).

mystical deer vanishes.

Wyatt's version is very different. His poem is about hunting, sex and property. It takes place in a royal hunting park, and Petrarch's deer is now a sexual quarry, almost certainly Anne Boleyn, drawing a wide field of competing pursuers behind her. There is at first nothing remotely mystical about this quadruped or what it stands for: passed through Wyatt's hands, an emblem shimmering with Christian symbolism emerges as a deer, and a woman, both unmistakeably real and living under systems of Tudor game laws and royal prerogatives. The diamond collar she wears is now prescriptive, not emblematic, turned into a real necklace with a clasp that kingly fingers can fumble, and instead of saying she is free, it says she belongs to the king (Caesar). Where Petrarch follows his deer in a state of illuminated wonder, we find Wyatt in his customary pose of resentful defeat, unable to go on, unable to give up. As the field with all its hullabaloo passes over him and away, his mind is in helpless pursuit. The revelation of the collar is a 'no trespassing' sign.

The strangest thing about this poem is the burden of its last two lines. The words on the collar – '*Noli me tangere*, for Caesar's I am' – are adapted from alleged inscriptions on the collars of Caesar's hounds. But for Wyatt they combine two famous biblical quotations: the 'touch me not' of the risen Christ to Mary Magdalene, and Christ's budgetary policy in Matthew 22, advising men to 'Render unto Caesar those things that are Caesar's' (and to God those things that are God's). The first half of the line allows Petrarch's Christian allegory to suddenly break the surface. The figure of the risen, renewed Christ flickers in the eyes of the deer-woman, immediately followed by the words 'for Caesar's I am'.

This matter – of exactly what things belonged to England's Caesar, and how much he could legislate for spiritual matters – was an issue of pre-eminent concern in the first convulsions of the English Reformation, and the one for which More and Fisher were to die. Read like this, the lines elide Anne Boleyn and the Church into a single entity belonging to the king. This allows an interpretation something like this:

I am the new Church. Do not touch me, for I belong to the king.

Solomon and the Queen of Sheba (*Hans Holbein the Younger*)

If these lines contain, as they seem to with the hindsight of history, a coded reference to the role of Anne Boleyn in the split of the English Church from Rome, it would make this an important piece of reformation literature, and the literary companion-piece to Holbein's audacious depiction of Solomon and the Queen of Sheba, thought to show, by a similar process of overlaid analogies, the very same thing: Anne Boleyn identified with Henry VIII's new Church.[17] It would also mean redating the poem from around 1526 or 1527, when Henry's interest in Anne began to be known in court, to some time after 1532, because the king was not 'Supreme Head of the Church of England' until then, and the question of his authority over the Church had not arisen. However, the later date would explain two scholarly puzzles. In the first place, it shows an extraordinary level of technical accomplishment for a work which, if the usual dates are applied, would be among the first sonnets that Wyatt – notorious for his metrical clumsiness in the longer line – attempted. In the second, there is the difficulty in reconciling a date around 1526-7 with the very high probability that Wyatt took his interpretation from a commentary that appeared only in 1533.[18] It was the first to advance the theory that Petrarch's deer could be a courtly lady pursued by suitors, but protected from molestation by Caesar's laws of marriage. In 1533, both Anne and her Church were legally bound to Henry.

[17] See Eric Ives, 'The Queen and The Painters', *Apollo*, 140 (July, 1994).
[18] Petrarch's vernacular poems were first printed in 1470. In the later 15th and 16th centuries, many editors and commentators began to interpret his often obscure verses. Their commentaries were frequently printed in the margins of the text, making their influence hard to elude. Close studies have shown that Wyatt consulted them for help when he was making his own translations. The most popular commentary of his time was Allessandro Vellutello's, published in 1525; but the commentary with similarities to Wyatt's "Whoso list" was written by Andrea Gesualdo and printed in 1533. There is not the smallest chance that Gesualdo was following Wyatt.

CHAPTER SIX

Wyatt's departure for Venice was a strangely precipitate affair. In the first days of January in 1527, he stepped into a boat on the Thames. There he got into conversation with a fellow passenger who was just setting off from London for some foreign destination. And where are you going? asked Wyatt. 'To Italy, for the king,' answered the man. Wyatt said, 'And I, if you please, will ask leave, and get money, and go with you.' 'No man more welcome,' was the reply. And Wyatt went to his father to get the money and the permission, and off he went. He was eager to get out of England.

The passenger's name was John Russell. He was 41 and an experienced diplomat, and another whose success had derived from his language skills. The tide of Russell's affairs had, quite literally, been taken at the flood one night in 1506, when a storm washed Philip, Archduke of Austria's ship onto the Dorset coast at Melcombe Regis. The young Russell, a kinsman of the house where Philip was hastily lodged, and a rare French speaker in that district, was sent for in a panic to give the archduke some company. This slender opportunity was not lost on Russell. He made himself so acceptable to the archduke that he ended up accompanying him to the English court, then at Windsor; and once he was there, he throve. He survived into Edward VI's reign and died as Earl of Bedford, enriched 'beyond all precedent' as one historian has put it, with abbey lands.

The circumstances that sent him to Rome in 1527 were these: in March 1526, the French king, Francis I, came to the end of

13 months of confinement as the prisoner of war of Charles V. The terms of his release were extravagantly disagreeable, and included the surrender of Burgundy and of French claims to the Italian lands that continued to obsess him. Nevertheless, he promised to honour them on his word as a prince and a knight, supplemented only with the provision of both his sons as hostages in his place. Father and sons embraced on a pontoon tethered halfway across the river Bidassoa, then the sons were handed over to the Spaniards and Francis returned to his own country. As soon as he was back in France, he began to look for a way out of his promise, and, luckily, found Henry and Wolsey pressing eagerly for an alliance in the name of universal peace.

Their last attempt at universal peace had occurred the previous year, when they had tried to invade a kingless France in concert with Charles V. This was Henry's final go at becoming King

John Russell, 1st Earl of Bedford (*Hans Holbein the Younger*)

of France, and it had foundered on Charles's lack of enthusiasm for the project. Now he and Wolsey decided that Charles had become too powerful, and began to look to France as a possible ally. They encouraged Francis to renege on his promises to Charles and join an anti-imperial league of Italian states, as counterweight to imperial power in Europe. This Francis had done 'in the name of Italian liberty'; but the pope, Clement VII, whose presence in the league was crucial to its effectiveness, had started to vacillate under pressure from Charles's imperial troops, now menacing him from the north. At the end of 1526, Clement began to lurch towards an imperial alliance: hence the dispatch of John Russell to Italy. Russell had with him 25,000 crowns of Henry's money to stop the pope from abandoning the league. After that, he was to go on to Venice for further negotiations.

There may have been a second motive for Henry's bribe, perhaps the same as Wyatt's motive for such a hurried departure: namely, Henry's relationship with Anne Boleyn. If this, as David Starkey maintains, had secretly turned into a commitment of marriage at the end of December (six days before Russell's departure), then Henry would have a new reason to fear the pope's defection to Charles. He needed the pope to annul his first marriage. Charles was his wife's nephew. As for Wyatt, he would have become one of the earliest auxiliaries to the king's scheme for marriage with a woman he himself had loved – an irony that he might later have appreciated, when all was known.

Wyatt and Russell set off for Paris, then on through Savoy to Rome. In Rome they were much admired as '*gallanti omini*',[1] mounted on the best horses in the Vatican stables, and generally fussed over. According to Wyatt's grandson, George (whose anti-papal credentials we have discussed), they were exposed to Romish customs when a couple of very beautiful prostitutes arrived for them, 'to refresh them withal after their long journey

[1] gallant gentlemen.

and absence from their wives', along with a 'plenary dispensation verbal' from the pope himself, for any resulting spiritual awkwardness. The Englishmen made their excuses and left in a state of moral indignation, with Wyatt reportedly taking the whole sordid episode as a sign of papal contempt for England and a 'prognosticke of the evil of their success'.[2] The embassy was, indeed, not a success. The Medici pope took Henry's money but, with imperial armies threatening Florence, the city of his family, it was not enough to stiffen his resolve. Russell fell off his superior horse and broke his leg, and the inexperienced Wyatt had to go on alone to Venice and Ferrara for further unfruitful negotiations, as the pope dithered and hesitated, hopping fearfully in and out of the league. Outside Bologna, Wyatt was captured by imperial troops, starving and mutinous after a winter of endless delays, and eventually ransomed for the enormous sum of 3000 ducats. The Duke of Ferrara paid the money, but the debt was Wyatt's. He still owed it to the king in 1532 and may never have repaid it.[3]

Wyatt and Russell got out of Italy at the beginning of May just as those imperial armies that the pope had stopped from sacking Florence, sacked Rome, and took him prisoner; creating the unorthodox situation of a pope imprisoned by his own protector, the 'Holy Roman' Emperor, Charles V. This caused a severe setback for Henry VIII's divorce.

*   *   *   *

While Wyatt and Russell were away there had been some developments in Henry's domestic life, and when they got back, in May, the cat was coming out of the bag. This was the month when Wolsey called a secret meeting to discuss the annulment, and on the strength of those findings the king went to Catherine

[2] Loades, op. cit.
[3] See Brigden, 'Wyatt in Italy', *Renaissance Quarterly*, no.58, 2005.

and divulged his concerns: he very much feared their marriage of 17 years was not legitimate. He told her to keep the matter secret, pending the necessary investigations; but Catherine, rightly fearing the result of quiescence at this point, took the opposite course. She immediately contrived to get a message to her nephew, Charles, and then she looked around for some ingenious ways to advertise her distress.

Spite asketh spite and changing change[4]
And falsed faith must needs be known.
The faults so great, the case so strange
Of right it must abroad be blown.

One of them was to commission a translation from Thomas Wyatt of part of a Latin work of Petrarch's entitled 'De Remediis Utriusque Fortunae' (Concerning the Remedy for Every type of Fortune).[5] This on the face of it was a gesture of kindly patronage for young Wyatt, a protégé of hers recently returned from Italy and known as a man of letters – but in fact it was a propaganda strike. A commission of this type was seldom motivated by desire to actually read the work proposed, and this was no exception. As everyone knew, Catherine's Latin was at least as good as her English, and besides, she already owned a translation of this particular work in her native Castilian. She requested it because its title and subject matter was germane to her case and would draw attention to her misery.

It is even possible that Catherine's choice of Wyatt, as the instrument of her grief, had a political edge. Through the latter part of 1527, court factions were beginning to take up positions on the divorce, and even though the king's relationship with Anne was half-secret, the Wyatts were going over to the Boleyns. Sir Henry Wyatt entertained the king and Anne at

[4] 'Blame not My Lute', Wyatt, XCIV, in Rebholz, op. cit.
[5] Literally 'Concerning the Remedy of Each Fortune'.[5]

Allington that summer, where, it is said in Allington lore, the king was walled into his bedroom at night as a security measure. In fact, it was here that Cardinal Wolsey first discovered his power was in decline. Returning from a diplomatic mission to France, he rode straight to the king – 'then in progress at Sir Harry Wyatt's house, in Kent... [It was] supposed among us,' wrote his senior household servant and biographer, George Cavendish, 'that he should be joyfully received at his home coming, as well of the king as of all other noblemen; but we were deceived in our expectation.'[6] In Wolsey's absence, the Boleyns, the Suffolks, the Norfolks – what Eric Ives calls 'the aristocratic heavy mob' had moved to supplant the Cardinal.

Wyatt, meanwhile, despite his diplomatic failures, his expense to the crown and his interest in Anne, was in such high favour that the king referred to him as 'our beloved familiar' in a letter concerning his ransom. For the queen to single him out as her first agent in a propaganda war was to ask what it now meant to be the queen.

None of this would be lost on Wyatt, now in an awkward position. He responded in a typically ambiguous way, by accepting the commission, attempting it and then giving it up as too repetitious and hard to translate into English because 'the labour began to seem tedious, by superfluous often rehearsing of one thing, which though peraventure in the Latin be laudable... yet for lack of such diversity in our tongue, it should want a great deal of the grace'. He presented instead a translation of Plutarch called *The Quiet of Mind*, proposing to the queen, as her most devoted and 'humble slave', that the substitution achieved 'the whole effect of that your highness desired of Petrarch', but 'without tediousness of length'.

If Catherine ever read this apprentice prose effort of Wyatt's, she would certainly have seen the wisdom of letting him start with something easier. But she would also have seen that it

---

[6] George Cavendish, *The Life of Cardinal Wolsey*, ed. Samuel Weller Singer (1827).

was not, as advertised, a more succinct and fluent rendering of Petrarch's arguments in *De Remediis*. Far from it. The piece she had wanted was one long re-echoing howl of misery 'often rehearsing' the single theme of inconsolable grief. The heaviest sorrows, it said, are far beyond the reach of puny reason or the consolations of philosophy. The piece she got took a more bracing attitude to the problem, emphasising the acceptance of fate, the comfort of reason and the futility of opposition to one's fortune. Bearing all in mind, we must wonder who Wyatt – who would certainly have consulted his father – was really working for, and if he had, with this, reversed Catherine's fire and produced the first salvo for the king's side.

Alone of Wyatt's works, *The Quiet of Mind* was printed in his lifetime. Catherine received it at New Year 1528,[7] the year when Anne would take up her public place at Henry's side, and the queen would come under ever-increasing pressure to go quietly. The king now went to her with his solution: she should regard herself as his brother's widow, and take the veil. He enlisted some heavyweight support for this idea: from Basel, Erasmus weighed in with a book and a letter explaining how her birth, exalted rank and 'her marriage to a most prosperous sovereign' were far less material to her true happiness than her inner resources. How rare it is, he enthused, 'to find a lady, brought up at court, placing all her hopes and solace in devotion' (which Catherine was not; she wanted to be queen and the wife of her husband). Hinting broadly at her questionable marital status, he soldiered on:

> would that others, *widows at all events*, would take an example from her, and *not widows only, but unmarried ladies*, by devoting themselves to the service of Christ. He knows what is expedient for all, and is often more propitious when He changes the sweet for the bitter. Every one

[7] New Year: it was customary to exchange presents at New Year, not Christmas.

must take up their cross; there is no entrance into heavenly glory without it. [Italics mine.]

It was true that this might have solved all Henry's problems, and was not an absolutely unreasonable proposal. Life in a convent was honourable, sociable, and not onerous. His wife was now too old to have children and must have been able to see that their single daughter – who would give the people a foreigner or an ambitious English baron for their king – put the whole Tudor project of sovereign unity in jeopardy. If Catherine had entered a convent then, the marriage might have been dissolved without affecting the succession. Henry would try for a male heir, Mary would keep her honourable place as a full princess of the realm, and all the obscenities of the Reformation – the smashed faces of the saints, the howling bonfires, Cranmer's hand in the flames – might have been averted.[8] But she was too offended. Henry's idea – that the book of Leviticus prohibited a man from marrying his brother's widow, and that their marriage was therefore an abomination in the eyes of God, and all their dead babies accursed – may have appealed to his own fixation with the points of the law, but it lacked the element of psychological cunning that might have made it acceptable to his pious, devoted wife. Catherine rejected it utterly, and took up her final lonely position of grievance and martyrdom.

Everyone began to adjust themselves to the strange unfolding situation. Cardinal Wolsey had been taken by surprise by Henry's determination to make Anne Boleyn his wife. He had not expected his French alliance would be made with the daughter of an English knight. He recognised, moreover, that his slowness on the uptake had allowed his aristocratic enemies – of whom the Boleyns were paramount examples – to gain the advantage and install themselves as the natural advisors of the

[8] Scarisbrick gives the argument as follows: 'if one spouse entered religion, he or she thus underwent a "spiritual death" and left the other free to marry.' Scarisbrick, *Henry VIII* (Yale, 1997).

king in this delicate matter. Seeing the king engulfed by love and surrounded by hostile nobles, he worked to reassure him that he was still the man for the job and could understand the king's preoccupations. At York House, his London residence, he threw dinners with more masquing, dancing, dressing up and frenchification than ever. Even the food was engaged in courtly pursuits, with roast beasts and birds coming to the table

> some fighting, as it were with swords, some with guns and crossbows, some vaulting and leaping, some dancing with ladies, some in complete harness, jousting with spears.[9]

Away from court, and fearful of Henry's shifting loyalties, he wrote to him in a new rhetoric, shamelessly adapted to appeal to his current priorities: 'There was never lover more desirous of the sight of his lady than I am of your most noble and royal person.' Here was a language the king could understand; and more and more people would be using it.

What of Wyatt? He was now an esquire of the body, an intimate of the king. Esquires of the body dressed and undressed the sovereign, and watched him day and night.[10] They had to look lively and be ready by 8a.m. 'at the furthest' to attend the royal pleasure. They shared the king's lodgings wherever he went and enjoyed a generous provision of beds (two) and horses (five), the *sine qua non* of court status.[11] But in autumn 1528 he left the court for Calais, fleeing 'the fire that me brent' – perhaps at Anne's insistence. He became high marshal there, the third most important position available. This, as the distinguished Wyatt scholar, Susan Brigden, says, 'was an office and honour, a recognised career for the gentry of Kent, but it was also exile'.[12] He came back two years later to find a changed

[9] Cavendish, op. cit.
[10] The Black Book, 1478.
[11] Eltham Ordinances, 1526.
[12] Susan Brigden, 'Wyatt in Italy', *Renaissance Quarterly,* 58 (summer, 2005).

administration – Wolsey disgraced, and Anne and her adherents in charge – but little progress on the king's 'great matter', as the divorce was known.

Henry's timing had been disastrous: the day that his bishops had decided to refer his case to Rome was, by an agonising stroke of ill luck, the same day that the pope had become Charles's prisoner. Since then, his agents had been trotting back and forth to Rome with pleas and threats. The Boleyns had shown enterprise, producing a brilliant young scholar, one Thomas Cranmer of Cambridge, who had proposed a mass consultation of the universities of Europe. This had been done. But in 1530 Catherine was still his wife and Anne not yet his mistress.

Anne would continue to hold out until the autumn of 1532 – *seven years* after he fell in love with her.[13] How did she do it? She did it with poetry. Which is not to say, by the agency of specific verses, but through practice of the cult of poetry and romance of which she and Wyatt were, in their time, the high priest and priestess.

---

[13] For the argument that it was Henry who held out against Anne, see G.W. Bernard, *Anne Boleyn, Fatal Attractions* (Yale University Press, 2010).

CHAPTER SEVEN

In 1530, when Cardinal Wolsey was dead and Henry's divorce suit moribund, Wolsey's gentleman usher – that is, the man who had had the management of his immense household – was summoned to Hampton Court to see the king. His name was George Cavendish. Arriving at the appointed time, he went to look for Henry.

> I found him shooting at the rounds [a circular archery target] in the park on the backside of the garden, and perceiving him occupied in shooting, thought it not my duty to trouble him, but leaned against a tree intending to stand there, and to attend his gracious pleasure.[1]

The king took his time, and Cavendish fell into some distant contemplation.

> [I] Being in a great study, at the last the king came suddenly behind me and clapped his hand upon my shoulder, and when I perceived him, I fell upon my knee. To whom he said, calling me by my name, 'I will', quoth he, 'make an end of my game, and then I will talk with you,' and so departed to his mark, whereat the game was ended. Then the king delivered his bow to the yeoman of his bows and went his way inward to the palace; whom I followed. Howbeit he called for Sir John Gage, with whom

---

[1] George Cavendish, *The Life of Cardinal Wolsey*, ed. S. W. Singer (1825)

he talked, until he came at the garden postern gate, and there entered; the gate being shut after him, which caused me to go my ways.

Cavendish is sometimes thought a simple creature, pre-occupied with cushions and the like, who failed to grasp the complexities of his master's situation;[2] but he was better than that. His biography of Wolsey shows a genius for the telling anecdote which has made him a lavish, if unreliable source of reference for historians – and for novelists, who can see that he is really one of their own. Years of directing the household had refined his sense of social choreography; and he has antici-pated the novelists' trick of setting his own mousiness as a foil for the actions of the great – never to greater effect than here, where the king's personality shows up in brilliant colours. This Henry looks like a real person: here is the charm (he remembers Cavendish's name!), the blast of geniality, the faintly bullying bonhomie, the billionaire's attention span as he sails into the palace, forgetting about Cavendish completely.

But Cavendish was not a novelist. He didn't write this to demonstrate Henry's character, but because any personal contact with the king was glorious and an occasion for record. In a system where all power and influence originated in the king, access to his person was all, and to flicker for even a mo-ment in the beam of his roaming attention was, as Shakespeare told us, to be gilded yourself.[3] And in Henry's case the opera-tion of that beam was swift, intermittent and arbitrary – and rarely as unpredictable as when it suddenly stopped moving and fixed its bulging intensity on one object. Cardinal Wolsey

[2] By the 19th-century historian J.A. Froude, for example.
[3] In sonnet 33, where the gilding effect of the early morning sun on the landscape is likened to royal favour:
  Full many a glorious morning have I seen
  Flatter the mountain tops with sovereign eye
  Despite climate change, the 16th-century English sun behaved much as it does in our own summers: radiant at dawn, completely clouded over by nine.

had had the measure of that.

'I assure you,' wrote Wolsey to another of Henry's ministers, 'I have often kneeled before him... an hour or two to persuade him from his will and appetite, but I could never bring to pass to dissuade him therefrom. Therefore Master Kingston, I warn you to be advised and assured that what matter you put in his head; for ye shall never pull it out again.'

In 1526, it fixed on Anne and stayed there, to the general astonishment, until 1536. She held him by the strength of her character, and her disputatious wit, and whatever phenomenal powers she had of interpretation, that enabled her to make the granting of Henry's 'will and appetite' a matter for Cardinal Wolsey, not her. But this particular personality would have been less interesting to him had he not had a proven weakness for the enchanted glades of courtly romance, and himself as an actor within them. He had played the knight in every role – the man of learning, the man of war, the man of God, the virtuous husband; every role, that is, except one, and that was the lover in full, formal, adulterous pursuit of an unobtainable lady. The love letters he wrote to Anne Boleyn – which make very sad reading when you know how the story ends – show clearly that this persona of courtly lover, as distinct from virtuous husband, was fully formed in Henry and had been signalling, somewhere in his psyche, for an answering adept to come and lift its latch. In Anne, he had her. She was the mistress of Petrarchan contraries: her blowing hot and cold at once made the perfect environment for the king's tender interest, so that it neither frosted nor burned but swelled amazingly on the spot.

Of heat and cold when I complain[4]
And say that heat doth cause my pain
When cold doth shake my every vein,

[4] Wyatt, CXIII, in Rebholz, op. cit.

And both at once, I say again
It is impossible.

He came out frisking. Into the lists in the Shrovetide games of 1526 he rode, bedecked with a motto of a heart not just on fire but in a press, and the words '*declare I dare not*' written below.

Whether he had dared to declare by then will always be a point at issue among historians, because the letters he sent her are undated. The first was probably written that year and certainly in the summer or autumn, as that was the hunting season, and it accompanied a gift of a buck – the king's own meat. The next letter is more instructive, being a deliberate exhibition of Henry's courtly expertise, intended to impress a better player than he. Naturally, he wrote it in French.

He recommends himself and his heart to Anne's favour, and hopes that absence does not lessen her 'affection to us'. 'For it were a pity,' he continues, 'to increase our pain, which absence alone does sufficiently, and more than I could ever have thought; bringing to my mind a point of astronomy, that the longer the days are from us, the further too is the sun, and yet his heat is more scorching; so it is with our love.'

This is a terrific bit of showing-off, centred upon the use of the word 'us'. This looks at first sight like the royal 'we' of Henry's official correspondence, but it isn't. The division of the heart and the self into separate entities was one of the finer points of courtly doctrine, and Henry, as a king, gets an extra mark for using the plural personal pronoun to mean himself and his heart, not the royal 'us' of majesty. To emphasise his understanding of this unique distinction, he reverts to the humble 'I' and 'my' of the servitor in the same sentence. Having done this, he is off onto an analogy between love and the orbit of the sun – showing the sorts of elevated conversation that Anne expected from him. She had made him raise his game.

The next letter continues with courtly love by numbers, and manifests the same anxiety about correctness that burned into every aspect of his life. 'I'm sure that the distance between our two persons annoys you a little,' he writes, and then, perhaps fearing that he has betrayed an imperfect command of the rules, he adds 'even though this pertains not so much to the mistress as to the servant ('*serviteur*').' Evidently, Anne has strategically removed herself from court and his advances, with the successful intention of making him miss her. It seems to him, he says, small reward for the great love he bears her that he must be separated from '*la parrole et la personage de la fame du monde que je plus estime*'.[5]

The original French is given for the sake of the old French word '*parrole*', which doesn't have an exact English equivalent, and has therefore been left out of the English translations. It means 'discourse' or 'teaching', and this is perhaps the key to Henry's perception of Anne. It shows he valued her conversation – but more than this, that he valued it as a required component in the courtly construct of their relations: the instructive discourse that a knight receives from a courtly lady. Right from the beginning he perceived her as an *authority*. That was a role she inhabited with ease – a fact one can only ascribe to her remarkable personality. It is a cruel blow to posterity that her own letters to the king are lost – probably destroyed along with their author – but the strength of her character is such that Henry's letters take the impress of it. Most of Henry's missives were decrees, like papal bulls, reactive only in the sense of adjusting their demands to information received. But these ones to Anne are entirely different: responsive, tentative, shaped to accommodate the fierce pressures of what was in Anne's lost letters. He was never in his life like this with anyone else. We see him trying to soothe and pacify her, enjoining her to patience (she out-impatienced

---

[5] 'the discourse and the presence of the woman whom I esteem most in all the world'.

him, the most impatient man in the world), calming some frantic accusation of abandonment, pleading undying loyalty.

> The knot which first my heart did strain[6]
> When that your servant I became
> Doth bind me still for to remain
> Always your own, as now I am;
> And if ye find that I do feign,
> With just judgement myself I damn,
> To have disdain
>
> If in my love there be one spot
> Of false deceit of doubleness
> Or if I mind to slip this knot
> By want of faith or steadfastness
> Let all my service be forgot
> And, when I would have chief redress,
> Esteem me not

We see him acceding resignedly to a now only guessable demand, or puzzling over her letters, struggling to comprehend some elusively worded statement of her intentions. 'Debating with my self the contents of your letter, I have put myself in great distress, not knowing how to interpret them, whether to my disadvantage, as in some places is shown, or to advantage, as in others I understand them.'

She was the same in the flesh. Licensed by Henry's passion, she showed a staggering hauteur in her treatment of personages, including himself. She railed at him for debating the divorce with his formidable wife: 'Did I not tell you that whenever you disputed with the queen she was sure to have the upper hand?' she snapped. Another time, she was in the king's privy chamber and, hearing that Wolsey was hovering importantly outside,

[6] Wyatt, XCI, in Rebholz, op. cit.

waiting for her dismissal and the commencement of men's business, she rapped out a message for him to come in and join them: 'Where else should he come, except where the king is?'[7]

As we see from this, she interpreted the role of courtly lady to the utmost of its potential. She became more powerful than any man. Paradoxically, once it was recognised that she and no other – not her father Thomas, not her uncle Norfolk – was now 'the true inheritor of that ultimate royal favour that had been Wolsey's strength,'[8] she attracted a degree of enmity more usually associated with hated male favourites than mistresses. Perhaps the manner of her operations – as an incarnation of the eternal feminine – aggravated her enemies' frustrations by making it impossible for them to compete. They were men. It was hardly in the Duke of Suffolk's remit to spring like a nymph onto the back of Henry's saddle and ride off in pillion with him, laughing and whispering into his ear. But Anne could. With her wit, her dazzle, her ludic, punning Burgundian manners, she melted into his dream of Albion.

One objective that was quite easy to achieve from this position was the thing that has most amazed the onlookers of posterity: keeping him off for seven years. As we have seen, convention demanded that the lady was chaste. Any insistence or coercion on the part of Henry – always a man with an eye on some cosmic end-of-term report – would show up in his knightly grades. He seems to have accepted early on that marriage was the price of her submission. However, the stroke of genius – in which she may well have had a part – was to incorporate Anne's virginity into the propaganda for the divorce. This had certainly happened by early 1528, as we can see from a letter Wolsey sent to his agents, Fox and Gardiner, in Rome, instructing them to correct the pope in his misapprehensions about the king's motives. Somehow, Clement VII had got the impression that Henry

[7] Ives, *The Life and Death of Anne Boleyn*, 2005.
[8] ibid.

was putting his wife aside 'not from fear of his succession, but out of vain affection or undue love to a gentlewoman of not so excellent qualities as she is here esteemed.' They were to put this matter right. They were to tell him that the king's marriage was an offence to God and a torment to his Christian conscience. As for the gentlewoman 'on the other side':

> the approved, excellent virtuous [qualities] of the said gentlewoman, the purity of her life, her constant virginity, her maidenly and womanly pudicity, her soberness, chasteness, meekness, humility, wisdom, descent of right noble and high thorough regal blood, education in all good and laudable [qualities] and manners, apparent aptness to procreation of children... be the grounds on which the king's desire is founded.[9]

From now on Anne's maidenhead was an article of Henry's case; she was quite safe. It would be nice to think she had a hand in this, and it was highly likely that she did. Not only was the divorce their joint project, but Wolsey's encomium, with its six different epithets for chastity and emphasis on childbearing, highlights those aspects of Anne's wifely potential that she liked to point out in herself. Among the surviving traces of Anne's existence is a page from an illuminated book of hours, on which she has written:

> *Be daly[10] prove you shalle me fynde*
> *To be to you bothe loving and kynde.*

Above this subscription is a picture of the Annunciation – a brilliantly concise expression of those otherwise inimical virtues, fecundity and chastity, which are reconciled in the (dark-

[9] Letter from Wolsey to Fox and Gardiner, February ?11, 1528.
[10] daily.

haired) figure of Mary at this moment of good news.

She writes in verse, the proper language of courtly love. Anne Boleyn was a judge of poetry: surely one of few women to make, as time would tell, literary-critical pronouncements from a condemned cell. Her court – both the unofficial one where she reigned as Henry's wife-in-waiting, and the formal one of her regency – was always a centre of its production. In accordance with the sentiments of the love-infected king, the fashionable courtiers set themselves to writing lyrics and sonnets, achieving patchy success and almost total incognito; so that nobody knows which poems were written by such courtiers as George Boleyn, Anne's brother, or Wyatt's friends, Sir Francis Bryan and George Blage, whose lyrics may now be swelling the 'doubtful attribution' sections of Wyatt's collected works. And just as the royal love affair bred poetry, so the poetry fed love. It gave expression to the king's overwhelming and semi-secret preoccupation:

Take heed betime lest ye be spied.[11]
Your loving eyes ye cannot hide
At last the truth will sure be tried.
Therefore take heed!

For some there be of crafty kind,
Though you show no part of your mind,
Surely their eyes ye cannot blind,
Therefore take heed!

For in like case theirselves hath been
And thought right sure none had them seen.
But it was not as they did ween.
Therefore take heed!

[11] Wyatt, CXVIII, in Rebholz, op. cit.

It substantiated Henry's desires and frustrations in his pursuit of Anne. It supported her right to refuse and his right to persist: fortunately for both of them in this protracted period of waiting, *renewing* one's suit was a staple of the genre:

> *For want of will in woe I plain* [12]
> *Under colour of soberness,*
> *Renewing with my suit my pain,*
> *My wanhope with your steadfastness.*
> *Awake therefore of gentleness.*
> *Regard at length, I you require,*
> *The swelting pains of my desire.*

Its resentful tone and theme of unrewarded merit gave a voice to the frustrations of Henry's Great Matter – which was itself a kind of secret suit, and he a suitor to Rome.

> *To wish and want and not obtain,* [13]
> *To seek and sue ease of my pain,*
> *Since all that ever I do is vain*
> *What may it avail me?*

> *Although I strive both day and hour*
> *Against the stream with all my power,*
> *If fortune list yet for to lour*
> *What may it avail me?...*

> *... For in despair there is no rede.*[14]
> *To want of ear speech is no speed.*
> *To linger still alive as dead*
> *What may it avail me?*

---

[12] Wyatt, LXXXII, in Rebholz, op. cit.
[13] Wyatt, CVII, in Rebholz, op. cit.
[14] no rede: no counsel, no saving course of action

The case progressed with terrible slowness –

Ever mine hap is slack and slow in coming.[15]

– and with a fitful, elliptical motion. Katherine of Aragon denied the authority of the English courts to try her marriage, and insisted the case be referred to Rome. Clement wavered and prevaricated and offered Henry defective assurances that raised and dashed Henry's hopes at once.

Assured I doubt I be not sure[16]
And should I trust to such surety
That oft hath put the proof in ure
And never hath found it trusty?

Wyatt's poems distilled the spirit of the rows and tears and makings-up that issued from Anne and Henry's chambers, sending a ripple of titters out through the European courts. She accused him of not loving her, of letting this go on and on while she grew old, of ruining her life when she could have made an honourable marriage elsewhere. He wrote that she should calm her unreasonable thoughts: what 'joy it is to me to understand of your comformableness with reason, and the suppressing of your inutile and vain thoughts and fantasies with the bridle of reason,' he wrote, with perhaps more hope than conviction. Wyatt caught such sentiments perfectly, down to the whiff of dignified reproof:

Accused though I be without desert,[17]
None can it prove, yet ye believe it true.
Nor never yet, since that ye had my heart,
Entended I to be false or untrue.

---

[15] Wyatt, XXI, in Rebholz, op. cit.
[16] Wyatt, LXXXV, in Rebholz, op. cit.
[17] Wyatt, LXVI, in Rebholz, op. cit.

Sooner I would of death sustain the smart
Than break one thing of that I promised you.

If this poem was on the programme of the pastime after one of Anne's meltdowns, the cognoscenti would know what it was for. All eyes would slide in her direction. Henry could look fervent and aggrieved. Something had been said, without exposure or loss of face. A poet like Wyatt, the master of grievance, reproach, disappointment and unrequited desire could make himself busy in this environment. Certainly his sense of being uniquely ill-used would have chimed with the king's.

Such hap as I am happed in[18]
Had never man of truth, I ween.
At me Fortune list to begin
To shew that never hath been seen
A new kind of unhappiness.
Nor I can not the thing I mean
Myself express

Was Henry not a good Christian? Had he not written an actual book in support of the traditional Church, and sent it to Clement's predecessor?[19] Was it not a relatively trivial thing to dispense for divorce?

Things of great weight I never thought to crave;[20]
This is but small, of right deny it not:
Your feigning ways as yet forget them not
But like reward let other lovers have,
That is to say, for service true and fast

---

[18] Wyatt, LXXXVII, in Rebholz, op. cit.
[19] Henry wrote his defence of the Church, the *Assertio Septem Sacramentorum* (In Assertion of the Seven Sacraments) in 1521, in response to Luther's criticisms. He may have had help from More and other divines.
[20] Wyatt, XXXV, in Rebholz, op. cit.

Too long delays and changing at the last.

There are some poems that show a more organised and deliberate way of being useful, and some of them give the impression
of having been written, or even recruited, as a gift to Anne's
campaign. One particularly interesting case is a Wyatt translation of a Petrarchan canzone set in an imaginary 'court of
love' (a regular feature of courtly entertainments).[21] The poem
is longer than most of Wyatt's verse, having speaking parts and
an air about it of an entertainment to be read aloud, with parts
taken by different actors. It is worth looking at with some care.
In it, the (personified but nameless) Lover states his complaint
against Love to Reason; whereupon a personification of Love
puts the defence.

The Lover's grumble concerns a youthful entanglement with
love which has caused him nothing but trouble: Love was 'aloes
and gall' to him, driving him abroad 'through froward people
and strait pressions',[22] with his nerves in pieces. 'Never bell
strikes/Where I am that I hear not,' he complains. Love then
replies with reproaches of his own for the Lover's ingratitude.
He, Love, took this fellow on as a protégé. He selected a very
special teacher for him:

> *Though he no deals worthy were,*
> *I chose right the best of many a million,*
> *That under the moon was never her peer*
> *Of wisdom, womanhood, and discretion.*
> *And of my grace I gave her such a fashion,*
> *And eke such a way I taught her for to teach*
> *That never base thought his heart might have reach*

---

[21] Wyatt, LXXIII, in Rebholz, op. cit.
[22] strait pressions: prisons; possibly a reference to Wyatt's capture near Bologna in
April-May, 1527.

For Petrarch this is his dead perfect love, Laura. Who is it for Wyatt? Another paragon, also a professor emeritus in the faculty of virtue, fidelity, patience, gentleness. So why does he complain? The last lines are the critical ones. The lover/Wyatt admits that, yes, Love may have given him this lady, but then look what happened:

> *'by and by*
> *Thou took her straight from me. That woe worth thee!'*
> *'Not I,' quod he, 'but price that is well worthy'*

Love replies – causing a forest of question marks to rear up among Wyatt's editors. What does that mean, 'Not I, but *price* that is well worthy'? It makes no grammatical sense, unless the word 'price' was once another word, *prince*, rendered as 'price' in the hand of the time but missing the mark, known as a tilde – ˜ – over the 'i' that transformed it into an 'n'. With this tiny alteration, the line would have read '"Not I," quod he, "but *prince* that is well worthy".' Henry, the worthy prince, took this prize of womanhood for himself.

This interpretation is very probably what Wyatt intended. It does give the only sensible reading, and it changes the burden of the poem entirely. Now the poem slides open to reveal a current story, with a cast of current characters: if the prince is Henry, then the peerless lady is Anne and the disappointed lover, Wyatt himself. In that case, the poem would carry a very specific message: it would say, *'I loved the king's mistress, but only in the prescribed manner of the courtly convention, as one of a number of suitors for a grand lady far above my deserts. I acknowledge it and my own unworthiness in comparison with the deserving winner.'* In other words, it is a masterstroke of damage-limitation and image-management: it clears the air over Wyatt's old association, acknowledging it, neutralising it and repackaging it as an elegant tribute to Anne's incarnation of female virtue – none more elegant in that society, as it assumes her into the character of Petrarch's divine, dead, chaste Laura, the courtly cult's queen in heaven.

Such an utterance on Wyatt's part was only possible in poetry. How else could he have said it? In conversation it would have seemed like indiscretion, in prose like an accusation. Poetry de-natured love, absorbed it into its conventions, made it all right. If the poem was a translation, so much the better. Translations provided safe passage for dangerous or delicate sentiments at this time. A clever translator could say more than he might dare in his own words. Behind the blind of another poet's words, he could declare and maintain what politicians call 'deniability' at the same time. He could – as Catherine of Aragon did – exactly translate a piece that fit his own predicament. But there was more. Small alterations in the text, undetectable to the general eye, would speak to the few alert adepts who, he knew, had read the originals. As in the poems of the pastime, it all depended on where you stood, and what you knew: whether you could angle the light so that its shafts slipped below the surface; and if, among the objects floating in that revealed dimension, you could see signs of disturbance and substitution. Move the light and the surface reseals, and all you have is another man's words – in this case a poem by a long-dead poet about a long-dead woman.

CHAPTER EIGHT

R eturned to court in 1530, Wyatt remained in good favour for the next few years. He is described in 1533 as 'one whom [Anne] loves very much'. He was always what his eulogist, John Leland, called 'friended' – a potent term in a client society, where your 'good friend' was a person who used their higher position on the social ladder to sue upwards on your behalf, in return for gifts, loyalty and useful information from below. But he was not a pre-eminent courtier. He remained – perhaps because of the legacy of his relations with Anne, the unorthodoxy of his marital position and the fact of his frequent, possibly related, absences from court – an outsider-insider. Though a favourite of both Anne and Henry and, later, Thomas Cromwell, who filled the king's chamber with his cronies, he never achieved membership of the inner circle of Henry's intimates, the gentlemen of the chamber. He was often away from court, and when he was there we seldom see his name appearing on any lists of favoured recipients of royal largesse – distribution of the king's clothes, for example – or grants of land or office, or starring in those catalogues of functionaries and courtiers whose names lent lustre to pageants, court entertainment and wars. He was not a top man like the gallant Sir Henry Norris, Henry's closest friend and most intimate attendant, or Sir Nicholas Carewe, the athletic phenomenon of the lists, or Sir Francis Bryan, a singularly adroit player in the markets of court favour, with a taste for huge stakes and a 20-year record of high returns.

Even in a court where it was normal practice to desert the

fallen ('Like lice away from dead bodies they crawl'),[1] Bryan showed exceptional cornering skills. He was the pre-eminent louse. He tracked the trajectory of the king's favour, then scudded ahead of it; so that when the golden beam settled on a new object, there was Sir Francis Bryan, already installed in the spot, ready to take advantage. When he appears in the *Letters and Papers* – the 21 great volumes of documents collected from Henry's reign – it is always as a man in the right place at the right time, always the principal ornament, the man most invited, topping the bill at every prestigious occasion. Here he is in 1518 as a guest of Cardinal Wolsey, lending his arm to Bessie Blount, the king's mistress and the woman of the moment. Here, in 1522, first to be knighted after some skirmish on the coast of Brittany. Here in francophiliac 1529 we see him at the ransom of Francis I's family from the Spanish, fully frenchified and offering his favoured person as collateral against the royal hostages; in 1530 we see him with his shoulder to the divorce, calling Anne 'my cousin' (she was cousin to almost everyone at court, and so was he); but just as conspicuous in 1537 at the christening of Prince Edward, the son of Anne's successor, when he was one of just four gentlemen officiating at the font.[2] If he felt the drag of moral queasiness on his manoeuvres, there is no sign of it. He had energy and rakish charm and one eye, and was obviously up for anything profitable or amusing, any momentary service for the king, no matter how seamy or ignoble. When Henry was curious about the true extent of his daughter Mary's innocence, Bryan volunteered himself for whispering sex-words in her ear and reporting back on the reaction. He has always been a slightly painful figure for the champions of Wyatt's high moral seriousness, for he was one of Wyatt's close friends. His nickname was the Vicar of Hell.

If Wyatt was not the pre-eminent courtier, neither was he the

---

[1] Wyatt, LXVIII, in Rebholz, op. cit.
[2] Hall, op. cit.

pre-eminent poet. That was Chaucer. The years since the death of Chaucer in 1400 had thrown up nothing to touch him, a situation that was as evident to the people then living as it is to us, and which remained unchanged until the time of Shakespeare. Anyone with a claim to poetry would be likened, optimistically, to Chaucer, for there was no other point of reference. Even Sir Philip Sidney, writing in 1583, marvelled at how curiously good Chaucer was 'in that mistie time', and how strangely hard it was for a man with all the intellectual conveniences of late 16th-century modernity to write as well. To conceive of the state of English literature in the mid-1500s we would have to imagine there had been no poetry to speak of between Wordsworth and Larkin, and none before Wordsworth either. Looking back from the present day, we can see that the aspiring poets-and-lovers of Henry's reign were treading the slack water between two towering waves of genius, but they didn't know that; they had no sense that a greater eminence was gathering; they could not foresee the centuries aloft, the confidence and spread of English letters; they only felt themselves washing down the glassy side of Chaucer's achievement, falling further from the crest of mastery. Inarticulacy or barbarism beckoned. No Europeans spoke English, and the idea of English as a language of love would have struck most French or Italians as highly comic. In this crisis of emotional inarticulacy, they groped behind them, for Chaucer.

In 1532, after Henry had declared himself head of the Church, a splendid single volume of Chaucer's works appeared with a preface written by Henry Wyatt's successor as treasurer, Sir Brian Tuke, and in this the great vernacular poet was claimed as England's Virgil and English itself as a glorious language. But this was really an effusion of anxiety about political isolation. All the humanist linguists thought that English in its current state (which was not the language of Chaucer) was a shaggy and hopalong means of expression. Wyatt's complaint about

Sir Brian Tuke (*Hans Holbein the Younger*)

'lack of diversitie in our tongue' was a concern for his whole generation.

It was lovers in particular who turned to Chaucer to recruit expressions for their feelings. *The Knight's Tale* – a story of love-rivalry and knightly deeds – and *Troilus and Criseyde*, his sublime love epic – were the favourite texts and principal emporia for the idioms of love, where an unconfident suitor could find a quality phrase to furnish his suit. The lovebirds of the 1530s held twigs of Chaucer in their beaks. Every line of Troilus' letter to Criseyde[3] turns up in the work of the 'courtly makers', as Wyatt and his contemporaries were later called.[4] At court, the leaders of fashion talked to one another in Chaucer – an affectation that some beheld with annoyance.[5]

---

[3] Sometimes called the '*Canticus Troilii*'.
[4] By Puttenham in *The Arte of English Poesie*.

Wyatt looked at all of this with an air of *de haut en bas*. He thought the general enthusiasm was well in advance of the general powers of literary discrimination, and witheringly observed that few could tell the difference between the 'Tale of Sir Thopas' – the parodic doggerel Chaucer gives himself in the *Canterbury Tales* – and the incomparable 'Knight's Tale'. His own use of Chaucer was more subtle and comprehending. The cynical sonnet to May, a kind of grumpy anti-tribute to the May morning conventions, gives some idea:

You that in love find luck and abundance[6]
And live in lust and joyful jollity,
Arise for shame, do away your sluggardy,
Arise, I say, do May some observance!
Let me in bed lie dreaming in mischance,
Let me remember the haps most unhappy
That me betide in May most commonly,
As one whom love list little to avance.
Sephame said true that my nativity
Mischanced was with the ruler of the May.
He guessed, I prove of that the verity:
In May my wealth and eke my life, I say
Have stood so oft in such perplexity.
Rejoice! Let me dream of your felicity.

May was often unkind to Wyatt. Captivity in Italy and the confirmation of his fears about Anne Boleyn and the king were the 'haps most unhappy' of just one unlucky May, and by no means his worst, as shall appear. No one knows when the astrologer Edward Sephame compiled Wyatt's charts; he may have been

---

[5] Thomas Wilson, author of *The Arte of Rhetorique for the Use of all suche as are Studious of Eloquence* (printed in 1553 but written much earlier) included Chaucerian in his list of unacceptable affectations of speech: 'the fine courtier will talk nothing but Chaucer', he complained.

[6] Wyatt, XXXIII, in Rebholz, op. cit.

using the fortune-tellers' trick of telling the customer what he already knows; at any rate the poem was written, probably in the late 1530s, for an informed readership who knew enough of Wyatt's CV to get the joke. Some of them – the more discriminating and refined types – would also understand the dissonances at work in the line 'Arise, I say, do May some observance!' This exhortation to honour the month of love was a commonplace even in Chaucer's time, enough so for Chaucer to make his own ironic use of it. His Knight plays it with a straight and manly bat, as one would expect, but in *Troilus and Criseyde* it is the great procurer, Pandarus, who enlists it in his campaign to pimp his widowed niece to Troilus. He chivvies:

> *Do weye youre boke, rise up, and lat us daunce,*[7]
> *And lat us don to May some observaunce*

Wyatt's sarcastic 'quote' puts a sour cast on the rituals of May morning as performed by Henry's courtiers: they may pretend to the gentility of the Knight, but their true presiding genius is Pandarus. This was a court where love was at the service of the scramble for position: there were other powers than Amor to propitiate, as he well knew. He wrote sarcastically to Bryan:

> *In this also see you be not idle:*[8]
> *Thy niece, thy cousin, thy sister, or thy daughter,*
> *If she be fair, if handsome be her middle,*
> *If thy better hath her love besought her,*
> *Advance his cause and he shall help thy need*

*   *   *   *

[7] *Troilus and Criseyde*, II, l.111-12, Benson, op. cit
[8] Wyatt, Epistolary Satire 3, 'Letter to Bryan', CLI, in Rebholz op. cit.

If Wyatt was not the top courtier or the most exalted poet, what was he to the court? He was their best shot. Anyone with a shred of judgement recognised that he was a cut above your usual courtier-versifier. The courtly cognoscenti appreciated his inferences, thought him very 'depe-witted' (much to the bafflement of later generations of literary critics), and when it was said that he 'reft Chaucer the glory of his wit',[9] it was not just because that was the sole honourable point of comparison, but because they knew he was the only one of them who could claim to be Chaucer's heir, not his customer. Indeed, he had customers of his own. In the British Library is a book displaying his clientele. It is now known as the Devonshire MS, and it was the facebook of the Tudor court. 'It shows,' says Professor Stevens, 'a group of courtly persons writing to, for and about each other… the poems are not merely written in courtly styles, they seem to refer, in stylised terms, to actual relationships.'[10]

As often with the traces of a lost society, one gropes for the exact purpose of the Devonshire MS. Even printed books were commonly circulated, being rare or in demand or fashionable, and the recipients would add personal interest by writing their initials or mottos on the flyleaf as a memento of their involvement, like the collectors' seals that accumulate on Chinese scrolls. This book went out with blank leaves. It was something between a game, a private club, a chain letter and a medium for social networking; and the currency was poetry. Poems conversed with one another, in 'answering' poems or verses, or by adding lines, or changing them. Whatever was said in a lyric was answered in another. It was a closed world, where prose had no authority to interfere.

The book seems to have returned at intervals to a young woman with strong Howard connections called Mary Shelton, who, it is thought, did things to it like alter misogynistic sentiments to pro-feminist ones. Some scholars have conjectured

---

[9] By the poet Henry Howard, Earl of Surrey.
[10] Stevens, op. cit.

from this that she was the organiser of the whole project, but that is rather uncertain. One thing we do know: the contributors had access to poems by Thomas Wyatt, and it was these, even more than Chaucer, that taught them 'what might be said in rhyme', as Surrey wrote. As there is no evidence that Wyatt himself ever handled the Devonshire MS, the fact that most of them – about 70 out of a 100-odd entries – chose poems by Wyatt is conclusive proof that he had no peer.

The Devonshire group was a self-selected, self-conscious elite operating at a high pitch of courtly affectation in the years around the mid-1530s.[11] The poet Surrey's name appears in the manuscript, and so does that of his sister, the Duchess of Richmond (wife of Henry's sole illegitimate son, Henry Fitzroy). Wyatt's brother-in-law, Sir Anthony Lee, was involved. The group also included the king's niece, Lady Margaret Douglas – the most eligible beauty of the day – and her lover, Lord Thomas Howard, who took a gamble on the king's weakness for true love and betrothed himself to Lady Margaret without Henry's permission. For this piece of *lèse-majesté*, he slammed them both in the Tower. It is thought that there, like those mating insects who continue to engage while their heads are being eaten, these privileged prisoners went on writing courtly poems in the Devonshire book, until Margaret was released and Lord Thomas died. The lack of any attested example of Howard's handwriting makes it impossible to prove that the book was in fact passed between them in the Tower; but no scholar has yet – despite strenuous efforts – been able to prove that it wasn't. Their predicament was unquestionably the focal event of this book, and not only that: it was a literal manifestation of the tropes of courtly love. It acted out their metaphors of imprisonment, suffering, dying, accusation, betrayal, concealment – indeed, the whole idea that one could die for love was now put to the proof: and the contributors to the

[11] Though it contains some poems that have been entered later.

Devonshire MS now found they could use the language of love to speak secretly of, about and to one another on a matter of high treason. It opens with the warning poem:

Take heed betime lest ye be spied[12]
Your loving eyes ye can not hide
At last the truth will sure be tried
  Therefore take heed!

For some there be of crafty kind,
Though you show no part of your mind,
Surely their eyes ye cannot blind.
  Therefore take heed!

Among this unnamed 'some' we might conjecture to find Anne Boleyn, who was queen when the book (and the affair) began, and had disapproved. Depositions taken at the time of the arrests revealed that 'divers times' when Howard had tried to 'resort unto her [Margaret Douglas]', he would have to 'watch till my lady Boleyn was gone, and then steal into her chamber'. As queen, she condemned impropriety. But some who remembered how she came to that estate might have thought disapproval was a bit rich, coming from her. The dig in the next verse was beautifully germane to the case:

For in like case theirselves hath been
And thought right sure none had them seen.
But it was not as they did ween,
Therefore take heed.

The Devonshire group were on the whole younger than Wyatt, and the clandestine potential of the Devonshire book excited them to the point where they risked defeating the whole

---

[12] Wyatt, CXVIII, in Rebholz, op. cit.

enterprise by impishly alluding to it. 'I write by this... I mean by that' wrote one scribe at the bottom of his poem, just in case his surreptitiousness had gone unnoticed. Accordingly, they were often attracted to those works of Wyatt's that could usurp their own apparent subject matter and turn into poems about the poems themselves. That may make Tudor courtiers sound like French doctoral students, which they were not; but they were young and self-involved and their poems were the vehicle for that most fascinating of all things, their own social drama. So of course the circulation of the lyrics – coded and secretive messages with thrillingly ambiguous constructive possibilities – became a source of interest in itself, for the whole group. It is also true – a truism, even – that any medium given half a chance will soon become its own favourite subject, especially when it is in the hands of a clique. What holds now for Hollywood or reality television held then for the courtly lyric, 500 years ago.

Me list no more to sing[13]
Of love nor of such thing
How sore that it me wring;
For what I sung or spake
Men did my songs mistake.

My songs were too diffuse.
They made folk to muse.
Therefore, me to excuse,
They shall be sung more plain,
Neither of joy nor pain.

This is a poem about the meaning of poems. Wyatt says his have been misconstrued; he acknowledges their ambiguity (his songs were 'too diffuse') and the consequence, that they made

[13] Wyatt, CXXXV, in Rebholz, op. cit.

folk 'muse'. Musing in Tudor times was a word with a dangerous undertow. When Henry VIII mused, there was seldom a happy outcome for the object of his contemplation. Though Wyatt claims to have been misunderstood, his real concern is to recall his poems from where they are, apparently, in circulation to stimulate or quicken rumours about such dangerous liaisons as that between Thomas Howard and Margaret Douglas. Or it may be just another layer in the game, a deliberate piece of stirring to intensify speculation: who are these 'folks' who had seen the poems? Why did they muse? What did they think they were about?

We can see from this that poetry-making and poetic interpretation were key courtly skills, and not just because they lent the participants polish, but because poetry was the hot vehicle for gossip and rumour. Anne Boleyn's court – both informal and formal – was a centre of production: 'pastime in the queen's chamber was never more,' wrote her vice-chamberlain to her brother, George, a few days after her coronation. With hindsight, one can see he may have been striking a note of caution. The pastime would be her undoing.

For now, it was her strength. She was wonderful fun. She was strong in conversation, joking, singing, dancing, repartee and general chat. The pastime had been her arena of operation from the start, and she had always used it to promote her cause and burnish her image. The following song – almost certainly *not* Wyatt's work – gives an instance of an amusement that she must at least have sanctioned, if not commissioned or even written, in the waiting years:

Grudge on who list, this is my lot:[14]
Nothing to want if it were not.

My years be young even as ye see.

[14] Wyatt, CCXVIII, in Rebholz, op. cit.

All things thereto doth well agree.
In faith, in face, in each degree
No thing doth want, as seemeth me,
If it were not

Some men doth say that friends be scarce
But I have found, as in this case,
A friend which giveth to no man place
But makes me happiest that ever was,
If it were not

Grudge on who list, this is my lot;
Nothing to want, if it were not

A heart I have besides all this
That hath my heart and I have his
If he doth well, it is my bliss,
And when we meet no lack there is,
If it were not

If he can find that can me please,
He thinks he does his own heart's ease;
And likewise I could well appease
The chiefest cause of his mis-ease,
If it were not...

... And here an end. It doth suffice
To speak few words among the wise.
Yet take this note before your eyes:
My mirth should double once or twice,
If it were not.

The obvious fit for 'it' is the king's cumbersome marriage to Catherine, obstructing Anne and Henry's happiness. In the

Christmas season of 1530, Anne had taken to dressing her servants in gowns embroidered with the same motto: '*groigne qui groigne*'.[15] 'A bold hypothesis... would suggest Anne as the performer of the song,' says her biographer, Ives. An even bolder one would suggest the word 'mirth' – a strange entity to 'double once or twice' 'before your eyes' – was a way of alluding to the one thing omitted from this checklist of Anne's qualifications, and the most important: her fecundity. Certain accompanying gestures could it make it very clear that what would double once or twice, 'if it were not', was of course her *girth* – and Anne, who was particularly fond of puns and rarely passed up the opportunity to make one, would have enjoyed the allusion to her francophone nickname *Asne* (mule) conveyed in the word 'girth'.

The king, meanwhile, continued to write love-verses of his own. Unlike most of his subjects' efforts these have come down to us with his name on, and we can see he was a stickler for poetic propriety, even by the standards of his own times. He was not mercurial. In the king's amorous doings there was always something deadly earnest, and so there is about these formulaic songs with their worthily respectful sentiments. One presses in vain on their surfaces for the double hinges and sliding panels of Wyatt's unstable lyrics – or even for any trace of credible human sentiment.

> *Whereto should I express*
> *My inward heaviness?*
> *No mirth can make me fain*
> *Till that we meet again.*
>
> *Do 'way, dear heart, not so!*
> *Let no thought you dismay;*
> *Though ye now part me fro,*

---

[15] *groigne qui groigne*: grudge on who list; literally, 'grumble who grumbles'.

We shall meet when we may.

When I remember me
Of your most gentil mind,
It may in no wise agree
That I should be unkind.

The daisy delectable,
The violet wan and blo—
Ye are not variable,
I love you and no mo.

I make you fast and sure;
It is to me great pain
Thus longë to endure
Till that we meet again.

It is strange that a man so suspicious – as Henry famously was – could be so *observant*. He did sometimes roll out a hearty double-entendre, heavily signposted. But he could never relate, for example, to the sort of sly mockery of chivalric values that thrived behind his back as the reign wore on and it became increasingly evident that virtue, here, was far from its own reward. A flash of this ribaldry comes down to us in a book that was doing the rounds of Wyatt's circle in the early 1530s, in which someone has written '*presto para servir*' (ready to serve) and others, beneath it, the doubtful coda '*forse*' (perhaps).[16] But the king would have no particle of sympathy for an ungallant sentiment like that. For him there could be no *forse* about his eagerness to serve. He was sincere in all his doings. If he were alive today, he'd be Canadian.

Nobody knows what Anne thought of Henry's personality,

[16] It was a book of French poetry from the previous century, belonging to George Boleyn. See Patricia Thompson, *Sir Thomas Wyatt and his Background* (Stanford, 1964).

or whether she loved this man who loved her, but we do know what she thought of his verse: not much. She was known to have laughed at his clothes and sniggered at his poems. The Spanish ambassador, Chapuys, who hated her, said at the time of her fall that the king had written some 'certain ballades' that 'the concubine and her brother laughed at as inept [gouffe], and which was held against them as a great crime.' Posterity, however, has upheld her judgement. Although Henry was powerfully clever and talented, and the only man at his own court with the full complement of troubador skills, both the poetry and the famous musicality are weaker under scrutiny than he might have liked. To Professor Stevens, much of Henry's own lyrical oeuvre looks suspiciously like borrowings from existing songs:

> The songs and instrumental pieces in the court songbook... are slight and exhibit a level of professional skill rather less distinguished. It is not merely that the king only seems to have one or two 'tunes'... it is a certain blundering about in the inner parts that betrays him.

Henry's contribution, he says, is often to add a part or voice to an existing piece – so often that it 'entitles us to wonder how much of the king's composing was of his own invention'.[17]

The fact that Anne's sharpness of discrimination was 'held against her as a great crime', shows how at her fall she was condemned for those very qualities which had especially recommended her to the king, and that her crime, far from being false, was to be too true to herself. She is unlikely to have scoffed at his poems in front of him, but the quality that enabled her to make the criticism was one he prized in her. Alone of his wives, she would talk to him about religion, and he would listen.

[17] Stevens, op. cit.

CHAPTER NINE

The break from Rome and the start of the English Reformation was the central drama of Henry's reign, and as the reign wore on the question of how to worship pressed increasingly on his subjects' lives. Broadly speaking, Wyatt was a reformer but, being a master of ambivalence in this as in everything else, the extent of his reforming zeal is still under review. In most studies of Wyatt you would expect to find his reforming beliefs examined in detail and his exceptionally dense religious poetry, the 'Penitential Psalms',[1] consulted for clues. But not in this one, which means to keep well clear of the subject, except where reform was interfused with love poetry: a narrow strait perhaps, but wide enough to admit two things – Wyatt's lyrics and Anne Boleyn's activities as the king's wife-in-waiting.

First, Anne: we have seen how Anne's authority derived from her assumption of a hieratic role in the courtly cult of love poetry. Now we can see how she flexed it in the service of the English Reformation.

*   *   *   *

Religious disputation was a particular talent of Henry's. He had practised it for pleasure and display long before the crisis of his divorce, and he continued to exercise it throughout the

---

[1] As with his other poetry, the Penitential Psalms are of uncertain date. Most scholars think he wrote them in 1541 or thereabouts.

reign. Anne – who must have been formidable in argument and astoundingly quick on the uptake – could hold her own with him well enough for this to become part of their repertory of exemplary courtly activities. Their common talent combined with their common interest to make the divorce a joint project. Henry told her everything. The letters he wrote her at this time, and the twinned and twined initials of their names in the *envoi* attest to a genuine partnership, an us-against-the-world complicity that powerfully recalls to the modern reader the letters of a later beleaguered king, Edward VIII, and the American divorcee who would cost him his throne. At the time, however, Henry's openness with Anne on these highly secret matters was evidently well known, and regarded by the king's supporters as something of a menace, thanks to the element of triumphalism in Anne that tempted her to 'leak' good news when she got it. A letter from one Robert Wakefield, a one-time supporter of Catherine's case and the greatest linguist of the day (hence a man who could excavate the scriptures for their truths), declares some nervousness on this score. He writes to the king to say he has changed his mind and will 'defend your cause or question in all the universities of Christendom against all men', but circumspectly begs the king to 'to keep the thing secret from all persons living, *both man and woman*',[2] for fear of repercussions if the queen's party found out. There was only one woman he could mean.

Both Anne and Henry put their hands to the pump. Despite his dislike of handwriting, he was inclined to write at moments of crisis or elation, and now he wrote. Wretchedly separated from Anne, he writes to her 'to advertise you of the great elengenes (loneliness) that I find here since your departing, for I ensure you, methinketh the time longer since your departing now that I was wont to do a whole fortnight. I think the

[2] Harpsfield, op. cit. (Italics mine).

kindness and fervence of love causeth it, for otherwise I would not have thought it possible for so little a while it should have grieved me'. He is able to console himself with the thought that he is 'coming towards you', and is also 'right well comforted, insomuch that my book maketh substantially for my matter, in writing whereof I have spent iiii hours this day, which caused me now to write the shorter letter to you at this time, because of some pain in my head, wishing myself (specially an evening) in my sweetheart's arms, whose pretty ducks [breasts] I trust shortly to kiss.' [3]

The identity of this headache-inducing opus of the king's has never been fully established, though he was evidently contented with its arguments in favour of 'the king's great matter', or 'our matter' as the codename went for operation: divorce.[4] Anne meanwhile, though writing no books herself, did something more effective: she found one that would tell the king what he wanted to hear, and used her special brand of authority to place it in his hands. The book was William Tyndale's *Obedience of a Christian Man*, a radical anti-clerical treatise that was widely trafficked in the literary underground in 1528-9. The manner in which it came into Henry's hands was through an elaborate process of courtly shenanigans, organised by Anne.

Having acquired a copy, Anne, whose untouchable position allowed her to read illegal literature, marked out certain passages ready for the king 'with her nail', but then, curiously, did not give it to him.[5] Perhaps she knew her man, and hesitated to drop transgressive ideas cold into such a temperamentally conservative vessel as Henry's mind. At any rate, she lent it instead

[3] Henry Savage (ed.), *The Love Letters of Henry VIII*, (Allan Wingate, 1949).
[4] It may have been 'The Glass of Truth', a readable and popular digest of the king's case intended for a broad readership and bearing the marks of Henry's interventions. It contains certain details of Queen Catherine's first marriage that would never have been released without Henry's permission. See G.R. Elton, *Policy and Police* (Cambridge, 1972).
[5] George Wyatt, *Life of Anne Boleigne*, op. cit. George Wyatt had this story from Anne Gainsford herself.

to Anne Gainsford, her gentlewoman, whereupon Gainsford's suitor, George Zouche, playfully snatched it from her 'among other love tricks' and refused to give it back. Zouche then took it away and studied it publicly enough to get it confiscated by the dean of the chapel royal and handed in to Cardinal Wolsey. As soon as the book was in Wolsey's possession, Anne went to Henry, her champion, to complain about her lost book and the cardinal's high-handedness. There were tremendous hints at what an interesting book it was. The king's interest was now thoroughly roused: he commanded the return of the treatise and Anne gave it to him to read, with all her instructive markings still in place.

The theatricality of this little episode, with its use of 'love tricks' to spirit the book from Anne to the king (and humiliate Cardinal Wolsey in the process), points to a set-up and shows an opportunistic and adaptive intelligence at work. Someone with perfect command of the courtly game had recognised its potential as a vehicle for weightier matters. Poetry was making something happen.

Now Henry read that clerical authority was contrary to God's law.

> Let kings... rule their realms themselves, with the help of laymen that are sage, wise, learned and expert. Is it not a shame above all shames, and a monstrous thing, that no man should be found able to govern a worldly kingdom, save bishops and prelates that have forsaken the world?

Godly kings should stop diverting their revenues into the papal coffers; they should desist from paying for the pope's wars; they should rise up and reform the church; they were accountable to no one but God. 'The king is in this world without law and may at his own lust[6] do right and wrong and

Anne Gainsford, Mrs Zouche (*Hans Holbein the Younger*)

shall give accounts to God only.'

Henry was as interested as Anne had predicted. 'This book is for me and all kings to read,' he said. He did nothing then to act against Rome, but he mixed these ideas into the general mulch of his musings against the pope; and when his minister, Thomas Cromwell, came to sow his own proposals, he found a receptive surface.

*   *   *   *

Now we have seen how love poetry was used to affect the course of Reform. Looking the other way, it is also possible

[6] lust: liking.

to see how the Reformation changed the way we thought about love. The place where this first registers is in the poetry of Sir Thomas Wyatt.

In most of Wyatt's poetry, love is represented as a bargain, or contract: the lover offers his service in the expectation that the lady will respond with favours, sexual or otherwise. Feminist sensibilities may note with distaste the element of coercion in the courtly lyric: how its emphasis on 'reward' and 'desert' exposes the posture of masculine obsequiousness as a blind for sexual entitlement and the courtly lady as goods for barter. Certainly, a courtly lover in full plain can sound not so much heartbroken as gazumped:

> *I see that chance hath chosen me[7]*
> *Thus secretly to live in pain*
> *And to another given the fee,*
> *Of all my loss to have the gain.*
> *By chance assigned, thus do I serve,*
> *And other have that I deserve.*

This ringing of tills is particularly loud in the poetry of Wyatt and his contemporaries. There is no such bargaining in the poetry of Petrarch, where the reward for the lover's service is the virtue and the dignity assumed in the crucible of its practice. As Wyatt's biographer, Patricia Thompson, has pointed out, no true Petrarchan could think he would 'spend his time in vain', like Wyatt in '*Whoso list to hunt*', just because he doesn't get the girl. Wyatt, meanwhile, has his own bone to pick with the courtly contract: he finds it too loosely drafted. He has been drawn into a rotten bargain where he is expected to pay, and pay again, to make all the suit, do all the begging, all the protestation of devotion, with no guarantee of satisfaction at the end. His is a life of continual exertion with no perceptible reward,

[7] Wyatt, CXXVI, in Rebholz, op. cit.

no increase of security, no reciprocity of affection.

> To *wish and want and not obtain*,[8]
> To *seek and sue ease of my pain*,
> Since *all that ever I do is vain*
> What *may it avail me?*

One may ask what this has got to do with the Reformation. The answer lies in the correspondence between the lover's relationship with his lady and late medieval man's relationship with God. Just as the lover strained to make himself acceptable to the lady, so the early 16th-century Christian strained to be acceptable to God. Hell gaped. How could one be saved? The traditional Church told him he could sue for God's favour with penances, pilgrimages, masses, prayers, good works and, notoriously, by purchasing time off purgatory with the little printed tickets, called indulgences, which the Pope had issued to pay for his building works. Nevertheless, in this enterprise as in the other, there was a presumption against success built into the system: in the case of the lover, his unworthiness of so great a lady, in the case of the Christian, the deeper unworthiness implanted by original sin. The state of grace – salvation – remained elusive, the state of uncertainty prevailed; indeed uncertainty, in both cases, was the spur for renewed efforts.

> For *want of will in woe I plain*[9]
> Under *colour of soberness*,
> Renewing *with my suit my pain*,
> My *wanhope with your steadfastness*.
> Awake *therefore of gentleness*.
> Regard *at length, I you require*,
> The *swelting pains of my desire*.

[8] Wyatt, CVII, in Rebholz, op. cit.
[9] Wyatt, LXXXII. in Rebholz, op. cit. (swelting: sweltering).

Like the lover, the Christian was not supposed to feel frustration or futility or hopelessness, but some did. The enormity of guilt overwhelmed them. How in a little life, with such puny materials, could one ever collect enough points to redeem the great debt? The early Protestants (as they were not known until 1529) found a remedy in removing the contractual element altogether. Salvation had nothing to do with deserts: belief in redemption through human merit was the consequence of years of error and malpractice in the Church. How foolish and impertinent, they declared, to think anything a *man* could do would be impressive to God, or influence His judgement. Man could never deserve salvation; only God could save, and because He was infinitely merciful, He would make mankind a free gift of His forgiveness. The Christian need do nothing but have faith; and even faith was a divine blessing proceeding from God's impulse to save his sinner. Everything then would emanate from God; God would pick up the Christian like an exhausted child and bring him to the place of unassailable safety. For Thomas Bilney, a student at Cambridge, conversion

> did so exhilarate my heart, being before wounded with the guilt of my sins… that immediately I felt a marvellous comfort and quietness… after this, the scripture began to be more pleasant to me than the honey or the honey-comb; where in I learned that all my fasting and watching, all the redemption of masses and pardons, being done without trust in Christ… to be nothing else but… a hasty and swift running out of the right way.

This beautiful idea had an obvious application to matters of love, and it isn't surprising that the first man to use it in poetry was the chronically unreciprocated Wyatt. His later love poems, probably to Elizabeth Darrell,[10] are the only ones to employ it,

[10] The late date and probable subject of this lyric are argued on p103.

and suggest that his relationship with her was of an entirely different order from the disputatious and speculative skirmishes of the courtly game. When he wrote of this lady that:

She from myself now hath me in her grace

what he meant by it was complete acceptance, analogous with the divine acceptance of the justified sinner. All the responsibility for being loved passes away from him, thanks to her; she will do it all for him: 'She *from myself* now hath me in her grace'; and – such is the layered genius of Wyatt's work – in the same lines that hint at their intimacy (and former intimacies, as we have seen), he shows himself also slack and held by his new lover in a posture of absolute trust. 'She hath in hand my wit, my will and all.' She is the author of everything, she will look after him, he has only to fall into her arms.

This slight song marks a momentous occasion in the history of relations between men and women: Wyatt has invoked the possibility of unconditional love and with that, he exits the Middle Ages. He leaves behind the medieval lover, that industrious model of masculinity who must always be doing something and whose counterparts are the warrior, the priest, or the clerk. He becomes an inward man whose feelings towards women are not expressed by a series of prescribed, public actions but communed in tunnels of intimacy, from heart to open heart, a 'quiet and comfortable' matter between lovers. He became the beloved.

*   *   *   *

More generally speaking, the Reformation affected love poetry by raising Christians' consciousness of words and what they meant. This affected all verbal communication at this time, because the new faith was, above all, a religion of the word:

the word spoken in sermons, sung in hymns, but especially the word that might be read by an ordinary, non Latin-speaking man, in his own language. 'What news of God's word?' was the question in every tavern. What about the English Bible? The reformers wanted a Bible in English so that English Christians could take instruction at the pure source instead of, as they saw it, through the polluting ministrations of a priest. To them, a priest was not the sanctified channel of divine mercy, but an impediment thrust between the Christian and his God. Matters were not helped by the low standards of oratory and exegesis prevailing, then as now, among the rank and file of the priest-hood. In the previous century, a small group of English enthusi-asts known as 'Lollards' had begun the work of translating the Gospels and had suffered the savage reprisals of the Church. But the work had gone on. For a long time the output was re-stricted to the amateur efforts of a few Evangelical activists, but then, in 1526, the exiled scholar William Tyndale published his translation of the New Testament and illegal copies came pour-ing into Britain on the wool routes, unstoppable and, thanks to the infinite reproductive capacity of the new printing presses, wholly resistant to such traditional controls as confiscation and book-burning.

Farewell, unknown, for though thou break[11]
My strings in spite with great disdain,
Yet have I found out for thy sake
Strings for to string my lute again.

The violence of the conservative response – the inquisitions, the purges, the searches, the burnings, the putrid invective of such as Thomas More – was not just the defensive reaction of a privileged caste under threat of redundancy. They really did believe the right to read and interpret God's word was too

[11] Wyatt, XCIV, in Rebholz, op. cit.

powerful a weapon to release into the hands of ordinary people, and that only those who had been purified by grace of orders were fit to receive and dispense God's undiluted word. What would happen if the ignorant, or women, got hold of it?

The translators themselves, meanwhile, were fully aware of the gravity of their task. The smallest adjustment of a word could lead the believer into righteousness, or set him on the road to hell. Furthermore, as the religious conservatives knew, the translators had the opportunity of embedding the tenets of the reform faith into the very Bible itself, by the use of this word as opposed to that. This had already happened with Erasmus's Latin translation (from the Greek) of the New Testament. For example, in Erasmus's version of Matthew, John the Baptist had cried out in the wilderness for mankind to 'repent' (*rescipiscite*) – an inward secret impulse from man to God – rather than to 'do penance' (*poenitentiam agite*) – a set of formal penitential activities dictated by the church.[12] An English translation based upon this would permanently enshrine the Evangelical position. In addition, the reformers would only accept doctrine for which scriptural support could be found; so the power of the written word to direct and influence spiritual matters became more and more worryingly apparent.

Anxiety spilled out onto writing of all kinds. Although the early 16th century is far from a golden age of lexicography, concern to establish the meaning of English words, especially in relation to their classical counterparts, resulted in a number of dictionaries being attempted, not without trepidation. English seemed coarse, limited, impliable; besides, there were few English texts of any consequence to support a definition by cross-reference. Latin words, by contrast, had depth and richness acquired, like the sheen on a lacquer bowl, through the layering of numerous and various usages in the ancient texts.

<hr>

[12] See Diarmaid MacCulloch, *Reformation* (Penguin, 2004), from which this example is taken.

How could an English word be expressive and definitive? How could it contain all that was implied in a Latin word, and seal itself against misinterpretation? The stakes were high: Thomas Elyot, the English humanist, first wrestled with the implications of mistranslating the language of governance in his '*Boke called The Governor*' of 1531. What, in English, was the *res publica*? Who were the *plebs*? (a tricky one, when the lowly origins of certain ambitious laymen in the king's inner circle were borne in mind). The subsequent undertaking of an entire Latin-English dictionary[13] nearly floored him. Reviewing the distinguished roster of those who had already tried, and 'remembering my dangerous enterprise (I being of so small reputation in learning in comparison of them, whom I have rehearsed,) as well as to the difficulty in the true expressing the lively sense of the Latin words, as also the importable labours in fetching, expanding and discussing' the terms of ancient writers, he was 'attacked by a horrible fear'. At the letter M he threw in the towel, and only resumed the task at the express intervention of the king.

The obstacles that Elyot encountered are articulated amongst the apologias and prefaces of the times, but perhaps nowhere so expressively as in the grammatical tics of the official writings to emerge from this struggle. Despite protestations to the contrary, early Tudor writers lacked confidence in English as a vehicle for complex ideas. Yet, they wished to be understood; so they devised a style of synonym-laden prose that is particular to them. When they feared a word was unequal to the burden of their import, they propped it up on one side or, in extreme cases, both, with a synonym or near-synonym, like reinforcements sent to the flank of an ailing platoon. A gate must be a 'portal or gate', a bag a 'pouche or sack'.[14] It was not enough that a thing be said; it must be declared, said, and spoken. It

[13] Published in 1538.
[14] From the introduction to William Caxton's translation of *The Book of the Knight of the Tower*, ed. Marguerite Y. Offord (Early English Text Society., OUP, 1971).

was not gracious enough to permit, one had to 'suffer and permit'; not responsive enough to be moved to do something, one had to be 'moved and stirred' to do it; not repentant enough to abolish (religious) abuses, what was required was

> the extirpation abolition and extinguishment of such abuses errours and enormities, as have long been violently maynteyned to the obtuscation [sic] of goddes holy and indeficiable[15] truth.

This peculiar double or even 'triumvirate' pattern produced a rather ponderous and hectoring style of prose that seems not so much to carry the reader as grind him into submission to its arguments. It also made things very long. Translations in English were always longer than the originals, sometimes by a large factor; it was cheerfully accepted that the task of the translator was expansion: Skelton actually defined translation as 'dilating matter'. In this context, then, Wyatt's own tendency to collection (even his prose translations were short) is especially remarkable, as he was going against the grain of the times. It took an unusual mind to produce a line with the proleptic concentration of

The stars be hid that led me to this pain.

The same mind found the sonnet could take, in the way that a song could not, a message made from a single unbroken conceptual thread. You can't expand a sonnet with an extra verse or lines, so you have to pack your meaning tight and deep. This suited Wyatt, who never achieved his emphases by extension or addition, but by an almost geometrical process of intensification – it was as though you could cut his poems through and read them in the cross-section. You read into them, not across.

---

[15] indeficiable: indivisible

He wasn't the only Henrician writer to pack his works with latent meanings; far from it: one might say this was the speciality of the reign. But this was mostly achieved by extensive citations from, and references and allusions to, biblical and classical texts. Wyatt was the one to see you could get something of the same effect by concentrating on the ambivalence of *words themselves*.

> *And I have leave to go of her goodness,*
> *And she also to use new-fangleness*

New-fangleness was a word for faithlessness, but in Wyatt's time it had been recruited by the enemies of reform as a term of abuse for the new religion. Its implications expand in the mind, not on the page. This is not just a matter of verse versus prose. Most of Wyatt's contemporaries thought the 'slipperiness' of the English language was the enemy of clarity. For Wyatt, words were window panes, but for most they were more like bricks to be piled defensively against some fatal breach or leak of meaning.

What really suited Henrician English was the drafting of laws, like the one passed in April 1533, called the Act of Restraint of Appeals. This was the Act that tore the English Church from Rome, and it contained the reign's most egregious instance of romance encroaching on realpolitik. It was a law about legal cases, resting on a fairy tale. It removed the right of contending parties – such, for example, as Catherine of Aragon – to have their case referred to Rome, regardless of whether the matter in hand be secular or spiritual. With this, the Church of England became an autonomous entity with the King of England as its head, enjoying 'plenary, whole and entire power, pre-eminence, authority, prerogative and jurisdiction'. The priestly caste were forbidden to acknowledge any legislative authority beside that of the sovereign monarch because, in the famous words of Cromwell's preamble to this, his most audacious piece of legislation:

> This realm of England is an empire, governed by one Supreme Head and King having the dignity and estate of a royal crown.

What was the basis for that assertion? It had been found in 'divers sundry old authentique histories and chronicles', that is to say, chivalric and Arthurian narratives like Geoffrey of Monmouth's *Historia Regum Britanniae* (History of the Kings of Britain) of 1136, a work of almost pure fiction that was essentially an adaptation of French romance poetry for 'historical' purposes. Here it was claimed that Ancient Britons were descended from Brutus, supposedly the grandson of Aeneas, that survivor of the fall of Troy whose settling in Italy led to the founding of Rome. The discovery of this common ancestor gave ancient Britain a cousinship with ancient Rome, and an equal claim to imperial status.

The humanist historians like Polydore Vergil reacted nervously when they found they were expected to cooperate with this travesty of their own historical rigour. Vergil had been quite unable to find any proof even of the historical existence of Arthur, let alone the immigration figures for characters out of Roman mythology. The king, however, despite his fixation with constitutional propriety and legal forms, had evidently enough of a stake in romance values to find these precedents acceptable, and he let this be the piece of legislation that made him answerable to his own authority and reconciled the requirement for perfect legitimacy with his other requirement, for a divorce. He ordered a set of commemorative tapestries depicting the life of Aeneas for Whitehall, the former palace of Cardinal Wolsey where Anne had long had her own rooms and a hand in the decorating. A tame historian (Wyatt's friend, John

Leland) was quietly found to write a defence of Geoffrey of Monmouth. When Polydore Vergil's *History of England* came out later in the year, it included the story of Arthur. The king's divorce was tried in England.

Speed was now of the essence. Anne was pregnant. Some time around the visit to Calais in the late autumn of 1532 she had succumbed to the king – or persuaded him to succumb to her, whichever version one prefers – perhaps hazarding that a pregnancy, and the fear that the longed-for son be squandered through delay, would outweigh the risk of his losing interest. If so, she was right. Henry married Anne Boleyn in the dark of an early January morning, in a service that 'for certain causes was thought more convenient to be performed somewhat privately and secretly', as George Wyatt put it in his defence of her, not saying that one of these causes was the persistence of the king's first marriage. Luckily, the means for its speedy dissolution were now at hand in the form of Thomas Cranmer, recently consecrated Archbishop of Canterbury. Cranmer was a known Boleyn protégé, avid for religious reform and already exhibiting that tendency to conciliate the king in all things that would be the enduring characteristic of his prelacy. He got to work straight away on the king's divorce, and on May 23, 1533, less than a fortnight after the opening of legal proceedings, he declared the Aragon marriage null and void. Six days later, Anne was crowned queen at Westminster Abbey.

CHAPTER TEN

She went to her coronation with her hair behind and her belly before, each in its own way an expression of her fitness to be queen. Although the order for these celebrations went out as soon as Cranmer's court adjourned, there were only 400 hours in hand to prepare for the greatest display of public pageantry since the visit of Charles V in 1522.[1] Thanks to the peremptory conditions of early Tudor party planning, it was possible in this short time to organise three full days of public entertainments: mobilise the 50 gold-clad barges that preceded the barge she sat in; smother whole streets with gold-thread tapestries; source, transport and caparison regiments of matching white palfreys; devise and make the river-going, firework-spitting monster that wriggled; execute the wine-flowing classical fountains; rehearse the musicians who sang to her triumph; fill the mechanical castle with declaiming allegorical figures; devise, cast and direct the tableaux on the theme of her virtues and supply instructive poetry on the same subject.

Wyatt had no hand in this. Courtier poets never wrote public verse. The commission went to two scholars: John Leland, the king's antiquary, and Nicholas Udall, soon to be famous for flogging schoolboys.[2] Wyatt's role at Anne's coronation was that of a senior courtier. He officiated as chief ewerer at the banquet, not in his own right but deputising for his father, Sir Henry, who, though elderly, had emerged from the recent

[1] Ives, *The Life and Death of Anne Boleyn.*
[2] See note, over.

scramble for position holding this covetable office. The ewerer provided the materials for washing the hands and face – most necessary in the infancy of cutlery – to the massive banqueting tables set up in Westminster Hall and overseen by men trotting up and down on horseback. At one end Anne sat alone under a cloth of estate, eating the 29 dishes of food that were served to her, while Henry looked on from a specially constructed viewing box where he was installed with the French and Venetian ambassadors.

It was said by her enemies that the people of London looked upon this in silence, that the occasion was 'cold, meagre and uncomfortable' (Chapuys), that no one cheered or raised their hats when Anne passed. Chapuys was rather disappointed that they had come at all, preferring for them to have stayed purse-mouthed in their homes, with the doors shut. In any case, the brilliance of the occasion failed to kindle much active

[2] Udall's activities as headmaster of Eton were broadcast in the next reign, as soon as his victims gained the unrestricted use of their pens. One sad alumnus was moved to verse composition:

From Powles [St Paul's] I went
To Aeton sent
To learn straightwaies
The Latin phrase
Where fifty-three
Stripes giv'n to me
At once I had

For fault but small
Or none at all
It came to pass
Thus beat I was.
See, Udall, see,
The mercie of thee to me
Poor Lad.

Udall's headship commenced very soon after the Coronation and may have been a reward for his contribution to the festivities. He stayed in post until 1541, when he was arrested on buggery charges and removed to the Marshalsea prison.

enthusiasm. The people were cool about her. They held her responsible for changes in religion and the ousting of the old, popular queen; they feared she might be French. Besides, she lacked the common touch that has always been held desirable in the consort of an English king, and always turned inwards for support to the sources of her power: the king, the court and her own self.

Her attitude to her family is a case in point. She was not, in fact, the sole author of her destiny: in the years of expectation, her father, brother and uncle had all put the hours in. Her brother acted as a go-between, her father as a pimp, enabling her assignations. One of Henry's letters chides Wiltshire, her father, for slacking in his duties. He had better arrange a meeting soon, he said, 'otherwise I shall think he has no wish to serve the lovers' turn as he said he would, or accord with my expectation.'

Wiltshire was also involved with strategy and image-management, as we know from an exchange he had with her when she was pregnant. He was overheard chiding her for letting out her dresses to hide her pregnancy, saying she should be proud of her condition. Anne, who was incapable of opening her mouth without making a pun, made one now on her 'condition', retorting that she was in a better state (condition, in the sense of social position) than *he* had wished her to be, that is to say, the Queen of England. This gives us a glimpse into a background of family confabulations over the timing of her pregnancy – strongly suggesting that Wiltshire had advised her to keep the king out, and thought her failure to do so would ruin everything, and had let her know it. But it also shows that she was prepared to defy him. Though she may not have always acted alone, she was not a counter in the power-play of an ambitious family, nor was she conspicuously grateful for their interventions. As far as she was concerned, she owed them little: she had noted their every act of self-preserving caution, every vacillation or hesitation, every failure of nerve, every point of divergence with her own programme, and now that she was queen, far from letting these little difficulties burn off in the general radiance of her zenith, she took this moment to present the account.

In some ways this was understandable: everyone at court was related by blood or marriage, one had to draw the line or be buried in the rush; but Anne was a bridge-burner by nature, not a conciliator, and a termagant to boot. As Henry's companion, she had never been one to cut her cloth. Henry's letters swim with mollification and – in response to some lost rebuff – the sort of shaken dignity one sees in a senior dog in retreat from an unexpected cat. When he tried to reconcile her with Wolsey, she never really accepted him as an ally and, despite his evident usefulness, went on behaving like a challenger for his post. Now as queen she was the same, maintaining old enmities and forging new ones. Princess Mary, the king's sister, who had refused to accompany Anne and the king to Calais, was also absent from her coronation proceedings.[3] Even in 1535, when her lack of sons had left her in need of friends, Anne sent the Duke of Norfolk, her senior kinsman, spinning from her room with 'shameful words that one would not address [to] a dog' (Chapuys), while he shouted back that she was a '*grande putain*' (great whore). *Semper Eadem* (Always the Same) was an apt choice for her motto, but consistency was, perhaps, the very last quality one needed for long-term survival.

As queen she chose a new one: The Most Happy. The phrase may have had some private resonance for Henry and her. We first found it in the lyric *Grudge on who List* (p146), where the speaker predicted she would become 'happiest that ever was,/ If it were not'. The subsequent appearance of these words on a medal, most probably struck to commemorate the expected birth of a son in 1534,[4] suggests that the unspecified 'it' was

---

[3] Mary Tudor may have been ill. She died later that month, but there is no reason to think she had softened her position on Anne.

[4] Ives, 'The Queen and The Painters', *Apollo,* July 1994. This unique medal, of curiously low quality, is in the British museum.

indeed the Aragon marriage. It also appears in a Wyatt poem that has never been included in the canon of his 'Anne Boleyn' poems, because it is usually thought to be about God, not Henry.

> After great storms the calm returns[5]
> And pleasanter it is thereby.
> Fortune likewise that often turns
> Hath **made me now the most happy**...
>
> ...Wherefore despaired ye, my friends?
> My trust **alway in him** did lie
> That knoweth what my thought intends,
> Whereby I live the most happy.

But the presence of Anne's distinctive motto among the words of thanksgiving gave an alternative, or parallel, identification for 'him': the king. Wyatt's inner circle knew who and what this phrase referred to, from its history in the pastime. For them – and only for them – the 'him' who 'knoweth what my thought intends', could combine Anne's intimate saviour, Henry, with an intimate type of God: one who will save on the strength of a man's inward thoughts, and therefore commend the new Church that Anne had helped to bring about. For a moment, Henry and God elide. After all, as the scholar Stephen Greenblatt has remarked, 'the two irascible autocrats [God and Henry] seem... to bear a striking resemblance to one another.'[6]

For Wyatt and Anne, to be 'happy' did not mean that condition which Americans strive for by right, or even the remission of pain. 'Prosperity, emotional contentment' was the primary definition, but the force of the word 'hap' was still alive in it: a noncommittal concept meaning 'fortune' or 'chance' or

[5] Wyatt, CXIV, 1st and 3rd verses, in Rebholz, op. cit.
[6] Stephen Greenblatt, *Renaissance Self-Fashioning* (University of Chicago Press, 2005).

'luck'. Hap could be good or bad, like weather. Like weather, it changed. You could have a lot of it, or not. Wyatt loved it for the way he could load it either way, for its manner of sly signalling to circumstances outside the frame of the poem.

> *Such hap as I am happed in*[7]
> *Hath never man of truth, I ween.*

And for the way it could be good and bad at the same time:

> *But spite of thy hap, hap hath well happed.*[8]

A verbal prestidigitator like Anne Boleyn would be well aware of this, and would enjoy the way her new motto alluded to her own audacity, with a sense that corresponds in modern English most closely to 'the most chancy'. She may have suspected that hap wasn't through with her yet.

Chancily, she sloughed off her uncle Norfolk for his conservative opinions on religion, and cast in her lot with his enemy, Thomas Cromwell, the king's new chief minister: a man of her own evangelical persuasion who had shown he could get things done.

> The said Lady Anne does not cease night or day to procure the disgrace of the Duke of Norfolk, whether it has been because he has spoken too freely of her or because Cromwell, desiring to lower the great ones, wishes to commence with him. (Chapuys)

Cromwell duly raised a forest of legislation round the turrets of her queenship. Historians sometimes point to this as the moment when neutrality ceased to be an option: 'If you weren't for

---

[7] Wyatt, LXXXVII, in Rebholz, op. cit.
[8] Wyatt, LXXXVI, in Rebholz, op. cit.

Henry and Anne, you were against them.'[9]

Cromwell's Act of Succession of 1534 introduced a capital punishment, as for treason, for even speaking against the king, the queen or the Boleyn marriage, asserted the illegality of the Aragon marriage, and established Anne's children as the only rightful heirs to the English throne. Every man had to swear the Oath of Succession, declaring the legitimacy of the new marriage.[10] So densely did he hedge Anne round, in fact, that when he wanted to be rid of her, there was no chink through which she might pass back into the world of Henry's subjects; and this is one reason why a radical solution had to be found.

Many explanations have been offered for Anne's fall, none of them wholly convincing. It is certain that the birth of a son would have saved her. The bonny baby girl born on September 7, 1533, and christened Elizabeth, offered hope for healthy boys, but two miscarriages followed, and the king, who had seen no prognostic of God's displeasure in the threats of excommunication that issued from Rome, saw one clearly now in the fact that he had no male heir and his wife was getting old. He had been promised a son; and now he had two daughters, each the product of a questionable marriage – for despite everything, the imperialists rejected the new marriage. At the second miscarriage Henry lost sympathy. 'I see that God will not give me male children,' he said, when he was informed.

Now everything started to fall away: Cromwell began quietly to unhook himself from Anne, and let it be known that he was no longer of her party. She disagreed with him on the allocation of funds from the newly dissolved monasteries, and besides, new developments in Europe had made him tend to favour an

[9] Derek Wilson, *In the Lion's Court: Power, Ambition and Sudden Death in the court of Henry VIII* (Hutchinson, 2001).

[10] This was the oath that Bishop Fisher and Thomas More refused to sign. More had no quarrel with the nominated heirs. His objections were reserved for the preamble to the Act, which stated that all Henry's subjects 'spiritual and temporal' rejected the right of the 'Bishop of Rome' as the pope was now called, to legislate in matters 'given by God immediately to Emperors and Princes'.

alliance with the Spanish, to whom Anne was anathema. At the same time, her traditional allies in France made it clear that, while Anne might look French to the English commoners, she was not French to France. The deaths in 1535 of More and Fisher, martyrs to the Oath, had scandalised Christian Europe and were widely seen as her doing; France joined in the general execration, adding some observations about her morals for good measure.

At court, meanwhile, another front was mobilising against her. She had shown that it was possible for the daughter of a mere English gentleman to become Queen of England. In doing so she had opened up a new swift passage to favour, a most interesting development for those still plying the old passages of service and farm produce. You could queue for days with your potted pears and never get a word in Cromwell's ear. But now courtiers were reviewing the ranks of their kinswomen in a new and thoughtful light. As Wyatt put it in a poem or 'letter' addressed to Sir Francis Bryan, and full of sardonic 'counsel' about how to get on at court:

> In this also see you be not idle:[11]
> Thy niece, thy cousin, thy sister, or thy daughter,
> If she be fair, if handsome be her middle,
> If thy better hath her love besought her,
> Advance his cause and he shall help thy need.
> It is but love. Turn it to a laughter.
> But ware, I say, so gold thee help and speed,
> That in this case thou be not so unwise
> As Pandar was in such a like deed;
> For he, the fool, of conscience was so nice
> That he no gain would have for all his pain.

[11] Wyatt, Satire 3, *Letter to Bryan*, CLI, in Rebholz, op. cit.

If Bryan had very little need of this advice, having done in earnest most of what Wyatt condemns in his satire, he was not the only one. The Seymours of Wolf Hall were excellent examples of this principle. Like everyone else, they had noticed that even with such an unhelpful harridan as Anne at the fore, the Boleyns had done well. There was the earldom, the lands and offices, the political heft, the diplomatic range, everywhere the sight of Boleyns stroking their beards at the council table. The Seymours had a likely daughter, the mild and pliable Jane. If she could pass where Anne had gone, the whole Seymour fleet would come cruising up in her wake. They had noted how Anne had forced this particular passage, and now they carefully coached Jane to do the same, in her own melt-watery way. Not much is known about Jane's character. Most likely her

Jane Seymour (*Hans Holbein the Younger*)

meekness was exaggerated in the official documents in order to draw a strong distinction between this gentlewoman-queen and the other one; but she was certainly compliant enough to do just as she was told by her brother and his wife; that is, to put the price of marriage on her virginity, and keep telling the king how the people abominated his present marriage and doubted its validity.

The king responded in exactly the way they thought he would: more like a serially divorcing bourgeois of our own day than a Renaissance prince, he serially allowed his choice of queen to be influenced by reaction against the most recent incumbent. He liked this girl, with her 'loving inclination and reverend conformity'. He failed to notice he was being led by the nose. The exact point at which the Seymour plan looked like it had legs probably coincided with the defection of Sir Francis Bryan to their camp.

> *But they that sometime liked my company*[12]
> *Like lice away from dead bodies they crawl*

Catherine of Aragon died in January of 1536, ostensibly clearing the last obstacle in Anne's path, but in reality depriving her of her last refuge. While Catherine lived, Henry could not remove his new wife without restoring the old, nor could Mary's supporters assert her legitimacy without touching on that of the Aragon marriage – the denial of which was the point where Henry stuck. With Catherine dead, none of these problems obtained. Henry could look elsewhere.

> *For though I have – such is my lot*[13]
> *In hand to help that I require,*
> *It helpeth not.*

[12] Wyatt, LXVIII, in Rebholz, op. cit.
[13] Wyatt, LXXXVII, in Rebholz, op. cit.

It is somehow characteristic of Anne's extravagantly 'happy' trajectory that this, the occasion of her highest ascent, concealed the impulse for the downswing. She and Henry put on yellow satin and danced for the old queen's death. Weeks later, she miscarried a second time. The beam of the king's protection swung away, leaving her in the dark.

CHAPTER ELEVEN

They flee from me that sometime did me seek[1]
With naked foot stalking in my chamber.
I have seen them gentle, tame, and meek
That now are wild and do not remember
That sometime they put themself in danger
To take bread at my hand; and now they range
Busily seeking with a continual change.

On April 24, 1536, Cromwell set up a commission to gather information concerning certain, unspecified, treasonable activities in Middlesex and Kent. On May 19, Anne was dead. How active he was in seeking her destruction is still a question in dispute, and probably always will be. In some versions, he plotted against her from the first. He needed her dead because she stood in the way of his new Imperial alliance, or disagreed with his religious programmes. He acted to remove her from fear that she would remove him first; moreover, her record of re-igniting the king's guttering interest meant she must be 'knocked on the head' like a bacterium, in case some insufficiently powerful strike at her should fail and cause her, and all her Boleyn adherents, to come raging back at him with newly invigorated strength. In other scenarios, the king was tired of her and he was serving the king's turn. Sometimes Henry appears as Cromwell's master, sometimes as his dupe. Some argue that the king believed in her guilt and others that he knew she

---

[1] Wyatt, LXXX, in Rebholz, op. cit.

was innocent. A very few think she was actually guilty of the crimes she was charged with. You can read these accounts one after the other and agree with all of them;[2] such is the ingenuity of our eminent historians; and this book has no intention of proposing a new solution, but to look from its own perspective at one generally accepted scenario (that of Eric Ives).[3] In this, Anne is innocent, Cromwell is both the *fons et origo* of the plot and the overseer of its details. Cromwell himself said he was the one to '*fantasier et conspirer*'[4] the said affair; there is no reason to think he was lying. He also claimed to have acted on the authority of the king. The point at issue – which determines Cromwell's autonomy in this matter – is one of timing. At what stage did the king authorise these proceedings? According to Ives, this was achieved only after Cromwell had 'tip[ped] Henry into crisis', with a scenario which, he knew, would act upon Henry's prejudices, egotism and suspicions with sufficient force to effect the necessary response. But how did he do it?

This is where poetry comes in.

*   *   *   *

In the days of May 1536, when Anne was imprisoned and awaiting execution, John Hussee, the delightful agent of Lord and Lady Lisle, wrote to his mistress, who was out in Calais and missing all this drama, about the gossip emerging from the court. From her point of view it can hardly have been a satisfactory letter, as it dwelt far too little on the details and far too much on how unsuitable they were for Lady Lisle's ear; but it was better than no news. 'Madam,' he began,

[2] For an account in which Cromwell acted on Henry's orders, see Suzannah Lipscomb, *1536: the Year that Changed Henry VIII* (Lion Hudson, 2009) For one in which Anne is guilty, see G.W. Bernard, *Anne Boleyn, Fatal Attractions* (Yale University Press, 2010).

[3] In the 2004 edition of his great biography of Anne, *The Life and Death of Anne Boleyn*.

[4] *fantasier et conspirer*: invent and conspire.

I think verily, if all the books and chronicles were totally revolved[5] and [those things] to the uttermost persecuted[6] and tried, which against women hath been penned, contrived and written since Adam and Eve, those same were, I think, verily nothing in comparison with that which Queen Anne hath done; which though I presume be not all thing as it is now rumoured, yet that which hath been by her confessed, and others, offenders with her, by her own alluring, procurement and instigation, is so abominable and detestable that I am ashamed any good woman should give ear unto.

I have italicised the first part of this long explanation, not because it shows scepticism (it doesn't. Hussee thinks Anne has confessed to most of it, as the second part shows), but because Hussee has stumbled on something central to the plot against Anne: that, though neither penned nor written, it was a literary construction. What Cromwell 'invented and conspired' was essentially a piece of poetic fiction, based on that familiar trope of romance poetry: a high lady, taken in adultery. He presented a courtly game as earnest, and such was the condition of the English court, unconfident in letters, uneasily balanced between credulity and cynicism in relation to chivalric mores, that it was able to persuade itself it was true. There was poetic justice in this, if no other kind, because Anne herself had risen on the same ticket. She had played the courtly lady for real power; Cromwell's idea was to use her own strength against her.

The events of the week of the arrests began on Saturday, April 29, 1536, when the queen had an argument with the groom of the stool, Henry Norris. Norris was an adherent of the Boleyns and the most influential man in the court, being Henry's most intimate body-servant and his closest friend. His

[5] revolved: turned over.
[6] persecuted: prosecuted.

beautiful manners and perfect pitch in matters of courtesy had earned him the name 'Gentle Norris'. In the course of this Anne said something rash; so rash, that when she realised they had been overheard she made Norris go to her almoner[7] and 'swear the queen was a good woman' – an uncharacteristically clumsy move that shows what strain she was under. It was highly counterproductive. Later that day she had been seen in conversation with a morose young musician of the chamber, called Mark Smeaton, who had been moping conspicuously around her. Meanwhile, the news of Norris' visit to the almoner had been wafted to the king, and on the Sunday, petitioners queuing for Cromwell in the courtyard at Greenwich had seen, through an open window above them, a curious, mute tableau of the queen holding out her baby daughter in a gesture of entreaty to an evidently angry king, who was standing in the window alcove and glowering down into the courtyard.[8] That night, Mark Smeaton was removed to Cromwell's house at Stepney for interrogation, and accused of adultery with the queen. By some accounts, he was grievously tortured. Strictly speaking, this was illegal, but, as a deracinated Fleming, a court entertainer without family or connections, he was torturable as none of the other suspects would be, and this may well ultimately account for the inclusion of this random waif in the line-up of Anne's 'lovers'. Cromwell could not proceed without a confession of some sort as a 'starter' for his brew, and he was hardly going to get one from Sir Henry Norris. With this little bit-player's confession, imaginatively deployed, he would get Norris anyway. It took some hours to get one even out of Smeaton.

The boy confessed. An hour before midnight, long-held plans for the king and queen to visit Calais in the first week of May – that is, the following week – were quietly cancelled.

[7] almoner: a personal chaplain in the queen's household.
[8] Eye-witness account of Alexander Ales, who sent it to Queen Elizabeth I in 1559. In Ives, *The Life and Death of Anne Boleyn.*

On Monday, the king and queen attended the May Day tournament. Anne's brother, George, Lord Rochford, led the challengers in the joust, Sir Henry Norris the defenders. Thomas Wyatt was on particularly fine form that day, according to the author of the *Cronica del Rey*, who added, 'This master Wyatt was a very gallant gentleman and there was no prettier man at court than he was.' The king is said to have offered Norris his own horse – perhaps to further obligate him for what was coming next. Anne, Queen of the May, spectated from her box, all graciousness and expertise, and everything appeared to be as usual until suddenly, at the end of the joust, Henry left the party with a small group including Henry Norris and, exceptionally, they returned to Whitehall on horseback, not by water. 'And of this sudden departing did many men muse, and chiefly the queen,' wrote Edward Hall. The queen was now left alone with the abandoned remnants of the festivities. She would never see Henry again.

On the long ride back, Henry examined Norris on the subject of the queen's adultery – 'and promised him his pardon in case he would utter the truth'. It is not known if, at this initial stage, the nominal price of his safety was an admission of his own guilt or just a confirmation of the queen's. At first, he said nothing; a little later, he was persuaded to make some kind of admission, which he withdrew at once. Thereafter he continued to protest Anne's innocence and his loyalty to the king.

> *Accused though I be without desert*[9]
> *None can it prove, yet ye believe it true.*
> *Nor never yet, since that ye had my heart*
> *Entended I to be false or untrue.*
> *Sooner I would of death sustain the smart*
> *Than break one thing of that I promised you.*

---

[9] Wyatt, LXVI, in Rebholz, op. cit.

Henry allowed him to be removed to the Tower the next morning, May 2. That same morning a body of senior lawyers and counsellors, including her uncle, the Duke of Norfolk, came to Greenwich to examine Anne, after which they took her away to the Tower, accused of adultery with three unidentified men. More arrests followed: five in all, including her brother, George, two other gentlemen with positions in the privy chamber – Francis Weston and Sir William Brereton – and Thomas Wyatt.

The reason for Wyatt's arrest has been much debated, because he wasn't charged along with the others, and he didn't die. It now seems that his presence there was more important than has formerly been supposed, and nastier. His experience of incarceration deserves a chapter to itself. In the meantime, we must return to Anne.

In the Tower, she lost command. Her custodian there was Sir William Kingston, constable of the Tower and well known to Henry's senior subjects as the Angel of Death. In 1530, when Cardinal Wolsey learned it was Kingston who had come for him, to escort him back to London, he knew at once his disgrace was terminal. See, soothed Cavendish, his gentleman usher, the king has sent 'gentle Master Kingston for you... willing also Master Kingston to remove you with as much honour as was due to you in your high estate'. But Wolsey grasped the portent of the name, and repeated it twice, with a heavy sigh, and said, 'Well, well... I perceive more than ye can imagine, or do know... all these comfortable words which ye have spoken be but for a purpose to bring me into a fool's paradise: I know what is provided for me.' Then his bowels liquefied.

Anne Boleyn in the same position was less philosophical. She was in shock and disbelief, and still thought she might set matters right. Learning who was in the Tower with her, she began to grope, aloud, for some rationale to the prisoners, looking for a case she could answer, a misunderstanding she could address; and in doing so, she gave Cromwell just enough material to dress up a case against her.

She dredged up her last contact with Smeaton. It wasn't much. He was over-familiar in her presence. She had seen him mooning around her and told him off for his impertinence, reminding him that the courtly game is a club with a closed entry: 'You may not look to have me speak to you as I should to a noble man, because you be an inferior person.' And Mark had said, 'no, madam, a look sufficed me, and farewell.' The details of the row with Norris were more fruitful. Anne had been talking to him about his betrothal to her cousin, Margaret Shelton, and why he had gone cold on the matter. His coolness may have seemed a sign of her own waning influence. It riled her enough to trip the regrettable outburst: 'You look for dead man's shoes,' she said. 'For if aught came to the king but good you would look to have me'. Norris was horrified by the imputation. Even before the Treason Act of 1534, this might have been enough to get him killed, as it encompassed the ancient crime of 'imagining the king's death'. He 'would his head were off', he said, rather than harbour such a thought.

As for Francis Weston, Anne could remember a conversation over a year before – again with Margaret Shelton at the centre of it. She had chided him for flirting with Madge, when Madge was betrothed to Norris. Weston had then said that Norris came to Anne's chamber more on account of Anne than of Madge, adding that he, Weston, also loved someone in her household better than Madge or his own wife: 'it is yourself'.

William Kingston took careful note and sent these terrified overspillings in letters to Thomas Cromwell; and when Cromwell received them he altered the charge against Norris from concealment of the 'truth' to adultery and the plotting of regicide. All the arrested men maintained their innocence, but Cromwell knew that the very fact of so many arrests would substantiate his case in a legal system when accusation was nine

parts of a conviction. Courtiers, recognising an opportunity to
dish their enemies and position themselves under the shower-
head of soon-to-be liberated possessions, came forward to depose or insinuate, with the results we read of in Hussee's letter.

Within a week Cromwell had confected, from this single in-
gredient of rancid courtly banter, the case for adultery, incest
and attempted murder, and tried the queen 'before a commission and two grand juries before the highest judicial tribunal
in the realm'.[10] It was audacious in the extreme. Even in fiction
it would be bold. Think of Desdemona in the high courts of
Venice, tried on the basis of a dropped handkerchief. To make
an indictment from such flimsy materials, you would have had
to forget, or pretend to forget, that there was any such thing as
courtly love. Cromwell may not have been an intimate of the
queen's chamber, but he had more cultivation than most who
were. He read poetry, collected pictures. He knew perfectly well
how the courtly bargain worked in the case of a queen: amorous protestations were paid in, and favours paid out in grants,
offices and promotions, not sex. Moreover, he knew the convention well enough to see that the tone of her chamber was
slightly risqué, and could be turned to advantage. Most of the
queen's 'lovers' were carefully plucked from the group where
the courtly game was played at a high pitch of suggestiveness,
balanced on a blade between earnest and game. Francis Weston
was 'but young, skant out of the shell'[11] and his life is well described in the debts he died owing: to his fletcher, his embroi-
derer, his tailor, his barber, his groom, his sadler, his shoemak-
er; to the woman who provided the tennis balls; to the top court
goldsmith, for losses at cards and dice to such as Francis Bryan,
Thomas Wiltshire, the king. If other gentlemen from this racy
set had been selected – Sir Edmund Knyvet, for instance, or Sir
Francis Bryan (who very nearly was, as we will see) – would

[10] J.A. Froude, *The Reign of Henry VIII* (1913).
[11] George Cavendish, *Metrical Visions,* ed. A.S.G. Edwards *(Columbia SC, 1980).*

she have had some similar indiscretion to recall? Very probably. Two of the conversations Anne remembered had taken place on the same day. It is reasonable to infer that they were not uncommon.

The four non-nobles – Weston, Norris, Brereton and Smeaton – were to be tried first, and then, some days later, the queen and her brother before a special court consisting of the English nobility in its entirety. These were the flowers of Henry's great Renaissance court and they swore on their honour, not on their oaths like commoners. If they felt themselves in some grotesque enactment of the *parlement*, or court of love, there was no sign of it. Besides, Cromwell had worded his indictment to frame Anne's crimes as a breach of courtly laws as well as nuptial ones.[12] He made her out as the active party:

> She, despising her marriage, and entertaining malice against the king, did falsely and maliciously procure by base conversations and kisses, touchings, gifts and other infamous incitations, divers of the king's daily and familiar servants to be her adulterers and concubines, so that several of the king's servants yielded to her vile provocations.[13]

Henry's nobles knew what to do. When people were called upon to 'prove' a crown case they were expected to affirm it, not test it. Many of them thought the Boleyn marriage was a political liability; all of them valued their lives. Failure to supply a guilty verdict would expose them to Norris's original charge of concealing truth, if not a worse one. At any rate, Cromwell was sufficiently sure of them to list specific, dated instances of the queen's adultery without bothering to check whether she

---

[12] Adultery of a queen was not a treasonable offence at the time of Anne's trial and didn't become one until 1542, when the law was inserted into the Act of Attainder condemning her successor, Catherine Howard, for the same offence.

[13] Anne Boleyn, indictment, May 1536, LP 10, 876.

and the named accessory had been in the same part of England at the time. In half the cases, they had not.

What about the king? Cromwell would have known that in this, as in the Oath of Succession, any niggling reservations of Henry's would easily dislodge in the cataract of judicial confirmation he was about to release. But he would never have got that far without the king's assent. There must have been a moment of anxiety at the presentation stage of this campaign, when he had to spin the 'evidence' to the king. The king's culture was deeply held; how could he possibly swallow it? Fortunately for Cromwell, he was exploding his feeble device on a point of the king's great weakness: his capacity for credulousness in matters of courtly love. The inclusion of Smeaton and Norris was a move designed to appeal to the king's outraged sense of propriety, not least because both represented stock figures in the cast of romance literature. Smeaton, the varlet – whose confession Cromwell had – was an untouchable in this system: for a queen to stoop to that was an abomination. Norris was the king's best friend. And was not Tristan, was not Lancelot, the king's best friend? Whatever part of him it was that had taken Anne as the embodiment of one romantic concept now took her as another: the adulteress, the sorceress, the betrayer of man. As soon as he was told, he believed everything. He wallowed in credulity.

For reasons that no one has ever been able to explain fully, Henry wanted her dead, though he may not have even known he did until the opportunity was laid before him, together with the materials for self-deception. Henry's behaviour betrays his assent, as we can see by comparing it with his reaction to similar news six years later, when he had a wife he adored. Then, his instinct was all for suppression, denial, punishment for the tale-bearers. When proof was brought that she loved another, he locked himself away in an extremity of humiliated grief. But in 1536, all his instinct was for promotion. He fostered his convictions by repeating every slander and adding some flourishes of his own. Anne had had 100 lovers, she had bewitched him, he was lucky to get off with his life. He revived a baseless rumour that she had tried to poison the late queen and the princess Mary. He even, if Chapuys can be believed, wrote it all up in a little 'tragedy' of his own devising which he would fish out from his pocket and wave about – an act that is psychologically consistent with his enduring need to support legislation with documentation. He said he had 'long expected the outcome of these affairs and had *before* composed a tragedy' on the subject.[14] He had always known.

This is not to say that Henry killed his wife because he had a weakness for courtly literature – of course not. Nor did Anne die because of the kind of poetry that flourished in her circle. The materials of Cromwell's plot were the Treason Act of 1534, which turned speaking against the king into a capital offence- and Smeaton's confession. But it needed a spark of an incident, and oxygen to thrive, and these were supplied by the king's susceptibilities and the goings-on in Anne's chamber. Here, as has been often said, 'pastime was never more'; but the peculiar suitability of those pastimes to Cromwell's purpose is what concerns us here. His plot relied upon the deliberate misinterpretation of a private language: in Anne's chamber they exulted in its shape-shifting shimmer, not realising that the wind might change. And here we must look to Thomas Wyatt, because he was the principal exponent of this, and his poetry its highest expression. Take another look at the central episode of his most famous poem:

Thanked be fortune it hath been otherwise[15]
Twenty times better, but once in special,
In thin array after a pleasant guise
When her loose gown from her shoulders did fall

[14] Letter from Chapuys to Charles V, May 16, 1536.
[15] Wyatt, LXXX, in Rebholz, op. cit.

And she me caught in her arms long and small,
Therewithal sweetly did me kiss
And softly said, 'Dear heart, how like you this?'
It was no dream: I lay broad waking.
But all is turned thorough my gentleness
Into a strange fashion of forsaking.

It was no dream. It was an axiom of love poetry that women made no advances and sexual fulfilment could occur only inside the iridescent envelope of a dream. In poems, the dreamer wakes alone. Not in this poem: *I lay broad waking.* This happened. It was a real girl, real pain, real betrayal.

For us, so adapted to confessional literature that even works of historical and scientific investigation must be floated to us on voyages of personal authorial discovery, it might not be evident what an outrage this was. But Wyatt's friends in the cognoscenti would have known it at once for an act of audacious and flamboyant rule-breaking. When this poem was read out, everyone would have known who 'she' was. There would have been tittering, glances, an intake of breath.

And yet. Is this really what it claims to be – a personal confession? We are ill-advised to take any of Wyatt's poems like that. What can certainly be said is this: nothing could be closer to the heart of his enterprise than these lines, where the treachery of the courtly lyric collides with the impulse to truth, and we are challenged to believe, or disbelieve, that a lyric poem can be a stage for personal revelation. We can also say that few things were less appealing to the king's own mental temper than an *unreliable narrator.* As Cromwell knew, Henry hated doubt.

CHAPTER TWELVE

When Anne Boleyn found out who was with her in the Tower, her first response was characteristic. 'They may well make pallets now,' she joked: a hysterical, inappropriate pun on pallet/ballade which shows that her head was already in a different place from the rest of her. As always with her, the point was well made. These refined courtiers had gone in a day from poetry-making to making their own beds with straw. Much good may their poems do them now; much good had they done all of them. Not that she could drop the matter, even now. The letter containing these almost unique instances of this vanished woman's utterance is badly damaged, but it appears that the next thing she said to astonished captors was, 'Only Wyatt can do it' – thus demonstrating a preoccupation with poetic excellence which is rarely found in prisoners on a capital charge, or English queens as a class. Lady Kingston, her attendant-cum-guard, agreed with this judgement and Sir William Kingston solemnly wrote it all down and sent it to Cromwell to swell his case as best he could.

Neither Anne nor Lady Kingston had any opinions on the reasons for Wyatt's presence in the Tower, though they obviously thought he was of a parcel with the other arrests. On the outside, rumour ran wild. Nobody knew when the arrests would end; the Duke of Norfolk heard he was in the Tower himself. John Hussee, busy in the mills of gossip, wrote to Lord Lisle in Calais on May 13,

Here are so many tales I cannot well tell which to write; for now this day some saith young Weston shall 'scape; and some saith there shall none die but the queen and her brother; and some say that Wyat and Mr. Page are as like to suffer as the others... But I think verily they shall all suffer, and in case any do escape it shall be young Weston, for whose life there is importunate suit made.[1]

This was of interest to Lisle for reasons beyond prurient curiosity: the arrested men were all in possession of extensive lands and offices, now about to come up for redistribution under the treason laws. Nor was it the done thing at the time to wait until detainees were convicted, before petitioning for their goods and titles. Ripeness was all. On May 2, the day after Norris's arrest, one Richard Staverton had got to hear of it and wrote to Cromwell:

Various offenders have been committed to the tower, among others Master Henry Norris, who has various rooms in the parts about me near Windsor, for which I hope you will have me in remembrance. He has the little park, the park of Holy John, Perlam Park, and the room of the black rod in Windsor castle, which I shall be glad to have, as I have 14 children.[2]

'Here is every man for himself,' wrote Hussee, and never more so than now. People who could, rushed up to London to make themselves conspicuous, and from those who couldn't, the letters came in so thick and fast that the treasurer had to make it known he was not planning to open any 'until this business be rid out of hand'.

Though Wyatt's arrest appeared to Hussee, as to Anne, of

[1] Muriel St Clare Byrne (ed.), *The Lisle Letters* (Penguin, 1985).
[2] Letter from Staverton to Cromwell, May 2, 1536.

a piece with the other arrests, historians have queried his presumption. It is thought that he may have been arrested on some other unrelated charge (which then became confused with the Boleynite arrests); or perhaps he was one whose connivance could not be relied upon, and he was put away to silence him. But among these, another, less complimentary scenario is beginning to emerge. In this, Thomas Wyatt was not arrested to keep him quiet, but to make him talk.

The events of that week, which I also extract from the account given by Eric Ives, proceeded like this. Anne, Smeaton, Norris and Anne's brother, George Rochford, were all in the Tower by the close of day on May 2. The next day, none except Smeaton had confessed 'to any thing' and the council were seeking further evidence to support the charges. Anne's babblings in the Tower resulted in the arrest, between May 4 and 5, of young Francis Weston, along with Sir William Brereton, a middle-aged groom of the privy chamber (whom she had not mentioned and whose inclusion is thought to be purely factional). But what she said was not enough on its own to condemn her, because it was not until May 9 that Cromwell felt secure enough of his case to call for juries. In the meantime, he continued his interrogations.

News of the first arrests reached Sir Henry Wyatt, now old and bedbound at Allington Castle but alert enough to see what danger his son was in. He wrote to Wyatt on May 7, urging him to assist proceedings in any way he could. He must get himself into the king's presence and stay there 'night and day'. That was no longer possible: Cromwell had blocked access to the king and had taken control of the investigation himself. Wyatt may have been trying to get to the king on May 7 or 8, when Cromwell called him in for questioning. He also summoned Sir Francis Bryan to come 'in all haste on allegiance' and another courtier, Richard Page, was called for in the same 'marvellous peremptory' vein that made them fear the worst. What happened then we do not know. Of Page little is known, but Wyatt and Bryan – here, as so often, one another's shadow – were both intimates of Anne's chamber and impeccable potential sources of information about her behaviour. Either would have done for a lover of Anne, or a witness. They were aligned behind different court patrons: Wyatt was a Boleynite, but Bryan, as we have seen, had already defected elsewhere. Certainly, Wyatt believed he was a victim of faction, and that the anti-Boleynite Duke of Suffolk, who hated him with an everlasting hate, had agitated for his arrest and execution. The night before his imprisonment, he must have sensed his head within the sights of the investigation, because he went straight to Suffolk and confronted him in desperate language, asking him 'to remit his old undeserved evil will, and to remember like as he was a mortal man, so to bear no immortal hate in his breast'.[3] By which he meant: stop, because you put your immortal soul in danger if you pursue your vendetta past this limit, and send me to my death. Suffolk persisted.

Whatever backstairs pressures were brought to bear, the upshot of it all was that Cromwell interviewed Page, Wyatt and Bryan, and he let Bryan go. The other two were conveyed to the Tower. The writer of the *Cronica del Rey*, the semi-literate busybody whose word is null on all historical matters except those in which Cromwell's nephew, Richard (whom he knew), played a part, takes up the story.

According to the *Cronica*, it was Richard who went to Wyatt and brought him to Cromwell's house. Cromwell then examined him and, once satisfied with his statement, he promised to 'stand as his friend', with the proviso that Wyatt 'would have to stay in the tower anyway'. Richard Cromwell then escorted Wyatt to the Tower in an informal manner, so that at first

nobody suspected that he was a prisoner; and when he

[3] Muir, op. cit..

arrived at the tower, Richard said to the Captain of the tower, 'Sir Captain, Secretary Cromwell sends to beg you to do all honour to Master Wyatt'. So the captain put him in a chamber over the door.[4]

That chamber was the upper bell tower, a relatively gracious lodging reserved for prisoners of high status. Wyatt was removed there on May 8, and the next day Cromwell made – finally – the first move to assemble his jury. By the 11th, Cromwell had drawn up an indictment in great secrecy,[5] and Henry Wyatt in Allington was gratefully responding to 'comfortable articles'[6] received from Cromwell, saying that his son was now safe but must remain in the Tower for the time being. On the same day, grand juries were called at short notice to assemble at Middlesex and Deptford in Kent – the sites of the alleged crimes – to decide *prima facie* on the offences alleged to Anne at Greenwich, and determine whether the charges would proceed to trial.[7] No charge this grave could ever be dismissed. The juries found for the bill. The following day, Anne's 'lovers' were tried at Westminster.

We can see from this that something happened after Wyatt's arrest, and whatever it was, it enabled Cromwell to draw up his indictment, muster his juries and commute the outcome for Wyatt from the death he foresaw to an honourable detention. Probably, Wyatt agreed to inform upon the accused. And if he did, he would be doing no more than was expected of him in a society where loyalty to the king cancelled all rival claims.

We cannot know what he said, though Cromwell appears

---

[4] Hume, op. cit.
[5] Letter from Sir William Poulet to Cromwell on May 11: 'My Lord of Norfolk showed me that he had no knowledge that the indictment was found.' Norfolk was on the 'special commission' for the trial.
[6] Letter from Henry Wyatt to Cromwell, May 11, 1536.
[7] Ives, *The Life and Death of Anne Boleyn*.

to have paid him £100 for saying it. It may be now that some of the more peculiar details of the indictment against Anne emerged. There was the strange charge of laughing at the king's verse 'which was made a great crime against them',[8] – a piece of plausible arcanum from the queen's chamber which the prosecution evidently valued. It lent colour to the charges, and can only have come from a source Anne rated as a judge of poetry, or why would she have shared this joke in front of him? Quite apart from the folly of it, very few people would get the joke. We already know from Wyatt that most of the court couldn't tell a good poem from a bad. But that is conjecture. If Cromwell made notes on the depositions, he destroyed them; if Wyatt wrote a letter – perhaps the seed of fact at the heart of all the proliferating myths about Wyatt and his letters to the king – it is gone. But we do have something left, slight enough to evade destruction: the poems.

*   *   *   *

The events of May 1536 were thought to have inspired no poetry until, in 1959, Wyatt's editor, working in Trinity College, Dublin, turned up a manuscript collection[9] of lyric poetry by Wyatt and mainly unnameable 'others', and discovered two lyrics on the subject that had been locked there for hundreds of years. But first, we will look at a sonnet that was circulating in the Devonshire MS in 1536 and 1537, and has been in full view ever since without attracting notice of this kind.

> *There was never file half so well filed*[10]
> *To file a file for every smith's intent*
> *But I was made a filing instrument*
> *To frame other, while I was beguiled.*

[8] Letter from Chapuys to Charles V, May 15, 1536.
[9] Usually known as the 'Blage MS'. See note on p198.
[10] Wyatt, XXXII, in Rebholz, op. cit.

But reason hath at my folly smiled
And pardoned me since that I me repent
Of my lost years and time misspent:
For youth did me lead and falsehood guiled.

Only one of Wyatt's editors, the fearless Rebholz, has been brave enough to try a paraphrase. His conclusion: 'the conceit and its implications are not entirely clear to me' speaks to all of us, I think. But when we think of Wyatt's interrogation and detention, and we bear in mind that the sonnet was going around the Devonshire group, most of whom were closely connected to the executed men, a little light sidles in. Is it a way of saying that Wyatt ratted on his friends? In the context of false charges, the 21st century eye mistakenly seizes on the word '*frame*',[11] but the telling verb in the 1530s was 'file', which then carried all of the following meanings: 'betray', 'charge with a crime', 'defile the honour of'. Wyatt was a filing instrument in all of these senses. Moreover, the last four of these lines (in bold) describe exactly what happened to Wyatt when he was at last released, as we know from a letter from his father to Cromwell, thanking him for getting Thomas off with 'favourable warnings [from the king] to his son to address himself better than his wit can consider'.

He, Sir Henry, has

sent for (Thomas) and commanded his obedience in all points to the king's pleasure, and the *leaving of such slanderous fashion as hath engendered unto him the displeasure of God and of his master. Found it not now to do in him, but already done.*[12]

If we go back to the poem and read the final four lines with a faintly sarcastic air, I believe we get something of what

---

[11] The definition 'concoct a false charge against' was not in use until the 20th century.
[12] Letter from Henry Wyatt to Cromwell, June 14, 1536.

Wyatt really felt about the matter. This was nothing to do with youthful folly or repenting of slanderous living, but a shameful episode for all concerned. He felt ill-used, and later on said so. He implies the same in the last verse of a much more famous poem, where he describes the bloody dénouement of this episode, which he watched from his cell in the bell tower:

Who list his wealth and ease retain,
Himself let him unknown contain.
Press not too fast in at that gate
Where the return stands by disdain,
For sure, circa Regna tonat. [it thunders around thrones]

The High mountains are blasted oft
When the low valley is mild and soft.
Fortune with Health stands at debate.
The fall is grievous from aloft.
And sure, circa Regna tonat.

These bloody days have broken my heart.
My lust, my youth did them depart,
And blind desire of estate.
Who hastes to climb seeks to revert.
Of truth, circa Regna tonat.

The bell tower showed me such sight
That in my head sticks day and night.
There did I learn out of a grate,
For all favour, glory, or might,
That yet, circa Regna tonat.

By proof, I say, there did I learn
Wit helpeth not defence too yerne,[13]

Of innocency to plead or prate.
Bear low, therefore, give God the stern,
For sure, circa Regna tonat.[14]

It's not a strong protest. To us, the burden especially reads like a collapse of nerve, burying the issue of this particular king's behaviour in a bromide about sovereign power. But it was still too critical for comfort. The last verse sees wit in the service of innocence crumple under the tanks of Henrician justice, and Wyatt leaves it open as to whose wit this might be. He packs the verse with legal and hunting terms, so a reading with a meaning something like this can come through: '*by the process of testifying, I learned that my wit was not required to plead a defence, (or) for preaching innocence.*' No other writing of the time would say as much, except perhaps a tiny, unnoticed lyric we will come to in a moment. Wyatt – whose watchword from now on was circumspection – left it out of his own manuscript; but it is thought that a young attendant of his, John Mantell, copied it unattributed into a collection of poetry he (and perhaps another before him) was making, and it was this that came ultimately to the stacks at Dublin.[15]

This is a haunting poem, emanating gusts of the unsaid. Though prison was hell for Wyatt as a man, for his poetry – always inclined to a condition of anguished immobility: help-less, paralysed, passive, stuck, immured by contrary forces – to be in an actual prison was something of a gift. As a poet, his life was gathering to this moment. There he was, pinned and miser-

---

[13] proof: 'testifying'; yearn: what hounds do when they are in full tongue. 'defence too yerne' is an oxymoronic construction for ironic effect, something like 'baying for acquittal'.

[14] Wyatt, CXXIII, in Rebholz, op. cit.

[15] This is the Dublin MS formerly known as 'Blage' after Wyatt's great friend, George Blage, who came into it after Mantell was hanged, aged 21, for taking part in an illegal hunting party. The identification of Mantell as the original compiler was recently proposed by Helen Baron, *The 'Blage' Manuscript: The Original Compiler Identified* (English Manuscript Studies 1100-1700, vol 1).

able, while events unfolded around him. Even the building looks
more perky than him:

> *The bell tower **showed me** such sight*
> *That in my head sticks day and night.*

The trials went on. The 'lovers' were tried first, and condemned, then the queen and her brother some days later. There
could now be no outcome for Anne but one, but she spoke well
in her defence, and so did her brother, who was still thought to
be in with a chance of his life; so much so that an enterprising
spectator opened a book on it, with odds on his acquittal laid
as good as ten to one, at one point. Rochford must have known
better, or he would have kept quiet when asked to respond to
a piece of evidence concerning the king's sexual potency. The
prosecution handed him a piece of paper and asked if his sister had ever said what was written on it. They told him to acknowledge it with a silent nod of assent, but instead, he read it
aloud, for the peerage of England to hear: Had the queen, to
his knowledge, told Lady Rochford that the king *'was unskilled
at sexual intercourse with his wife, and had neither vigour nor
staying-power'*[16] in bed? Why no, he declared. The queen had
said no such thing. The jury convicted.

Sitting in his cell, Wyatt was witness, in every sense, to a
cataclysmic event, one of those gashes in our history that tears,
as Rilke said, the 'till then from the ever since'. The world of
his youth was ended. The lightness had gone out of love, the
old gallants had become sanctimonious and obtuse, his own
gift to 'mark and remember everything he seeth', having started
him off so well, had commended him as an informer. Here, in
a week, was a world where nothing was innocuous, not even a
compliment, and the king's best friend and his darling, the great

---

[16] Letter from Chapuys to Charles V, May 15, 1536: '*Nestoit habile en cas de soy
copuler avec sa femme, et qu'il n'avoit ne virtue ne puissance*'. It was claimed that
Anne had said this to Lady Rochford, Rochford's wife.

untouchables – were snatched from the earth.

Ou sont les gracious gallants[17]
Que je suivoye ou temps jadis
Si biens chantans, si biens parlans
Si plaisans en faiz et en dis

wrote Francis Villon. Wyatt knew where his were:

The bell tower showed me such sight
That in my head sticks day and night.

These lines do their own sticking in the head, but without revealing their secret. Since the discovery of the poem, no one
can agree on what, exactly, Wyatt saw. As ever with Wyatt, the
salient fact, 'the thing', is on the outside of his poem and all
we can see is its shadow, like something approaching from behind. Recent commentators have thought it was Anne's lovers,
executed on the scaffold site at Tower Hill; others have thought
it was Anne herself, beheaded inside the Tower grounds on May
19. Nor does a visit to the bell tower itself resolve the mystery.

The bell tower is a round turret on the south-west corner of
the Tower of London, used in the 16th century for important
or politically sensitive prisoners. It contains two rooms, one on
top of the other. The lower chamber – said to be the cell of Sir
Thomas More – is almost below ground level and has arrow-
slit windows that couldn't show anyone anything. The upper
chamber, where we are to assume Wyatt lodged, is a large room
with a high ceiling, well appointed with a large fireplace and a
garderobe.[18] In its present state it has big handsome windows
– later replacements of the old two-light windows – but none
of them face into the Tower grounds. They are on the outside

---

[17] Francis Villon, *Selected Poems*, ed. Hale (Penguin, 1978).
[18] separate wardrobe and privy.

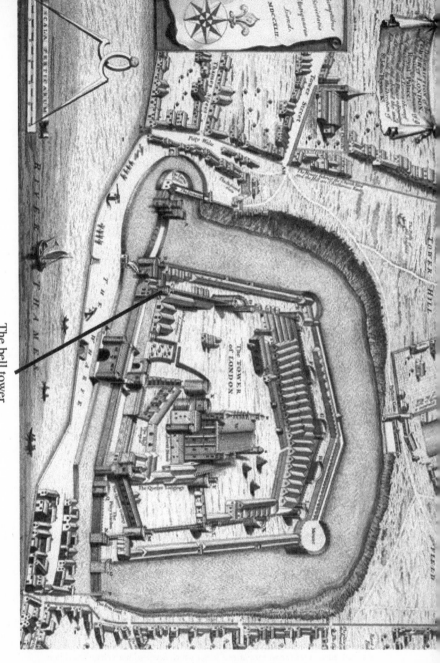

The bell tower

Map of the Tower of London, 1537

of the tower, and open to the south-west, towards the Thames and Tower Hill. Unfortunately, that doesn't settle the matter, because these windows do not command a grandstand view of the Tower Hill site where Norris and co. died; it's much too far away.[19] From one of them Wyatt could, at most, have made out some activity in the distance, like a crowd forming around the raised scaffold, but he would have needed a powerful telescope to see anything of the action. He would have seen very little through a grate. And yet, the poem says something completely different. It gives an impression of a highly visible event, some distinct horror repeating on the retina.

There is another possibility. We don't know how the cluster of buildings containing the bell tower was internally configured in 1536. The 'lieutenant's house' that adjoins it on the east side in the 1597 plan was not then built, and we don't know the shape of the earlier building it replaced. Given the circumstances of Wyatt's detention, he may have been allowed access to a north-facing window somewhere in the vicinity of his cell.[20] The author of the *Cronica del Rey*, who claimed to be the only foreigner present at Anne's execution, said Wyatt was seen there, watching 'from a window of the tower, and all the people thought that he also was to be brought out and executed'. That would be consistent with the emphasis of the lines

> *The bell tower showed me such sight*
> *That in my head sticks day and night.*

and not just for reasons of proximity. The couplet contains an allusion to Chaucer's *Knight's Tale*, and this is probably the key to what Wyatt saw. As everyone knew, the action of the *Knight's*

[19] I am grateful to Major General Keith Cima, resident governor of the Tower, for allowing me access to the bell tower so I could confirm this for myself.
[20] Geoffrey Parnell, the keeper of Tower history, informs me that there was once a staircase turret on the east face of the Tower which accessed both chambers, but it was 'eroded' by the addition of the precursor to the 'lieutenant's house'.

Tale turns on an incident involving a knight, a tower and a May morning, when Palamon looks down from his tower cell and sees the lovely Emilia walking below. From that moment, he is smitten. He can't get her out of his head. This was not an unusual occurrence in romance literature. One might almost say it was part of a knight's job to be smitten by girls out of tower windows. In Chaucer, it happens like this:

> *And so bifel by aventure or cas* [21]
> *That thurghe a window, thickke of many a barre,*
> *Of iren greet and square as any sparre*
> *He caste his eye upon Emylya*
> *And therewithal he bleynte,* [22] *and cride, 'A!'.*

In Wyatt's case, it was also a May morning. Wyatt took, as we have seen, a darkly ironic view of May's 'observance' as applied in his own case. What, then, more ironic than the grotesque perversion of that courtly scene which now occurred beneath his own window: the vision of Anne Boleyn walking to her death? She was the queen, she had once been the beautiful girl he loved, she was the living incarnation of courtly culture in his time. Well may he blench. It couldn't be proved even if more were known about the bell tower complex, but it is psychologically and artistically consistent with what we know of Wyatt, and has support from the sources. With the nod to the *Knight's Tale*, these lines become exceptionally rich: they allude to the queen's rise as well as her fall, and show her beginning in her end, and her end in her beginning. When she made her pun about ballades and pallets, she got a sharp reproof from her attendant: 'Such desire as you have had to such tales has brought you to this.' But it raised her to glory first.

If Wyatt saw Anne Boleyn's execution, he was one of about

---

[21] Chaucer, *The Knight's Tale*, op. cit.
[22] bleynte: blenched.

2000 people to do so. There was a special swordsman brought from Calais, as a measure of the king's clemency. On the scaffold she spoke a few words – characterised by some as 'bold', that is to say, without acknowledging her guilt – and prepared herself for death. A pathetic detail shows her fastening her clothes 'about her feet' – a measure of modesty to prevent the crowd from looking up her skirt if her headless body, convulsing, should splay her legs.

As soon as she was dead, Sir Francis Bryan took horse and rushed off to bring the good news to Henry and Jane Seymour, and after that no one spoke of her again. She became a cipher in the squabble for the Church, but she ceased to be a person. When it was absolutely necessary to refer to her, some embarrassed locution was used, like 'that other one'.

As for her lovers, they were not entirely forgotten. Another poem in the Dublin MS, almost certainly *not* by Wyatt, shows how they were remembered. Because the poem is quite long, the important lines are in bold:

> **In Mourning wise** since daily I increase
> **Thus should I cloak** the cause of all my grief;
> So pensive mind with tongue to hold his peace.
> My reason sayeth there can be no relief;
> Wherefore, give ear, I humbly you require,
> The affects to know that thus doth make me moan.

It sounds like a love poem. Here are all the usual ingredients of the love lyric: lament and circumspection, but then:

> The cause is great of all my doleful cheer
> For those that were and now be dead and gone.

This is a poem for the dead. It goes on:

What though to death desert be now their call[23]
As by their faults it doth appear right plain.
Of force I must lament that such a fall
Should light on those so wealthily did reign,
Though some perchance will say, of cruel heart
'A traitor's death why should we thus bemoan?
*But I, alas, **set this offence apart**,*
Must needs bewail the death of some be gone.

As for them all I do not thus lament
But as of right my reason doth me bind.
*But as **the most doth all their deaths repent***
*Even so do I by force of **mourning mind**.*
Some say, 'Rochford, hadst thou been not so proud
For thy great wit each man would thee bemoan.'
Since as it is so, many cry aloud,
'It is great loss that thou art dead and gone.'

Ah, Norris, Norris, my tears begin to run,
To think what hap did thee so lead or guide,
*Whereby thou hast **both thee and thine undone**,*
That is bewailed on court of every side.
In place also where thou hast never been
Both man and child doth piteously thee moan.
They say, 'Alas thou art far overseen
By thine offences to be thus dead and gone'.

Ah, Weston, Weston, that pleasant was and young,
In active things who might with thee compare?
All words accept that thou didst speak with tongue,
So well esteemed with each where thou didst fare.
*And **we that now in court doth lead our life**,*

[23] Wyatt, CXCVII, in Rebholz, op. cit.

Most part in mind doth thee lament and moan.
But that thy faults we daily hear so rife
All we should weep that thou art dead and gone.

Brereton, farewell, as one that least I knew.
Great was thy love with diverse, as I hear,
But common voice doth not so sore thee rue
As other twain that doth before appear.
But yet no doubt but thy friends thee lament
And other hear their piteous cry and moan.
So doth each heart for thee likewise relent
That thou giv'st cause to be thus dead and gone.

Ah, Mark, what moan should I for thee make more
Since that thy death thou has deserved best,
Save only that mine eye is forced sore
With piteous plaint to moan thee with the rest?
A time thou hadst above thy poor degree,
The fall whereof thy friends may well bemoan.
A rotten twig upon so high a tree
Hath slipped thy hold and thou art dead and gone.

And thus, farewell, each one in hearty wise.
The axe is home, your heads be in the street.
The trickling tears doth fall so from my eyes
I scarce may write, my paper is so wet.
But what can help when death hath played his part
Though nature's course will thus lament and moan?
Leave sobs therefore, and every Christian heart
Pray for the souls of those be dead and gone.

This is a very strange poem, and quite a brave one. Again, it seems maddeningly vague, full of botched opportunities for protest, and retreats into generalised pieties; more like a poem that is trying *not* to say something and entangling itself in its own cover-ups. But it has to be read in the context of Cromwell's Treason Act of 1534, which had made it, for the first time, a capital offence to even speak against the king: a stricture that was open to the widest interpretation. The executions had made everyone jumpy and careful. Letters passing from the court at this time say little and sign off with the inexplicable conclusion 'news here are none'. The poem captures the atmosphere: the court's a place where people say what they don't think and think what they don't say, where people are fed the official line till it chokes them, and keep quiet: 'Most part *in mind* doth thee lament and moan/ but that thy faults we *daily hear* so rife.'

We don't know which of those who 'lead our lives in court' wrote this. It seems to have been composed before the severed heads decomposed. Unfortunately, the date of Wyatt's release can only be dated to some time between May 19 and and June 14, when Sir Henry wrote his account to Cromwell of his interview with his repentant son. It is commonly assumed that Wyatt was banished to Allington for the rest of the summer, but there is nothing to prove it and he may have been back in court very quickly. Against that, the style is very unlike his. But whoever the poet was, he was dangerously off-message with his denial that the interests of a subject are identical – as they were supposed to be – to those of the king. A properly loyal subject would not '*set (the treason) apart*' and grieve the dead, with the unacceptable implication that the king's enemy could be one's friend. The treason should cancel the friendship and obviate the grief. Less wisely still, he questions the king's justice: by asserting that Mark Smeaton '*hath deserved best*' his death, he implies the other deaths were not deserved. It suggests the poet knew of Smeaton's lonely confession, and we might infer from this censure that his real crime – for which he deserved to die – was to inculpate the others.

In any case, a hierarchy of sympathy is established. The

court grieved least for Smeaton, most for 'gentle' Henry Norris. It was known that Norris, alone of them all, had had the chance to buy his life and had chosen death over disloyalty to Anne. In other words, he died for the chivalric principles that everyone else chose to forget: an egregious position in the circumstances, as Wyatt knew better than anyone.

> But all is turned thorough my gentleness
> Into a strange fashion of forsaking.

When they came for Norris's possessions, they found preserved among his textiles the costume he had worn at the Field of the Cloth of Gold.

*　　*　　*　　*

As for everyone else, the impulse to self-preservation is well described by one last chilling, ventriloquistic little poem tucked in a corner of the Devonshire MS:

> To counterfeit a merry mood
> In mourning mind I think it best,
> But once in rain I wore a hood
> Well they were wet that barehead stood.
> But since that cloaks are good for doubt[24]
> The beggar's proverb find I good:
> Better a path than a hall out.[25]

We can see what sort of creepy behaviour is commemorated here, but not the occasion for it, specified only as 'once in rain'

[24] doubt: both 'uncertainty' and 'dangerous situation'.
[25] Although the sense is self-evident, there is nothing quite like this in Alexander Barclay's collection of contemporary proverbs. The nearest I can find is 'Beggar is woe that another by the door shall go'.

(certainly a pun on 'reign'). The full sense of it only comes through when we notice that the second line 'In mourning mind I think it best' is flashing a connection to 'In mourning wise' – the first line of the ballade we've just read, about Anne's lovers and the events of May 1536. It's an answer poem, in other words, mocking the pieties of a poem *that isn't there*, except in the heads of the readers. Whoever the author was, he certainly knew 'In mourning wise' and he expected the co-contributors of the Devonshire to have seen that poem in circulation, recognise the cross-reference and get his meaning: it's pointing at someone who dodged the axe by guile. We can only guess at whom. The allusion to proverbs may be significant: both Sir Francis Bryan and Sir Thomas Wyatt had a brush with the investigation; both were known to use proverbs in their speech. What we can know for sure is this: the makers of the Devonshire book knew exactly who was meant. They all knew what it was to stand 'barehead' in May 1536, and they knew who among them had ducked to avoid the same fate. The connection between the two poems was made in their heads, not in the book. It was then lost with 'In Mourning Wise' until the discovery of the Trinity MS in 1959 brought the two poems together again, and with them this unique insight into the secret thoughts of the court – the closest thing we will ever have to an admission of skulduggery.

CHAPTER THIRTEEN

After the king and Anne, Sir Henry Norris had been the most important person at Henry's court. His gentle heart was not the sole reason for bewailing his demise 'on every side', as the ballade had it: a man in the position of Norris was at the fount of a widespread system of benefaction, irrigating even those places 'where thou hast never been'. Now he was dead and gone, all this had dried up in a single moment, leaving his clients to find another patron quickly, even while the court was reordering and offices were unassigned. Cromwell took charge of the reshuffle. People in remote postings, lacking information and reliant on agents and tides to carry their appeals, came off especially badly. John Hussee wrote to Lord Lisle in Calais, to say that he had failed on his behalf with John Russell, the anti-Bolyenite courtier promoted in the new regime:

> as touching your suit to the king, Mr Russell saith he moved his Grace concerning your Lordship's preferment, and that his grace should say that it was too late, for because all things were disposed long since... The truth is, as I of late wrote your Lordship, Mr. Russell is a right worshipful and a sad discreet gentleman, but my mind giveth me plainly that he shall never prefer your lordship for your advancement. I pray God take Mr Norris to his mercy, for you have made an unlike change.

He advises Lisle to send quails and wine to Russell, along with 'some loving letter; and likewise unto Master Secretary, though he do you little good and promise much'.

> *Such is the fortune that I have[1]*
> *To love them most that love me least*
> *And to my pain to seek and crave*
> *The thing that other have possessed.*
> *So thus in vain alway I serve*
> *And other have that I deserve.*

Wyatt, on the other hand, had had what one might call a

Thomas Cromwell (*Hans Holbein the Younger*)

---

[1] Wyatt, CXXVI, in Rebholz, op. cit.

'good' crisis. He had emerged from it traumatised, sobered and balding rapidly. Nevertheless, from a practical point of view he was well placed. Russell admired him and Mr Secretary had for him the nearest thing to a soft spot that he could manage.

One thing was for certain: he was now Cromwell's man. Cromwell it was who had saved him. When Sir Henry Wyatt – old and ill but always a shrewd investor in political stock – wrote to thank Cromwell for his help in the matter of the arrest, he effectively bequeathed him his eldest son.

'And I have charged [Thomas]' he wrote 'not only to follow your commandments from time to time,[2] but also in every point to *take and repute you as me*.'

And this also was not now to do in him, but already done.

Cromwell's rise had been inexorable and unostentatious, and these years were the culmination of his power. He came, as his enemies said, 'from the dunghill'[3] – that is to say, a mushroom man. The traditional routes to eminence were blood and the Church, but he rose without either and subdued both – a consummation more to be admired in our secular, egalitarian age than it was in his own.

From what can be discerned of his early years, he seems to have gone as a soldier with the French army and worked with Venetian traders. Having acquired the law in the London courts, he went to work for Cardinal Wolsey – and it was here, working to dissolve some of the dimmer monastic houses and funnel the proceeds into one of the cardinal's projects, that he had perceived the potential of the idea. A proper account of his doings is beyond the pretentions of this study, except to say that for sheer executive competence he was a phenomenon on the scale of Mozart or Shakespeare: a man who seems to have moved in his own element of decelerated time to achieve a week's work in

[2] from time to time: not 'occasionally' but 'on all occasions'. Cf. 'Men have died from time to time, and worms have eaten them, but not for love.' (*As You Like It*, 4.i.)

[3] Attainder of Thomas Cromwell, LP 15, 498.

a day. Somehow he had found the hours to learn four languages and read deeply in poetry, religion, ancient and humanist philosophies, to collect paintings and savour old manuscripts. He was first with the latest books.

Merriman, his (Catholic) biographer and the editor of his letters, alleges he was conscious of an intellectual inferiority to More and Fisher, the churchmen he destroyed, and so 'avoided having any conversation with them' in his campaign against them; but that is to judge him by standards in which he himself had no interest. He was a man of business, not an intellectual, and he did nothing for its own sake. It was said that he had charm. Though this is not always apparent, a letter written to him in July 1522 by one John Creke, who had evidently spent some time with Cromwell and another man, Wodall, shows how much. Creke addresses him as '*carissimo quanto homo in questo mondo*', and goes on:

> the great *amicitia* that hath been between us cannot out of my memory, the affection was so perfect; and if ever I come above you shall know it. My love toward you resteth in no less vigour than it did our last being together. My heart mourneth for your company and Mr Wodall's as ever it did for men. As I am a true Christian man, I ne'er had so faithful affection to men of so short acquaintance in my life; the which affection increaseth as fire daily. God knoweth what pain I receive in departing, when I remember our gosly[4] walking in the garden; it make [sic] me desperate to contemplate. I would write larger; my heart will not let me.

It was not Creke but Cromwell who 'came above', and in the process ceased to be the person who had inspired such thoughts

---

[4] gosly: no one seems to know what this is. Perhaps an MS error for 'gaily'.

of reciprocal love. His own attitude to friendship was now quite a different matter; more like a leasehold agreement mined with hidden reversion clauses. Famously, he was the only friend to his old master, Wolsey, remaining to plead his cause with Anne and the king when everyone else fled his disgrace. A letter to Wolsey from that time shows all the marks of the kind of friendship Cromwell would come to perfect:

> I am informed your Grace hath in me some diffidence, as if I did dissemble with you or procure anything contrary to your profit or dishonour. I much muse that your grace should so think or report it secretly considering the pains I have taken... I reckoned that your Grace would have written plainly unto me of such thing, rather than secretly to have misreported me. But I shall bear your Grace no less good will... Let God judge between us. Trewly your Grace in some things overshooteth your self; there is regard to be given what things ye utter and to whom.[5]

One notes the tone of reprimand, the menace in his disappointment, the accusation of disloyalty, the reversion of blame to the accuser; but the crucial words are the first three: *I am informed*. Wolsey had made the mistake of going behind Cromwell's back, and his servant had found out about it, as he always did. He would soon come to control a wide network of informants through which it was extremely hard for any letter or message to pass; many recipients of letters from Cromwell had hoped to be hearing from someone else. He stood in every man's light; and yet he was invisible, with no apparent agenda or will of his own, lacking the caste loyalties of a noble or a churchman, acting only as master secretary, the pure-running faucet of the king's own will. For which reason it was very hard for his

[5] Letter from Cromwell to Wolsey, October 1530, Roger B. Merriman, *Life and Letters of Thomas Cromwell*, Vol 1 (Oxford, 2006).

enemies to dislodge him: how could you get a purchase on a man whose interests conformed in every point to those of his master? That is the position Cromwell took and the standard he imposed on all the king's subjects. He made a fetish of ingratitude; for him all dissent was disloyalty. Unlike Wolsey, he was not a man to spend hours trying to dissuade Henry from his will, on his knees or not. He could see how the years of Anne Boleyn had killed the king's taste for dispute, and he would never presume to instruct him: he appeared above all as a facilitator. In fact, it is possible to view Henry's choice, not only of wife but of chief minister for these years, as a reaction to the personality of his second wife; and the well-known commendation of Jane Seymour would almost do as well for the minister: Jane was, as we have seen

> In every condition, of that loving inclination, and reverend conformity, that she can in all things well content, satisfy, and quiet herself with that thing which [the king] shall think expedient and determine.[6]

Cromwell had the further advantage that he could make that thing happen; and also, by manipulating the king's increasingly suspicious and paranoid nature, he could guide his determinations, unnoticed.

There was an Achilles heel. The language of Creke's letter is the language of love, but in reality no man spoke to man like that unless they had a very particular shared interest: the new religion. Master Secretary was, in the words of a historian of the Reformation, a 'highly motivated evangelical'[7] (as Protestants of that time are called by historians), and so was Creke, whom Cromwell later installed in the household of Thomas Cranmer. He was never a firebrand – a wonderful word meaning 'one who lights his own pyre with troublemaking', and nor was this side

[6] Letter from Henry to the Duke of Norfolk, June 12, 1537.
[7] MacCulloch, op.cit.

always uppermost in his dealings. He could subsume it to the king's business, and sufficiently dissemble to treat with the religious conservatives at court when it suited; as, for example, in the plot to get rid of Anne Boleyn, when he let them believe he would reinstate the princess Mary in return for support in the coup. But he pushed forward a programme of reform throughout the 1530s, turning opportunity into advance. The Catholic-led uprising in Lincolnshire and Yorkshire at the end of 1536 gave him the chance, in its dreadful aftermath, to suppress the larger religious houses and complete the destruction of English monastic life; and he continued to work on the production of a Bible in English, with the aim that one be placed in every church. It was a fatal, unforeseen divergence of this programme from the king's interests that did for him in the end.

But that is in the future. In 1536 – and even more in '37, when the near-success of the northern rebellion had given the king a nasty shock – the combination of Cromwell's policies and his methods were turning the court into a place where loyalty was not assumed in default of any evident treasons. From now on, the prudent courtier made a focal point of loyalty in whatever way he could. This was certainly the case with Thomas Wyatt. After his release from the Tower he did everything he could to demonstrate desert for whatever efforts had been made to extricate him. In the 'commotion time' of the northern rebellion of 1536-7, he went at the head of 150 Kentish men he had raised for the king's cause,[8] and may have provided 200 more for the king's own bodyguard. A sherrifhood of Kent followed. In 1537, he was knighted[9] and he obtained a good marriage for his one child, Thomas, so that his son would be able to claim kinship with every one of Henry's English queens. Soon

---

[8] But was later countermanded and returned. Wyatt, *Defence*, in Muir. op. cit.
[9] The date of Wyatt's knighthood is uncertain. I am grateful to Susan Brigden, who argues that the knighthood was conferred when he went as ambassador to Charles V in 1537.

he was boasting of his rehabilitation into the king's good graces and 'the confidence and credit the king had me in' as soon as he was released.

The Wyatt Holbein commission was an aspect of this campaign. Between 1536 and 1537 the Wyatts ordered a large number of works from Holbein – more than any other English family except the king and the Howards. The purpose was to show the Wyatt family *redux* and mustered behind not just the king but his chief minister too: for Cromwell was Holbein's greatest English patron, ultimately responsible for a great many of Holbein's commissions, including the royal ones.

The whole family sat to Holbein. The preparatory drawings for the surviving portraits of Wyatt's father, sister and son are lost; whereas for Wyatt himself the painting is lost and what survives is the famous image of him, almost frankly full-faced but with swivelled eyes, as though to look at something, or someone, passing behind the painter. Dendrochronological investigations into Sir Henry Wyatt's panel in the Louvre show that it was now that he sat with his motto '*Oublier ne puis*' [I cannot forget] showing in his broken mouth, so no one else could forget he had been barnacled for the sake of the Tudors.

Sir Henry died soon after, and his son enlisted Holbein's help in another piece of family propaganda: a new coat of arms. Coats of arms had become very important in the 1530s – perhaps even more so than in the high period of English chivalry – for this was the era of the forgotten undertaking known in the world of heraldry as the 'Period of Heraldic Visitation'. Its operations, unique to England, lasted from 1530 to 1686, and meant that all grants of arms became conditional upon their use. That is to say, if a gentleman of England wished to keep his right to bear arms, he had to show his appreciation of that honour by displaying them widely – in windows, lintels, on buildings, on banners, on shields, tombstones, plate, seals,

Thomas Wyatt (*Hans Holbein the Younger*)

armour and so on – or else it would be repealed. Heralds went out in a county-by-county programme of 'visitations', or inspections of property, to satisfy themselves that the bearers of arms were assiduous in this matter. They may not have needed much persuasion, but still, it was a case of 'use it or lose it' – a fact perhaps too little considered in the general lamentation for the way that parish church interiors, in the post-Reformation years, exchanged their saints and candles for the banners and shields of the local gentry.

Through the dates of the various 'visitations' of Kent, we learn that Sir Thomas Wyatt added the device of the horse-barnacle to his coat of arms in 1537, or thereabouts. It would act as a useful reminder in these awkward times of what the Wyatts had endured for the regime. No doubt Wyatt took full advantage of the promotional opportunities imposed by the visitation, though nothing remains. The one place where the arms can still be seen today is, however, intriguing. There is a sketch of them on the back of a Holbein drawing of a female sitter, identified in a later inscription as: *Anna Bollein Queen*. Art historians have long rejected this identification, but David Starkey[10] has reopened the case for it on the grounds that the author of the inscription, Sir John Cheke, tutor to Edward VI and a habitué of Henry's court, was more often accurate in his superscriptions than had formerly been supposed.

If it is a picture of Anne Boleyn, it gives a very different impression of her from the one of common conception, with the Modigliani face, the black hair and pearled French coif. The drawing shows a woman in an informal robe, without jewellery or headdress. This plainness could be the deliberate expression of an unconventional, humanistic approach to portraiture, but that contention must be placed against the queen's known love of finery, the general dazzle of ornament in all surviving royal portraits, the shared lack of sympathy for decorative restraint and the unlikelihood that the king – whose policy was to assert his wife's legitimacy by every possible means – would allow her to be shown in her dressing gown. Moreover, she shows here as a mild-eyed, slightly horse-faced blonde with a pronounced and plump dewlap beneath her chin. If this is really Anne, then the hostile account of her with a high collar at her coronation – allegedly worn to conceal a swelling or goitre on her neck – would be more than spiteful speculation, as it is usually now

---

[10] By David Starkey and John Rowlands in 1983, and reasserted by Starkey in 2007 in *Lost Faces: Identity and Discovery in Tudor Royal Portraiture*, (Philip Mould).

assumed to be; on the other hand, it would contradict accounts of her as thin, long-necked and dark, make Wyatt's name of 'brunet' into a mystery and her well-known comment on prospective decapitation, 'I have a little neck', into another sort of joke altogether.

The Wyatt coat of arms *verso* has been thought variously to bear or not to bear on the matter. The arms are those of a man. This means they can't be used to make a positive identification, but it also constitutes (in my opinion) a powerful argument *against* the sitter being Anne. Holbein was not in the habit

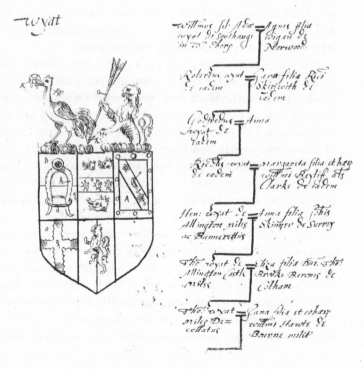

The Wyatt coat of arms in the 17th century, showing the barnacle in the top left section

of drawing on the back of his portrait sketches – in fact, this is the sole instance of any kind of design, mark or drawing on the back of his English portrait sketches.[11] Both artist and patron were known for their circumspection. Given this, and given the present circumstances of Wyatt – a man who had barely emerged from prison in connection with the queen's adultery, and who had commissioned new arms to assert his recovery from that regrettable incident – it is inconceivable that these would have ended up on the back of a picture of Anne Boleyn. Quite the reverse: he had put her behind him.

There is another possible identification for the sitter. It may be that this is a picture of Elizabeth Darrell, who was probably intimate with Wyatt at the time of the events of 1536 and was certainly so by the summer of 1537. Wyatt had long been separated from his wife. Elizabeth Darrell had hair of 'crisped

Unknown Woman – 'Anna Bollein' (*Hans Holbein the Younger*)

[11] I am grateful to Dr Susan Foister for this point.

gold' – the very same hair of the drawing, showing the suppressed kink typical of smoothed-down wavy hair; the informal dressing gown would be more suitable to a woman of whatever uncertain status attached, in the early 16th century, to the mistresses of married knights than to a queen of England. The fact that the arms on the reverse are masculine and 'can't be those of the sitter' has been used to refute the idea that the picture is connected to Wyatt. This would obviously present no obstacle if the sitter was Elizabeth Darrell, and it would more naturally arise for Holbein to sketch them on the back of a drawing if that drawing was destined for the same client as the arms. In fact, the need for a new design for arms and a drawing of Besse would more than plausibly have arisen from the same contingency. In 1537, Wyatt was to go away on a diplomatic mission. He would need plate for his residence, and arms for his plate. (It seems there was a pool of diplomatic plate, supplied by the jewel house and recycled from ambassador to ambassador. When an ambassador was recalled, this plate returned to the jewel house to be struck with the arms of his replacement.)[12] At the same time, he may well have wished for an image of his mistress to take away with him. He didn't want to go. Before his arrest he had been looking for a post in Calais; now things were different. His father had died, leaving him large estates to manage. He was in love, and that may have diminished his appetite for distant postings. But he owed his life to Cromwell, and Cromwell had plans for him. If Cromwell had known their ultimate consequence, he may have made other plans.

[12] In 1533, for example, a cup was returned to one of the king's regular goldsmiths, John Freeman, with instructions that 'the arms of the said Sir Francis (Bryan) may be taken out, and the striking the same vessel with the arms of Master Wallop, who was deputed ambassador to the French king in April last'. Accounts of Plate, January 10, 1533, LP 6, 32.

CHAPTER FOURTEEN

Thomas Cromwell had a habit of writing down his 'remembrances', that is to say, to-do lists for the business of the moment. They are very interesting documents, showing how nothing was beyond Cromwell's competence, and nothing beneath his notice. He never let dignity get in his way. The remembrances for the beginning of 1537 read:

> Item: to remember the execution of the clipper of money, to be done to the example of other... to send to my lady Wallop a kirtle cloth... the sending of such as shall go to the Emperor, the French king, the king of Denemark, and other German states.

Cromwell was particularly interested in the matter of the resident ambassador to the imperial, or Spanish court of Charles V. He had been contemplating a new Spanish alliance since April 1536, but he recognised that events of recent years – the divorce from Catherine, the split from Rome – had left a certain awkwardness in relations still to be overcome. There had been an English ambassador in Spain during this time, but he had not been expected, as this new ambassador was expected, to promote an alliance with the empire (the secular arm of the papacy) – while holding the king's line on the matter of the royal divorce, the royal supremacy[1] and the illegitimacy of the

---

[1] The assertion that the king was supreme head of the English Church. Henry VIII had formally taken the title of Supreme Head in January 1535.

Princess Mary, who happened to be the emperor's first cousin. These were uncharted waters. Cromwell and the king must have thought highly, then, of Sir Thomas Wyatt to send him there on his first resident posting, with a mission to achieve the near-impossible. Why, when there were far more experienced diplomats to hand, did they send this almost untested individual on this most sensitive mission?

The answer, at least in part, is: because he was their best poet. Wyatt's career has often appeared to divide into two distinct halves, with the courtier-poet supplanted by the sober diplomat of the late 1530s. This perception is an inevitable consequence of the unbalanced source material available to his biographers: his life after 1537 is told through diplomatic letters and involves him in the events of European politics. But it is wrong to think of his poetry and his diplomacy as antithetical: Wyatt's diplomacy grew out of his poetry, and his poetry sustained his diplomacy.

*   *   *   *

In the first half of the 16th century, diplomatic recruitment took a new direction. The effect of humanism on diplomacy was to change, over time, the profile of the ambassador from the clerical model – the walking repository of canon law, trained to counter precept with precept – to the courtly model, where a courtier would embed himself in the foreign court and use his own charm and advocacy to influence policy. Crucially, he was to speak in *propria persona*, not just as the incumbent of his office but as a considerable person in his own right, with opinions of value in themselves. Wyatt was sent as 'a personage of wit and reputation'. His instructions were very clear on this point: in policy discussions he was not to seem to parrot the party line but to make his proposals 'as of yourself' – in his own words, as though they proceeded from his own deliberations.

A poet would be good at this, and it is worth mentioning that Wyatt's opposite number in France, Sir Francis Bryan, was also a poet; as was George Blage, who came out to join him the next year. A poet was a linguist, familiar with the nuances of foreign languages. A poet was a rhetorician, used to pressing his suit in ingenious ways, skilful with language that confected an atmosphere of hope, not certainty, as Wyatt was instructed to do. The language of diplomacy was as coded and formal as that of poetry: a poet could work it to deliver his message without disturbing the surface and causing affront, as sometimes happened when inept diplomats shoved too hard with their masters' interests. As for courtly skills, there was no shortage of these with Wyatt, one of the few Englishmen in history to be held suspiciously smooth by a senior French diplomat.[2]

This new kind of diplomacy obviously raised the stakes for the envoy himself. The snag will have been noted, that the ambassador who speaks 'as of yourself' [i.e. himself] isn't really giving his own opinions, just presenting his instructions in a carefully personalised package. Nevertheless, the fiction of his autonomy meant he could be held responsible when things went wrong, even though diplomatic outcomes were inevitably decided by complex pan-European initiatives well beyond his control. Doubtless this was one of the reasons for Wyatt's reluctance. By his own account: 'I never begged the office, and but for th'obedience to my master I would utterly have refused it… as well for I knew my own unhability whereby I should be wondrously accumbered (as) for that I was given to a more pleasant kind of life.'[3]

There were, in fact, plenty of good reasons for not wanting to be an ambassador. To begin with, you were on your

---

[2] After scoring a diplomatic point against Wyatt, the French ambassador Castillon wrote, 'And so I had won against Mr Hoyet, who will return as he came, paying me so many compliments that I esteem myself wiser than I thought.' Letter from Castillon to Montmorency, June 4, 1538.

[3] Wyatt, in Muir, *Life and Letters*, op. cit.

own: there was no official structure of support, and you had to create all the lines of contact and information with your own resources 'and no council but my own foolish head',[4] as Wyatt said. The extent of the misinformation in ambassadors' letters suggests that these lines were often imperfectly laid. Then there was the business of leaving your own affairs in the hands of surrogates, paid agents of questionable perseverance or 'friends' at court who would, it was hoped, press for your interests, but were usually more diligent on their own behalf. Then there was homesickness and the sense of emotional exile. But worst of all, there was the expense: for the new courtier-diplomat was also expected to pay his own expenses 'as of himself'. This was far from a fiction: ambassadors' 'diets' – the allowance for the expenses of living – quickly ran out in the cost of reflecting one's sovereign's dignity in one's own estate; soon they needed all their diplomatic skills just to write home for money. It was the same all over Europe. In 1528, Jean du Bellay, the French ambassador at Henry's court, put it most wittily in a letter to his superior on the subject of the 'sweat', a now-vanished plague that killed within hours:

I found the ambassador of Milan leaving his lodging in great haste because two or three have been attacked… if all ambassadors are to have their share of it, you will not have gained your cause; for you will not be able to brag you made me die of hunger, and the king will only have gained nine months of my service for nothing.[5]

A few days later, he wrote to say that was it, he was off, he would rather die of the sweat than stay as an ambassador. As for his replacement,

[4] Wyatt, ibid.
[5] Letter from Du Bellay to Anne de Montmorency, June 18, 1528.

In any case, don't send a man who will not spend money, or else matters will not mend. I do not speak without reason.

On this point Wyatt also scored. He had always had a predisposition to spend money, and this, since the death of his father, was floated on the recent inheritance of lands so extensive that he appeared to be one of the richest men in England. The lands were indeed valuable – Wyatt himself alludes to it[6] – but, as Cromwell also knew, things in that quarter were far from rosy. Wyatt was hopeless with money and already had substantial arrears to set against his inheritance. As the treasurer, Tuke, observed to Cromwell, he was 'the king's debtor to no small sum', including the outstanding 'extraordinary' debt from his ransom a decade before, and numerous others besides. Tuke asked him to pay the debt now, before his departure. When Wyatt refused, he went to Cromwell for advice on how to proceed. Cromwell decided to let it lie for the moment. From time to time he pondered taking envoys' debts out of their diets, but as there was no way of doing it without cramping diplomatic scope, he found a use for the unpaid debts in keeping up the pressure on an often reluctant workforce. In the meantime, it suited him if Wyatt's extravagant side was to the fore.

Wyatt left for Spain, via Paris, in the first week of April 1537, taking with him a crew of retainers of various degrees of competence, and a vast and splendid new wardrobe, which got no further than Zaragoza before it was seized and taxed by the Spanish customs. After him came urgent requests from his brother-in-law Cobham, demanding money for the upkeep of his sister, Wyatt's wife, now landed on his own hands:

---

[6] Letter from Wyatt to his son, April 15, 1537: 'I call not that honesty that men commonly call honesty, as reputation for riches, for authorities, or some like thing, but that honesty that I dare well say your grandfather had rather left me than all the lands he did leave me.' The comparison would lose its point if the lands were modest.

Desiring him to remember his poor wife and give her something reasonable towards her living, for Mr Palmer sent her to be at Cobham Hall, saying Mr Wyatt would not find for her any longer. I used every effort to make him grant her some honest living, but he would promise nothing.

Poor Elizabeth Wyatt, her fate was dreadful. An adulterous game had cost her her husband, her child, her dignity, her position and usefulness in society, and now she was just an expense that nobody wanted to pay. What had she done? Perhaps slept with some lowly groom or footman, a man like Mark Smeaton who 'most deserved [his] fate'. She might have been forgiven a nobleman. As it was, Wyatt was implacable:

I wrote to Sir John Russell to speak to him[Wyatt],' [wrote Cobham to Cromwell] 'and he said he would give her something, but soon after told my servant he would not. I also got Sir William Hawte[7] to break the matter to him, and Master Henry Wyld and his brother, but all to no purpose.

She must have been on his mind as he passed through Paris. He touched on the matter in a homiletic letter he composed for the benefit of his only child, the newly married Thomas.

Love and well agree with your wife, for where there is noise and debate in the house, there is unquiet dwelling. And much more when it is in one bed... Such as you are unto her such shall she be unto you. And the blissing of God for good agreement between the wife and husband is fruit of many children, which I for the like thing do lack,

[7] Sir William Hawte was the father of Jane Hawte, who had married Wyatt's son, Thomas, in 1537.

and the fault is both in your mother and me, but chiefly in her.[8]

One learns quite a bit about Wyatt from this beautifully compressed pen sketch of a happy family, wiped out. First, that marital rape was distasteful to him; second, that he mourns the loss of domestic happiness and feels bereft of children; third, and perhaps most unusual for a man in his circumstances, he acknowledges his own part in it. He was an honest man, and couldn't quite drown his responsibility in righteous indignation at his wife's behaviour. As so often with Wyatt, he seems here to lack the moral impermeable that everyone around him possessed, that kept the truth off. He can lie and cheat as well as anyone, but he can't completely suppress his sense of how things really were.

Looking at this from Cromwell's point of view, there was virtue in an envoy with a radar for political humbug, but danger too: this person must be carefully kept on-message. Accordingly his letters to Wyatt are sharply doctrinal. Evidently, though, he thought well of him, and believed he would impress the Spanish. He arrived with letters recalling the old ambassador, the chaplain Dr Pate, and praising his great 'learning and fidelity' to the Spanish authorities.

Wyatt was going to need all this learning. In the time between Cromwell's first overtures to Spain and his dispatch of the new resident ambassador, an alarming development had taken place in European affairs. After decades of fighting one another in an apparently endless squabble over contested Italian lands, the French and the imperialists were inclining to peace. Charles V was losing his appetite for fighting the French. Turks in the east and Lutherans in the north threatened the unity of the empire; now was the moment to ally with Francis in the name of the

[8] Letter from Wyatt to his son, April 15 , 1537. Muir, op. cit.

established Church and mount a grand crusade, backed by the pope, against the infidel and the heretic in Christendom. As for Francis, the prospect of gaining Italian land through alliances, not expensive wars, interested him strangely.

This was the scenario that the schismatic Henry VIII dreaded most. If English foreign policy had one consistent aim, it was to get between France and Spain and prevent them from joining forces against her, as they now threatened to do. Henry's recent actions – the brutal suppression of the Catholic uprising, the deaths of More and Fisher, the desecration of shrines and holy objects as the great abbeys were brought in hand – made him an object of abhorrence to Catholic Europe, a 'most impious king', and a worthy recipient of chastisement. The horrible prospect now arose of imperial blockades on the trade routes, starving the people and emboldening England's religious conservatives to regroup and rise in concert with the invaders. Henry would be overthrown and England divided between France, Spain and France's old ally, Scotland. In addition, there was a man at work in the courts of Europe with that very objective in mind. His name was Reginald Pole, an English nobleman of Plantagenet descent with a cleaner claim to the throne than Henry. His and Wyatt's lives were about to collide.

Pole had once been Henry's golden theological protégé. In the king's magnanimous early years he had raised Pole's Yorkist family from disgrace and paid for a Paduan education for their elegant, brilliant son, with the aim of producing a pearl of scholarship to rival any in Christendom. Pole would be a credit to English culture, and perhaps, later, Henry's Archbishop of Canterbury. He had excelled in all, and achieved such an international reputation for learning that he became an obvious person to recruit for the king's divorce project. Henry wrote, requiring him to set down his opinions of the case in favour of the divorce and the supremacy. Pole dawdled; Henry's agents urged him to get on with it. It needn't be a large book, they assured

Reginald Pole (*Sebastiano del Piombo*)

him, just 'the most effectual reasons briefly and plainly stated'.

In May 1536, Pole's opinion arrived. It was a very large book indeed, and its contents 'most contrary to the king his purpose', as Cranmer observed, with some restraint. It contained a lengthy denunciation of Henry's case and his headship, addressed to him personally and couched in terms most unpleasing to Henry's intellectual vanity. Henry was a Nero, he was a tyrant governed by a whore. The tone as well was condescending. He (Henry) was to think of him (Pole, Henry's protégé) as 'your mother'. As Henry's mother, Pole lamented the decline of that intellectual promise 'that shone in you especially in the first years of your letters'. Henry's 'intelligence, learning and prudence' could never be compared to that of

Fisher and More, whose deaths had moved him to speak his mind as 'the only man left'.[9] In conclusion, the sooner that Henry was deposed, the better for England, and he himself would welcome that day. He called upon the sovereigns of Christendom to exert themselves in that cause.

The production of this treatise, known as *De Unitate*, recast Pole as Reformation England's premier traitor, principal ingrate and most wanted man. Remaining in Italy against all entreaties for him to come back to England and 'debate' the matter with Henry, he had thrown in his lot with Rome and received an immediate cardinalship 'specifically for use against England'. Accordingly, the spring of 1537 found him on an urgent papal legation to France and Spain to drum up support for a coordinated attack on schismatic England. Wyatt's job was to stop this from happening.

He was to go first to France, and meet up with the ambassadors there: Stephen Gardiner, Bishop of Winchester, and Sir Francis Bryan, at that moment engaged in a battle for French hearts and minds against Reginald Pole; for Pole was also in France, agitating for invasion. Bryan, for his part, was supplementing oratory with action. Although no-one had actually told him to murder the cardinal, he had instructions to get 'the said Pole by some mean trussed up and conveyed to Calais,'[10] which amounted to the same thing; and he would have succeeded in ambushing Pole if someone had not given Pole the tip-off. Pole escaped. The king's disappointment was great.

From Paris, Wyatt was to proceed to Spain. They arrived in Valladolid, the capital, on June 21, and everything seemed to go well. 'The fairest lodging in the town next to th'Emperor' was dislodged for them, and Wyatt went immediately to the emperor to set out his business 'not with pompe and setting forth of himself, but with sober and discreet words, like a wise man',

[9] From *De Unitate*, quoted in Thomas F. Mayer, *Reginald Pole: Prince and Prophet* (Cambridge University Press, 2000).
[10] April 25, 1537, LP 12, 1032.

as his servant, John Briertonne put it.

His instructions were threefold: first, he was to judge the sincerity of the emperor's protestations of friendship to England, and gauge the extent of his commitment to the French peace, preferably in such a way as to retard or unseat that process. 'Feel the deepness of his heart,' wrote Cromwell, 'Fish out the bottom of his stomach.' If the Franco-Spanish peace was really happening, Wyatt must secure for England the inexpensive but sheltered role of mediator between them. It must not go to Rome.

There was a contingency plan. If the worst happened and France and Spain did join forces against Henry, England could seek an alliance with an archipelago of Lutheran states in the north of Europe, whose princely rulers had declared for the new religion and had leagued together against the surrounding immensity of the empire. For a reformer like Cromwell, this alliance had obvious attractions, but for Henry VIII it had only the appeal of a last resort. He was never a Lutheran and anyway, he had his doubts about these princes, that they were not quite out of the top drawer. To treat with them might dim his lustre in the eyes of such as Charles V and Francis I, whom he felt were more his natural peers. Cromwell nevertheless kept relations with the Lutherans at a quiet simmer while waiting to see what Wyatt's embassy could achieve.

Apart from his own skills of persuasion, Wyatt's tools were few. He had in his diplomatic bag a letter that Cromwell had composed in the name of the once 'Princess', now 'Lady' Mary, acknowledging the illegality of the Aragon marriage and her own illegitimacy. There was a signature, extracted under threat of abandonment and death. Wyatt was to show this demonstration of family unity to the emperor at once, so he could see how his cousin renounced her claim to the succession, except in default of 'legitimate' heirs. Unfortunately for Wyatt, this errand conflicted with the third aim of Wyatt's embassy: to negotiate imperial marriages for Mary and the other English daughter, the baby Elizabeth, whose illegitimacy had never been in doubt for the Spanish. Henry's council had spotted this flaw, and ordered some hasty investigations as to what, if anything, could be done to make the king's daughters a more brilliant marital prospect: 'The king has two daughters, not lawful, yet the king's daughters,' – here was the rub – 'and as princes commonly conclude amity and things of importance by alliances, it is thought necessary that these two daughters shall be made of some estimation, without which no man will have any great respect to them.' Might it not then be desirable to 'advance [Mary] to some certain living decent for such an estate, whereby she may be the better had in reputation?'

What was at all costs to be prevented was an alliance between a French prince and the emperor's gorgeous niece, the recently widowed duchess of (the eternally desirable) Milan 'which the French king thinks thus to get into his hands.' If that happened, 'the French king and the Bishop of Rome [the pope] would join together by all likelihood against us, so that the king would be destitute of friendship on all sides, and his daughters remain unprovided for, and no prince of honour would desire the king's amity by mean of either of them'.[11]

A problem indeed for Wyatt. The imperial councillors were not at first especially interested in Henry's offer, except to see how much hard cash might be got out of him in lieu of legitimacy. But then in October 1537, Jane Seymour, the English queen, gave birth to a boy and then died, altering the English succession and bringing Henry himself onto the marriage market. At this, European ears pricked up. Now the king and all three of his children could be packaged into an altogether more alluring bundle of marriages. In France, Sir Francis Bryan pressed his inquiries about French princesses and likely dukes. In England,

[11] The King's Council, April ?3, 1537. LP 12, i, 815.

a search begun, somewhat in the style of Cinderella, to identify all ladies, foreign and domestic, who might make brides for the king. The delegate tasked with this, John Hutton, resented the assignment and complained to Cromwell that 'I have not much experience among ladies, and therefore this commission to me is hard.' That may have been disingenuous on Hutton's part. But if it was true that Hutton was no judge of women, then his continued employment as bridefinder general was a curious (and rare) oversight on the part of Cromwell, who should have known his master better. Possibly the success of the Boleyn and Seymour women, girls of unexceptional looks, had brought him to think that Henry could be led to service in any stall; if so, it was a mistake. The king repeatedly protested that he could not.

No trace of performance anxiety troubled the face of the negotiations. On the contrary: the legend of the English king's 'amorous complexion', much insisted upon during the debacle of his second marriage, became a very useful implement for negotiating his fourth. In discussions for a French alliance, politics were disguised as love. The famous royal inclination was used to justify an urgent suit for the particular French princess, Mme de Longueville, who had just been betrothed to James V of Scotland. The picture had begun to form -in imperial as well as English minds – of what damage a Franco-Scottish alliance could wreak: an invasion of England through her Scottish border could pick up strength in the mutinous north and, descending on London, place the newlyweds on the English throne and establish French control of the Channel. The English now pressed Henry's preference for the beauteous princess.

Full of apologies and assurances, Francis regretted that the promise to the Scottish king, 'whom he thinks of as his own son', must be honoured. On St Valentine's Day, 1538, Henry put forth a characteristic suggestion, in which amative and political concerns were so entwined that the ends of both were lost: what if Mme de Longueville herself *preferred* to marry him? He told the French ambassadors to 'reply to the Scottish king that if the lady is not willing, [he] cannot constrain her to accept him, for marriages must be free'.[12]

No one, as Henry well knew, was ever less free than a royal princess of the early 16th century. What he meant was that Mme de Longueville be compelled to prefer him. It was a perfect example of the uses of love in achieving other ends. Yet it contained a truth about the disposition of the English king, whose amorous complexion was not libidinous but delicate. He knew he was no Francis I, to father annual children on an ugly wife, or watch the arrival of a new wife from an open window, arm in arm with his mistress. He knew an unattractive bride would have acute dynastic repercussions; and besides, he was uxorious by nature. Marriages ending in divorce and murder had failed to bruise Henry's marital idealism; to himself he was still the *preux chevalier* of 1509:

I love true where I did marry

and he still hoped that the peace of nations might be sealed with a union of chaste and fervent hearts. He could not see the matter as purely one of diplomacy; consequently the French brush-off affronted his vanity as a man as well as a monarch. How could Mme de Longueville prefer James of Scotland, not just a lesser king but, so Henry's ambassadors had told him the year before, an inferior man with hick manners and laughable jousting skills?

'The said king (of Scotland) lieth at the Tournelles, daily assaying his horse and harness, so I assure you he had need to do, if he intend to get any honour here,' they soothed. 'He is a right proper man, after the Northern fashion.'[13]

---

[12] Letter, February 14, 1538, in Jean-Baptiste Louis Kaulek, *Correspandance Politique de MM de Castillon et de Marillac, ambassadeurs de France en Angleterre*, 1537-42 (Paris, 1885)..

[13] Letter from Sir John Wallop to Lord Lisle, December 14, 1536.

Likewise, when Henry asked for a line-up of French ladies to be conveyed to Calais with the Duc de Guise for inspection, there was urgency in the request. Marriage to him was 'a thing whereof the pleasure and quiet, or the displeasure and torment of the man's mind doth much depend'.[14] 'By God,' he said, 'I trust no one but myself. This thing touches me too near.' The French need not fear dishonour: if not himself, he would send a delegate from the English court of equal rank to the Duc de Guise.

The French ambassador, Castillon, doubted there was such a person at the English court, and said so. As is well known, he responded with a withering assault on Henry's manners. Why stop at a beauty pageant, he asked. Perhaps the king would like to mount these princesses in turn, and see which suited him best? The insult was well turned for its complimentary implications. Henry retreated abashed, but not affronted. Privately, however, the foreign ambassadors had an inkling of his shortcomings. At the time of Henry's third marriage, Eustace Chapuys – in a dispatch that exceeded even his usual standards of bitchiness – had speculated on the unlikelihood of Jane Seymour's being a virgin, adding 'perhaps this king will be only too glad to be so far relieved from the trouble'.[15] Rochford's words[16] about Henry's performance were over the Channel in a trice. So it was perhaps with this frailty in mind that later, in a more conciliatory mood, Castillon changed his advice on this matter and urged his master to arrange a princess-viewing at Amiens, despite the breach of protocol. A political interview between the two kings could furnish the excuse, so that 'your honour will be saved in letting him see the ladies'. In reverse of the usual priorities, here was love disguised as politics.

---

[14] Instructions to Sir Thomas Wyatt from the king, June 1538. *The Works of H.H. Earl of Surrey and of Sir T. Wyatt the Elder*, ed. George F. Nott (1815).
[15] Letter from Chapuys to Antoine Perrenot, May 18, 1536. 'si elle [Jane Seymour] ne tiendroit pas a sa conscience de n'avoir pourvu et prevenu de savoir que c'est de fair nopces'.
[16] See p199.

CHAPTER FIFTEEN

If Castillon was prepared to accommodate Henry's little *faiblesses* in respect of amatory matters, it was largely thanks to the strategies of Sir Thomas Wyatt in the imperial court. Wyatt had been negotiating hard for an alternative package of marriages on the imperial side, and made it known that this would include the marriage of Henry to the Duchess of Milan, with Milan settled on Henry's daughter. The prospect alarmed the French sufficiently to make them press their own alliance with more enthusiasm. The emperor had, of course, also promised Milan to Francis's negotiators. It was a time of mutual and multiple deception, double-dealing, backsliding, wavering and craft that bred an anxious paralysis in all the courts of Europe.

> *Each man me telleth I change most my device*[1]
> *And on my faith me think it good reason*
> *To change purpose like after the season.*
> *For in every case to keep still one guise*
> *Is meet for them that would be taken wise;*
> *And I am not of such manner condition*
> *But treated after a diverse fashion*
> *And thereupon my diverseness doth rise.*

Legates from all parts toiled to find out the true intentions of foreign kings, while their own kings kept them in the dark. Wyatt had to keep all diplomatic contingencies alive, suggesting

---

[1] Wyatt, sonnet XXX, in Rebholz, op. cit.

everything but promising nothing, comporting himself with such ambivalence that both Spanish and French legates were held in a state of expectant uncertainty, and he himself always flexible, ready to alter with alteration of policy.

> It may be good, like it who list.[2]
> But I do doubt. Who can me blame?
> For oft assured yet have I missed
> And now again I fear the same.
> The windy words, the eyes' quaint game
> Of sudden change maketh me aghast.
> For dread to fall I stand not fast.

Charles V, the Holy Roman Emperor, played at great advantage in this game. In addition to his vast territories and unique position of influence in Christendom, he possessed the physical characteristics that were perfectly adapted – as though by some equally rare effort on the part of evolution – to thrive in the environment of Renaissance politics. Just at the time when foreign legates were instructed to form personal relationships with kings, and distil intelligence from 'manner of speech and countenances', a benevolent Nature had formed Charles V to frustrate any such attempts. He was impenetrable. Unlike Henry VIII, whose moods rippled over his face like a baby's, the emperor's face showed nothing except the genetic misfortune of his underbite. English envoys checking his waxy face for the rising and sinking colour that was 'wont... to bring a man certain word how his errand is liked or misliked', checked in vain. His blue eyes were blank, his voice low and quiet. 'There is in him almost nothing that speaketh beside his tongue'[3] – and that barely, for half his words went astray in the cavern of his underhanging jaw.

---

² Wyatt, LXXXV, in Rebholz, op. cit.
³ Moryson on Charles V: Hardwicke, State Papers, Vol I, in Nott, op. cit.

Charles V (*Flemish School*)

The opacity of his opinions did not, of course, prevent him from holding them, and his opinion of Sir Thomas Wyatt was good. He spoke easily to Wyatt, so that no other envoy was 'so meet to fill that room'.[4] As the year wore on and the court journeyed from palace to palace on an endless progress through Spain, Wyatt rode up with the emperor, chatting easily. The French, fearing the disappearance of Milan into this rapport, retaliated by viciously misrepresenting it to Henry as treason. In the spring and summer of 1538, a French delegation arriving at the English court began a whispering campaign against Wyatt, saying Wyatt was more the emperor's man than Henry's, and that Wyatt and Cromwell, not the king, were dictating English policy in Spain.[5]

'Alas, who shall men trust?' said the king.

---

[4] Letter from Bonner to Cromwell, October 15, 1538.
[5] Spanish Calendar, June 17, 1538.

It was an easy thing in 1538 to obtain short-term gain by working on the king's suspicions. Cromwell was the master at this, but everyone did it: diplomats, ministers, courtiers and prelates, all of them briefing against one another and working the king into a ferment of distrust, without, apparently, foreseeing the ultimate disadvantage of this strategy. The result of it was that Henry soon came to divide his servants into those who were suspect because they may be papists, and those who could not be trusted because they may be heretics. Maddened by this, fearful of radicalism at home and foreign plots abroad, he and Cromwell began to send their own delegates out to spy upon one another in the course of their diplomatic duties.

Take heed betime lest ye be spied.[6]
Your loving eyes ye cannot hide.
At last the truth will sure be tried.
Therefore take heed!

For some there be of crafty kind,
Though you show no part of your mind
Surely their eyes ye cannot blind.
Therefore take heed!

There was an admirable economy in this, and a further advantage, that it brought home to those who were used as spies the likelihood that they themselves would be spied on in future – and kept them in a state of perpetual fear. Wyatt would protest that 'The king should send who he trusteth or trust who he sendeth'. But the king would do neither.

For in like case themselves have been
And thought right sure none had them seen
But it was not as they did ween.
  Therefore take heed!

[6] Wyatt, CXVIII, in Rebholz, op. cit.

To judge from Wyatt's experience, there may have been some idea of setting reformers on religious conservatives, and vice versa. Cromwell had sent Wyatt to Paris to inform on the ambassador there, Stephen Gardiner, the (conservative) Bishop of Winchester; now it was Wyatt's turn, they sent the Archdeacon of Leicester, Dr Edmund Bonner, soon to be Bishop of London.

As Bonner was one of the great trimmers of Reformation history, one cannot securely say what his religious convictions were in 1538. Famous under Mary as a diligent burner of Protestants, he was now, before 'the change of the world',[7] Cromwell's creature, and enough of the good evangelical, so it seemed, to invigilate the production of the English Bible in Paris. Yet Cromwell, who knew everything, may already have had some inkling of the views that would emerge from Bonner at the moment of his fall (whereupon 'not a good word could Bonner speak of Cromwell, but used the vilest and bitterest that he could speak, calling him the rankest heretic that ever lived')[8] – opinions that would incline him to mistrust Wyatt and make him a good sniffer-out of misconduct in that quarter.

Bonner may have made a proficient spy, but he was a useless ambassador: devious without subtlety, charmless, affected, peremptory and oleaginous in turn; so that the chief legacy of this peevish, vain and contumacious little man's diplomacy are the letters from his co-diplomatists begging for his recall. In fact, it is quite hard to explain Cromwell's persistent deployment of Bonner in these delicate months except, perhaps, as the secret weapon in some subtle counter-scheme of his own to encourage anti-English sentiment throughout Europe, leaving England no option but alliance with the Lutherans and the rapid advance of reform. As for Bonner himself, it grated on

[7] John Foxe, *Acts and Monuments,* ed. Hobart Seymour, 1837-41
[8] *ibid.*

his self-regard that his career as an ambassador should come at the exact moment when diplomatic prestige was draining away from the clergy and into the hands of the likes of Wyatt. He was not the resident ambassador. The instructions for him and his sidekick, Simon Heynes, Dean of Exeter, make this painful development very clear. There is nothing here about counselling the emperor in *propria persona*. He is not to speak up like Wyatt, 'as though it proceeded from your own head'; but, on the contrary, as though it proceeded from the deliberations of better theologians than himself. He and Heynes were to submit those points of religious doctrine that supported Henry's supremacy, while 'acknowledging themselves unmet[9] for such a charge'. They may refer to letters written by superior clerics and, worst of all, they must 'confer with Sir Thomas Wiat before having an audience'.

But Bonner did not see himself in this unglamorous role of a clerical functionary. He had eminent longings. To himself he was a person of exalted learning, culture and refinement, something of a horseman, something of a ladies' man, cutting a dash through the courts of Europe. For this purpose he had kitted himself out with Italian poetry. It was he who had asked Cromwell to lend him some Petrarch and that *sine qua non* of courtly sophistication, Castiglione's *Il Cortegiano*, 'to make me a good Italian', as he coyly explained. He had had eight years to study it, and was determined to put into practice what he had learned. Whatever that was may have been acceptable in England, but in France and the Burgundian courts of Spain, it was grotesque. It appalled Wyatt to think of this fat, self-important little priest hectoring the emperor, or having to have him in tow on his social rounds. He hardly knew which was worse, Bonner's rudeness or his *politesse* that made him, as Wyatt later said, 'a laughing stock to all men that came in your company; and me sometimes to sweat for shame to see you'.[10] But he kept up relations.

[9] unmet: unmeet, unworthy.

Illustration from Foxe's *Book of Martyrs*, showing
Bishop Bonner torturing a Protestant

Conscious of Bonner's prickly vanity, he horsed and harnessed
him in style, and lodged him at least as well, so he said, as he
himself was lodged, and put up with him sitting 'on my right
hand', at 'the upper end of the table' when they ate together.
Nevertheless, when it came to actual negotiation, he and John
Mason, his co-delegate, were genuinely fearful that Bonner's
involvement would make matters worse than they already were
for England, and tried to offload him. Once, they did manage
to slip through some loose end in an arrangement and leave him
and Heynes fuming outside the audience chamber. Wyatt had
no idea what a catastrophe this would bring upon himself.

As far as foreign policy was concerned, one struggles to see
how matters could be much worse than they were in the summer of 1538. Francis and Charles had drawn closer than ever.
The French and imperial fleets were making ready to sail down

[10] Wyatt, in Muir, , op. cit.

the Mediterranean for a magnificent floating peace conference at Nice. Now all that was left for England was the 'mayning' or mediation of the peace, as we have seen. That was in the gift of both the peacemaking parties, but Cromwell had preferred that it should come from the emperor; and now didn't hesitate to lay all responsibility for the outcome at Wyatt's door, reminding him of assurances he had made at an earlier stage of negotiations.

Mr Wyatt, now handle the matter in such earnest sort with the Emperor, as the king (*who by your fair words hath conceived as certain to find assured friendship therein*) be not deceived.[11] [Italics mine]

But though both France and Spain had made gestures of offering the mediation to England, they had always intended to vest it in the pope; and so they did. Rome was named mediator and England was roundly 'left out of the cart's arse'[12], as Wyatt expostulated – and potentially under the cart's wheels, if this Catholic confederacy turned on her.

In May of that year, 1538, Wyatt and Mason sailed with the imperial fleet to the meeting at Nice and made their first contact with Bonner and Heynes, just arrived from Paris, as crowds poured into the coastal towns. The English contingent consisted of themselves, their crew and enough of Wyatt's attendants – 16 all told – to make a decent show for English diplomacy.[13] Among the company were the 21-year-old John Mantell, 'the handsomest and best bred man in England', later to be hanged for his involvement in a murderous hunting party,[14] and George Blage, who was Wyatt's particular friend, known at court for

[11] Letter from Cromwell to Wyatt, March 1, 1538, Merriman, op. cit
[12] Wyatt, in Mui, op. cit.
[13] Letter from Bonner to Cromwell, August 1538.
[14] For John Mantell, see Baron, op. cit.

his wit. As both of them are associated with the making of the Dublin MS[15], it is very possible that they used some of the heavy waiting-around time to look at Wyatt's poems, maybe learning them by heart;[16] but that was hardly their priority. Now they had a crisis on their hands. They were desperate for anything they could lob under the wheels of the peace process to prevent Charles and Francis treating without Henry. Wyatt to this end 'trotted continually up and down that Hell through heat and stink, from counsellor to ambassador, from one friend to another',[17] trying to get a purchase on imperial intentions. Finding only a general chill from all sides, he was moved to propose a desperate measure to the assembled group as they sat at dinner racking their brains. He could send his companion, John Mason, to seek out Cardinal Pole (whose enormous beard was conspicuous in the papal train) and 'look if he could suck out any thing that were worth the king's knowledge: which they all there thought good'. This was a mistake, as he would find out, but as he had run out of suggestions, he decided to go ahead anyway.

Wyatt, meanwhile, continued to prosecute the marriage alliances, now so configured as to tie the three parties so close together that no one could move. But these, alas, had just the wrong amount of purchase: not enough to deflect the kings from their peace, but enough to get Wyatt sent back to England, supposedly to thrash out the details, four days before the arrival of the French at Nice. As a sop to the impossible position Wyatt was now in, Charles promised to conclude nothing without him, but only if he returned within 25 days.[18]

It was summer in the Alps. It may have been just possible to

[15] The MS known as 'Blage', see p198.
[16] Some scholars think Wyatt took his own MS of his poems, the 'Egerton MS', with him to Spain.
[17] Wyatt, *A Declaration*, Muir, op. cit.
[18] Cromwell says 25 days (Merriman,op. cit); Wyatt later claimed he had only 16 days (Wyatt, *Defence*, in Muir, op. cit.

make the journey in that time, but Wyatt was delayed by bad weather on the return crossing. When he got back, it was too late. After a rocky start at Nice, when some almost intractable precedence issues – each monarch asserting his own superiority – had prevented the contracting parties from leaving their respective boats, the pope had indeed negotiated a ten-year truce between them; and now he, with the ubiquitous Pole, was off to Aigues Mortes, on the Carmargue coast, to celebrate with the two kings.

England was nowhere in this, and her envoys were made to feel their redundancy right away, in very immediate manner, as all around them people stopped paying them any attention. In the French fleet, Sir Francis Bryan applied himself to the card tables in a bid to get himself noticed, and lost a lot of money as a result. He wrote a furious letter to Henry on the topic of this sudden demotion, complaining that the French king 'took no notice of him as if he did not know him'. ('I think Bryan made this despatch after dinner,' said the French ambassador, imperturbably.)[19] As for Wyatt, there was nothing left to do but to send the king copies of the agreement 'wherein he was not mentioned contrary to th'emperor's promise and to the French king's letters.' French and imperial marriage prospects receded, and Henry's petulant threat to take himself elsewhere and 'not to marry unless the emperor or the king my brother prefer my friendship to that which they have together' did nothing to restore them.

In London, Cromwell began to review the various possibilities for a German alliance.

[19] Letter from Castillon to Francis I, July 25, 1538.

CHAPTER SIXTEEN

In England that autumn, the first fears of invasion arose. The king realised he must anticipate a joint attack from these Catholic princes urged on by Cardinal Pole – the status of whose disloyalty was now raised to 'lewd and extremely ingrate'... 'rebel and cankered traitor'.[1] This fear made him trust his overseas orators less and suspect them more of leaguing with his enemies. Wyatt, Bryan, Stephen Gardiner – Henry picked at a suspicion, never quite proven, that they were all in cahoots, nudging one another on in some ulterior Roman enterprise. He already suspected that Gardiner, a religious conservative, was the one who had tipped off Cardinal Pole when he was in Paris the year before, and let him escape Bryan's henchmen. Wyatt had been there at the time. And now, it seemed, they were sharing information in a way that Henry didn't like. Cromwell wrote to Wyatt 'his Majesty doth much marvel that you send your letters open to my Lord of Winchester',[2] allowing the bishop to read their contents as the diplomatic packet passed through France to England. 'For albeit he doth not mistrust him, yet he noteth some folly in you to do it without his express command'.[3]

As distances between courts were long, the speed of travel slow, and all ambassadorial negotiations were delicately and critically interrelated, it seems that a case could be made in

---

[1] Letter from Henry VIII to Wyatt, Feb 13, 1539.
[2] open: i.e. not sealed. Winchester: Stephen Gardiner was Bishop of Winchester from 1531.
[3] Letter from Cromwell to Wyatt, April 4, 1538, Merriman, op. cit.

favour of the king's ambassadors perusing one another's dispatches; but in 1538 all was subsumed to fear of treason. To Henry and Cromwell, all contact made breeding places for conspiracy, and they looked around for a means to break up what they saw as a too-cosy, potentially pro-imperial cabal. The means that they found was to recall Gardiner and promote Edmund Bonner as French Ambassador in his place – 'By God!' said Henry to Castillon, 'I will not write [to France] until there is another ambassador there called Dr Bonner. The others have deceived me and let themselves be seduced by Wyatt, with whom I am not pleased.'

The advancement of Bonner – soon to be promoted to Bishop of Hereford[4] – seems a less than obvious solution when his abrasive personality and linguistic deficiencies are considered.[5] That Gardiner was as aware of his shortcomings as Wyatt had been in Spain is evident from his visible dismay when he learned that it was Bonner who had come to replace him ('The flesh in his face began all to tremble')[6], and the insulting detail in his list of handover instructions. These included such elementary advice as what to wear, how to hand over a packet of letters (wrapped in *clean* paper) and how to converse with the king: 'neither in communication too sharp, whereby you should exasperate him, nor duller in language than the case should require' – a tip apparently tailored to Bonner's special oratorical gifts.[7] Bonner had, however, a good grasp on one important tenet of service to the second Tudor: he understood very well that in times of high suspicion, favour becomes a fixed commodity; and that the only way to get it is to take it out of another man's store. Accordingly, when Gardiner had gone back to England, Bonner sat down at his desk to write a letter to Cromwell, in his

[4] Bonner was elected to the see of Hereford in October of 1538.
[5] For Bonner's linguistic shortcomings, see letter from Cromwell to Bonner, June 8 1538, Merriman, op. cit.
[6] Letter from Bonner to Cromwell, August 1538.
[7] Gardiner, Instructions to Bonner, LP, 12 (ii), 143.

minute, ink-sparing hand, on the subject of Sir Thomas Wyatt.

The letter he wrote is known to historians as 'Bishop Bonner's Accusation'.[8] It is mainly a catalogue of the ways Wyatt failed sufficiently to admire the writer, Dr Bonner, written by one with a touchy mania for his own dignity. He begins with a sop to Cromwell's known liking for Wyatt: what a pity it is that he 'should mislike any thing about such an excellent wit as Mr Wyatt hath, with singular and many great qualities'. But then he overcomes this reluctance in time to mislike Mr Wyatt over ten separately numbered headings, each beginning afresh, 'I mislike Mr Wyat.'

He misliked Mr Wyat because Wyatt went to the emperor without him and Heynes; because Wyatt went to his first minister, Grandvela, without them; because Wyatt told everyone that Heynes and Bonner were not proper ambassadors; because Wyatt said he would go with them for their audience with the emperor but then gave them the slip at the last minute, sending them in alone (and unable to speak French, the language the emperor spoke, so not showing at their most effective); because Wyatt wrote letters to Mason but wouldn't show them to Bonner; because he was obviously 'desirous to have had us gone'; because he wouldn't let Bonner ride his horse, and so on.

There were some more general reproofs of Wyatt's conduct while they were at Nice and Aigues-Mortes: he had heard Wyatt complaining about his posting and the expenses of it; he had grumbled openly about his previous imprisonment; he was a spendthrift 'given all to pleasure, and spending unthriftily upon 'nuns';[9] he was much too pally with the emperor; he thought too highly of his companion, Mason, 'as glorious and malicious a harlot as any that I know, and withal as great a papiste where he dare utter it' – and too little, correspondingly, of Bonner. It

[8] John Bruce, 'Recovery of the Lost Accusation of Sir Thomas Wyatt, the poet, by Bishop Bonner', *Gentleman's Magazine* (June, 1850).
[9] nuns: Bonner means 'prostitutes'.

was a feature of the bishop's rhetoric at this time to let the scarlet word 'papist' flare up here and there on the page. The fact that Wyatt was a known evangelical seems not to have deterred him from this tactic, but obliged him to use it more diffusely, throwing it anywhere it might stick – hence at Mason, and even, rather desperately, at the emperor and Cardinal Grandvela,[10] whose papism could hardly have come as a surprise – in the hope of tainting Wyatt by association. He ends his letter with a nauseating assurance of his continued diligence as an informer 'though it were against mine own brother', and requests that a particular individual, Philip Hoby, be the one to come out and be 'a witness of all my doings' in France. In other words, he tries to influence the roster of surveillance and protect himself from people like him.

Cromwell received this letter at the beginning of September. He must now have been quite familiar with Bonner's invective style, having just received an almost identical letter from him about Stephen Gardiner. Gardiner's crimes against Bonner were in much the same elusive vein as Wyatt's and included a particularly delicious crime of having misled him into thinking he was invited to dinner. When Bonner had turned up in expectation of a welcoming feast, Gardiner had let him sit at the table, 'making merry communications all supper while, but nothing at all yet speaking to me, or giving anything to me, saving, at the coming of the fruit, he gave me a pear'.[11]

What did Cromwell think? He was a man with no vanity to wound, and held it as a weakness. Did he sigh at having to rummage in these pitiful expectorations? Did he laugh? Certainly the letters are funny in retrospect, because they show Bonner as uniquely blind to the obvious explanation for all these evasions: that his co-ambassadors thought him an atrocious bungler and

---

[10] Nicholas Perrenot de Granvela, Charles V's chief minister for foreign affairs from 1530.
[11] Letter from Bonner to Cromwell, August 1538.

general liability, and would run a mile to avoid contaminating their diplomatic efforts with his. But Bishop Bonner was not such an idiot as he seems, and was content to sacrifice his pride to vengeance. Enumerating these humiliations, he phrased them so that they could, with a very small adjustment of interpretation, be turned into something much more sinister. Gardiner was suspected of being the one who tipped off Pole in Paris: that was a grave suspicion. Looked at maliciously, all this avoidance of Bonner might have meant that the king's ambassadors were conspiring in secret, negotiating out of sight of the faithful cleric so that 'they may tell after what they list, and so in likewise write and deceive their Master'.[12] This is what Bonner meant Cromwell to think, as Cromwell knew.

Cromwell now had enough to move against Wyatt and Gardiner, should he want to. He called in Mason, who was in England, preparing to return to Spain, and took him in for questioning before the council. He wrote to Wyatt saying Mason was detained due to illness, not caring that this was a transparent and lazy lie, and that Wyatt, his friend, would certainly find it out. Then he let the matter drop, and put the letters away.

*   *   *   *

In Toledo that autumn, Wyatt had a good idea that something was up in England. All had not been well with him in this mission from the very start. He had begun with ' a great fear lest anything should quail through my fault' and had often cause to wish 'a meeter man than myself in the room'.[13] Though Bonner's account shows him as an effective thriving man, primed with friends, well connected, buoyant and nimble on the diplomatic stream, the letters he received from Cromwell show how all this time the air was slowly squeezing out of him.

Those letters themselves were part of the problem. Cromwell

[12] Bonner, *Accusation*, in Bruce, op. cit.
[13] Wyatt, Defence, in Muir op. cit

had a method for keeping his overseas men in line: he kept them in a state of permanent unease, threatening and chiding them, anticipating the king's displeasure, promising to advance their affairs but always retarding the outcome, typically blaming any delay on some negligence of their own – so that they felt themselves keenly indebted to him, without actually having received anything. Obviously, men on diplomatic missions hoped for reward on their return; and to manage this expectation Cromwell operated a system of 'credit', or favour, which was indeed very like a simple banking mechanism, wherein he kept a mental account of every man's successes and failures. If a man's balance rose to the requisite level in my Lord Privy Seal's[14] head, it could be converted into valuable offices or grants, and this encouraged everyone to work harder and harder in the king's interests; and yet the level never seemed to rise sufficiently for anything to be done, because the minister was eating away at it in the other column, making constant deductions for perceived shortcomings and misdemeanours. To make matters worse, the commission itself was always represented as an immense favour, so that the envoys felt the depth of their indebtedness even before they had arrived. Cromwell was often moved to remind his diplomats that this was the correct construction of events, as they tended to take the opposing view. One wrote insistently from Antwerp: 'Yow think I am in paradise, and I thinke in purgatorie; purgatorie I fynde it.'[15] Cromwell was robust about such complaints.

To wish and want and not obtain [16]
To seek and sue ease of my pain
Since all that ever I do is vain
What may it avail me?

---

[14] Cromwell had occupied this office since the summer of 1536.
[15] Letter from Stephen Vaughan to Cromwell, April 13, 1536.
[16] Wyatt, CVII, in Rebholz, op. cit.

Although I strive both day and hour
Against the stream with all my power,
If fortune list yet for to lour
What may it avail me?

His letters to Wyatt are a perfect demonstration of this system. From the very first letter scolding him for being 'slack and negligent to write unto me', every post carries a fresh entry for the debit column. He has always done something wrong. *Item*: delay in the execution of instructions ('It is much marvelled that you have not delivered my lady Mary's grace's letters. It was a part of your instruction, and very negligently thus pre-termitted'). Deducted. *Item*: a lax household left in England ('For all the haste I would not omit to advertise you that some of your servants be called and named common stealers of the king's hawks'). Deducted. *Item*: impertinent request for money: ('I marvel that you would put the king to the charge of your interests. The precedent were too evil to be admitted'). *Item*: the king misled by Wyatt's too-encouraging words. *Item*: money imprudently lent to Sir Francis Bryan, to tide him over his gambling debts. Deducted. Deducted. Deducted. And in all of these accounts, it is only by Cromwell's intervention that the calamity of the king's displeasure is averted – more deductions for the trouble, and a more pressing sense of indebtedness for Wyatt, with further proofs and protestations of loyalty required.

The knot which first my heart did strain[17]
When that your servant I became
Doth bind me still for to remain
Always your own, as now I am
And if ye find that I do feign
With just judgement myself I damn
To have disdain

[17] Wyatt, XCI, in Rebholz, op. cit.

If in my love there be one spot
Of false deceit or doubleness
Or if I mind to slip this knot
By want of faith or steadfastness,
Let all my service be forgot
And, when I would have chief redress,
Esteem me not

But if that I consume in pain
With burning sighs and fervent love
And daily seek none other gain
But with my deeds these words to prove
Methink of right I should obtain
That ye would mind for to remove
Your great disdain

And yet Cromwell was not all disdain. He held his client in true affection. Though the letters are dark with threats and chidings, they are shot through with shafts of avuncular concern, out of his normal mode. He takes a kindly interest in Wyatt's English affairs; which was just as well, as Wyatt had none of his father's talents for administration and deputising, and his people were surprised to see how poorly he had provided for his own absence. Young John Mantell, returning to England with letters, marvelled, 'How slenderly Mr Wyatt's matters have been handled here.' 'Since I came,' he wrote to John Mason, 'no man but my self solicited Mr Wyatt's matters to my Lord' (Cromwell). And Cromwell himself often referred to the disarray of Wyatt's interests:

> your agents here, *if you have any*, be very slack to call upon any man for you. Your brother Hawte was not thrice here sithens you went, and the rest I hear nothing of unless it be when nothing is to be done. I never saw man

that had so many friends here, leave so few perfect friends behind him. Quicken them with your letters and in the mean season, as I have been, so shall I be both your friend and your solicitor.[18]

One of Wyatt's least 'perfect' friends at court was Thomas Wriothesley (pronounced 'Riseley'), a satellite of Cromwell's whose power was on the wax. His speed into the trough of grants, perks, offices, honours and the rest had collected admiring glances from the start; and now that the monastic properties were coming on stream, through the newly opened Court of Augmentations,[19] he was punctual in that quarter. It was for this that Wyatt had mobilised him, perhaps in return for Spanish horses, as the state of English horseflesh was very run down after years of wars and underinvestment. As Cromwell's 'clerk of the signet', Wriothesley drafted much of his correspondence, so he knew all about Wyatt's case. He wrote to him soothingly, reassuring him of the king's favour, leaning on him not to write in cipher unless absolutely necessary, and spare him the trouble of decoding it. Unlike Cromwell he was always bonhomous and emollient, apparently mindful of their common enterprise; like him, he tended to emphasise his own industry and friendship, and the virtue of patience, but with no guarantee of results. He wrote to Wyatt:

I nearly got you today 13s 4d a day increase in diet; and no doubt it will come. In your other great suit I have small courage; but, perhaps, among the rest, we may get a morsel... I think as much how to relieve you as any friend you have here... I will shoot so long for you till at the last I will surely hit somewhat, a fat or a lean.[20]

[18] Letter from Cromwell to Wyatt, April 8, 1538.
[19] The Court of Augmentations was set up in March 1536, to collect the revenues of the suppressed abbeys and dispose of them in a manner most profitable to the king.
[20] Letter from Wriothesely to Wyatt, February 15, 1538.

Thomas Wriothesley (*artist unknown*)

I see that chance hath chosen me [21]
Thus secretly to live in pain
And to another given the fee
Of all my loss to have the gain.
By chance assigned, thus do I serve,
And other have that I deserve.

Wyatt sent him the horses.

*   *   *   *

On November 13, 1538, Wriothesley wrote to Wyatt with word of a significant development at court. Passages of important news coming out of Cromwell's office were always expressed

---

[21] Wyatt, CXXVI, in Rebholz, op. cit.

with the emphases of the party line in place, so that the recipient would know exactly how to convey it onwards. In this case, the news was big enough for Wriothesley to remind him of the practice:

> I write this unto you because you may peraventure hear somewhat hereof, and the thing percase be sinisterly interpreted. Now that you know the truth, you may declare the same upon my poor word, and so you may make answer accordingly.

The big news was the arrest of the Marquis of Exeter and the Earl of Montague, brother of Cardinal Pole, on treason charges. Enraged by the publication of Pole's *De Unitate* in Rome, the king decided to move against Catholic faction and as many members of the Pole family as he could. The resulting series of arrests, attainders and executions of the so-called 'white rose conspirators' swept away the last of Henry's subjects with a legitimate claim to his throne. With them went Pole's poor old mother's head, his brother Geoffrey's wits and the life of Sir Nicholas Carew, Henry's (religious conservative) master of the horse.

Carew was a lifer in the Henrician court, a genius in the jousting lists and one of Henry's oldest and closest friends. There is a portrait of him after a lost Holbein, looking spindle-shanked and resentful, not at all like a man who could trot a horse into the tiltyard with a young tree in his spear arm. He was one of the two or three top courtiers of the reign, and despite his open support for first Catherine, then Mary, he had kept his place for two decades. Cromwell had made a fool of him in 1536, when he had bought Carew's cooperation in the plot against Anne Boleyn by leading him to believe that Mary's reinstatement would follow. Now the opportunity arose to dislodge him in a torrent of anti-Catholic suspicion released by the Exeter 'plot'.

Sir Nicholas Carew (*Hans Holbein the Younger*)

Cromwell found against him on the basis of some letters 'which the said Carewe ... afterwards, to conceal their treason, traitorously burned',[22] and for the prior existence of which there is no evidence at all. On December 31, Sir Nicholas Carew – who only the month before had sat on the jury against his co-accused, Lord Montague – attained the special distinction of the reign: *equitus decollatus*.

Wyatt had words for these reversals:

Stand whoso list upon the slipper top [23]
Of court's estates, and let me here rejoice
And use me quiet without let or stop,
Unknown in court that hath such brackish joys.
In hidden place so let my days forth pass

[22] Indictment of Sir Nicholas Carew, February 14, 1539. LP 14, 290.
[23] Wyatt, XLIX, in Rebholz, op. cit.

That, when my years be done withouten noise,
I may die aged after the common trace.
For him death grip'th right hard by the crop[24]
That is much known of other, and of himself, alas
Doth die unknown, dazed, with dreadful face.

A translation from Seneca, as this is, was a safer place for protest than most. As Hamlet said to Claudius as they took their
seats for *The Mousetrap*: 'the story is extant, and written in
very choice Italian'. The poem was extant. Like Hamlet, Wyatt
could insert in it some small additions of his own. With a few
tiny changes, a word pinched out here or let in there, he takes a
Senecan passage about self-knowledge and gives it back lined, as
it were, with a piece about self-preservation under the Treason
Act. Wyatt's advice about 'using me quiet', living 'withouten
noise' and not being 'much known of other' carry a warning to
the talkative. Seneca recommends the subjugation of pride and
a humble death, like 'a common man'; Wyatt's concern is with
an *un*common man's *lifespan*. Only the silent die in their beds
'aged after the common trace'.

It was one of Wyatt's peculiar transliterative gifts that
he could translate poems not just into English, but into
England. Italian *strombotti*, Horatian satire, Hebrew psalms,
French *chansons* and *ballades*; *canzoni* and *sonnetti* and *ron-
deaux* and Latin epigrams all passed through his transforming
hands and landed with their feet in the Thames. All his materials are English: he used Anglo-Saxon words and English proverbs, he changed Virgil into Chaucer and Provence into Kent. It
was all quite deliberate and nourished a conscious ambition to
be an English poet for a culturally independent English court.
But it also meant that his poems of instructive vein, like this
one, could turn a moral into a health warning and abstraction
into something bordering on demonstration. So here, where we

[24] crop: throat.

actually *experience* the courtier's progress: he appears to be going *up*, passing the poet in his (either humble or tacit) retirement. But the last lines reveal the truth of his trajectory. He lost his footing on the 'slipper top' of the first line, and has tumbled down the poem, past the quiet poet, into the abyss.

> For *him death grip'th right hard by the crop*
> *That is much known of other, and of himself, alas,*
> *Doth die unknown, dazed, with dreadful face.*

Almost every word is Anglo-Saxon, and the last four are his own addition. In the Latin, mortality 'lies heavy' on the man who doesn't know himself. Here, death itself drops out of the sky. The sense of speed is awful: no time to settle accounts. Here is the surprise of the tap on the shoulder, the surprise at finding oneself dead, and nothing between: 'dazed, with dreadful face'. A row of Anglo-Saxon monosyllables, equally weighted, sound like an axe on wood: hím/ déath/ gríp'th /ri′ght/ hárd /b′y /the cróp'. Chip, chop. Chip, chop. Here comes a chopper to chop off your head. Certainly, this was England.

CHAPTER SEVENTEEN

When Wyatt received Wriothesley's letter, he felt his own foot slip, and for two reasons. As Wriothesley guessed, news of these arrests would have percolated into Spain through various couriers, and fragments of the Exeter furore would find their way to the king's envoys. Thanks to the work of dedicated historians, we now know that the actual crimes of the 'conspirators' boiled down to some indiscreet grumblings against the state of the realm; but these were made to seem much more incriminating when added to the meatier charge of contact with Montague's brother, Reginald Pole. Now they could be worked up into 'crimes of lese majesty traitorously imagined and uttered as far as they durst against the King's royal person, his issue, his council and the Whole Realm' – with, as so often with Henry, an accompanying book on the subject, rushed out of Cromwell's propaganda department and circulated, so it was imagined, as a counterweight to that of Pole.[1] Wyatt would soon be getting one in Spain, with the idea of getting it seen in the imperial court.[2] But in November, rumours reaching Wyatt would certainly establish that the principal charge was contact with Pole. This was bad. He himself had made contact with

---

[1] In fact, Pole had never wanted *De Unitate* to be widely circulated, nor was it. When he discovered it had been printed without his consent, he bought up the entire edition.

[2] In February 1539, Henry sent Wyatt a copy of 'An invective against the Great and Detestable Vice, Treason, wherein the Secret Practices, and Traitorous Workings of them that Suffered of Late are Disclosed', the work of Cromwell's most brilliant propagandist, Richard Moryson.

Pole, when he sent Mason to find him at Nice. No matter what the motive, the fact was there, and he had discussed it all in front of Bonner. Moreover, he knew he was already in trouble from that quarter. When John Mason returned from London, he had told him the truth about his detention and questioning, and Bonner's part in it. Probably they discussed the matter and deduced the sort of suspicion they were under from the line of Mason's interrogation. The meeting with Pole was obviously a problem. Was Cromwell also looking to link it with Wyatt's 'open' letters to Gardiner, and Pole's escape in Paris the previous year? Since Mason's return things seemed to have settled down. This new commotion over Pole would rake it all up again.

There was worse. When Wyatt departed for Spain he had left Elizabeth Darrell behind him. This Besse, or Bessy, held conservative opinions on religion. She had been a lady-in-waiting to Catherine of Aragon, and was one of the few who had kept stout faith with her. Like Thomas More and Bishop Fisher, Besse refused to sign the Oath of Succession; her survival at court can only be explained by her being a woman, and obscure. When Catherine died she left her the great sum of £200 'for her marriage'.[3] Was she already involved with Wyatt? Intriguingly, her name 'Besse Darrell' appears in Cromwell's brief 'remembrance' from the time of Anne's execution, where a large payment to Thomas Wyatt (of £100) is also recorded. Both may be connected with reward for Wyatt's testimony in the Tower. If he was placed to receive such sums, he may have tried to pass a Cromwellian crumb in Besse's way as well. Her father and brother were both dead, she had had no place since Catherine's death: the 'marriage' referred to in Catherine's bequest never happened. She had thought of applying for a place with Princess Mary and, failing that, with one of Henry's subsequent queens – most likely her kinswoman Jane Seymour. When none of this had come to anything, a place was found for

[3] Muir, op.cit.

her – perhaps by Cromwell – among people of the old persuasion, where she would be comfortable. Her new employers were the sort of conservatives who dismissed any servant found reading the Gospels in English: the Marquis and Marchioness of Exeter, now arrested for high treason.

It seems strange to us that Wyatt, an evangelical, would freely choose a woman with conservative beliefs. Doubtless he thought they would be subsumed to his own in important matters, like the temper of his household or the education of his children. But aside from this, it must be remembered that reform had come for the Wyatt generation halfway through their lives. They had already forged friendships and affiliations, made marriages, pursued patronage and protection along other lines of interest. They weren't like Montagues and Capulets. They weren't yet tribal. Most had friends on both sides, and for much of the time they worked and played alongside one another, not really distinguishable in their habits or aims in life until, as occasionally happened, some tremendous event occurred to make beliefs stand apart and bristle, like a passing magnet raising iron filings from shale. And as the reign progressed it became, if anything, harder to practise what we would call 'religious profiling' upon a careful courtier, thanks to the baffling inconsistencies of a religious policy that pulled in both directions at once. In the late 1530s, Henry suppressed the last religious houses, burned relics, set up the English Bible in every parish church and pursued a programme of fervent anti-papism such that 'there is not a village feast nor pastime anywhere, in which there is not something inserted in derision of the Holy father;'[4] but as far as doctrinal matters were concerned, the moving spirit was one of retrenchment and reassertion of traditional Catholic practices. Thanks to these dislocations of policy, it was hard to say which camp you were in. Even a loyal subject whose one wish was to

---

[4] Letter from Marillac to Montmorency, July 13, 1539, in Kaulek, op. cit.

fix himself to the official line and stay there had to be fairly gymnastic to keep up, both faithful and flexible at once.

> *The windy words, the eyes quaint game*[5]
> *Of sudden change maketh me aghast*
> *For dread to fall I stand not fast*

Elizabeth Darrell had tried to do just that. Under interrogation she had turned witness against the Marquis of Exeter and his excitable friend, Sir Geoffrey Pole, citing some spirited protestations they had made to her about the sorry state of the world and the persecution of Sir Geoffrey's brother, Cardinal Pole. It seems Mrs Darrell knew quite a lot of diplomatic gossip. She knew the name of the assassin sent for the cardinal in Flanders at the time of his first legation. She had told it to Sir Geoffrey Pole. She knew 'there was one of the privy [council] with the French King, very familiar with Sir Francis Bryan, which gave Cardinal Pole warning that it was intended to slay him': a sensational allegation. Then she knew about a poison they had in Spain, 'which put on an arrow head, and the same pricking a person, he should die; and the remedy was the juice of a quince or peach'. Wyatt had told her that the previous year on his brief visit to England. She knew Wyatt had sight of Cardinal Pole at Nice, but he 'spake not with him, nor one of them would not look on another', from mutual antipathy.

In all probability she hoped these depositions would prove Wyatt's loyalty as much as her own; but they also showed that she and Wyatt were leaky. Details of the plans to murder England's premier criminal had passed through her into the household of Pole's friends. What she had told Sir Geoffrey Pole had gone straight to his brother, the Cardinal, as a warning.

Wyatt, catching scraps of this in Spain, would have guessed as much and conjectured horrors. He knew servants of Exeter

---

[5] Wyatt, LXXXV, in Rebholz, op. cit

had been arrested. Was Besse Darrell one of them? How could he explain? What could he say without incriminating himself? Why had he heard nothing from Cromwell? Silence in that quarter was the sound of a door shutting.

> *Such hap as I am happed in*[6]
> *Had never man of truth, I ween.*
> *In me fortune list to begin*
> *To shew that never hath been seen*
> *A new kind of unhappiness.*
> *Nor I cannot the thing I mean*
> *Myself express*

Cromwell was silent for almost a month; then, at last, came a strange letter. Strange to us, that is, because it seems to be answering questions when none have been asked. It addresses some of Wyatt's personal concerns as though in answer to a letter, but without referring to any letter. There is the pressing matter of £200 lent to Sir Francis Bryan, for example; and it offers reassurances of his own and the king's continued goodwill, when none have been solicited. 'It is well known you want no good heart and alacrity and his majestie considereth well and *continueth* your gracious and benign Lord. For my part ye may be certain that I bear unto you *no less good will and sincere affection tha[n] I was wont*'. [Italics mine]. Also, the letter conveys, with emphatic reticence, an important detail about the Exeter arrests: Exeter and Montague have been 'commanded to the Tower' along with 'a sort of their adherents *of mean estate and no estimation greatly*'. That is, not anyone you need to worry about, and not Elizabeth Darrell, daughter of Sir Edward Darrell of Littlecote. This is crucial information, too sensitive for names and addresses.

[6] Wyatt, LXXXVII, in Rebholz, op. cit.

Nor I cannot the thing I mean
Myself express

All of this makes sense if there are missing letters from Wyatt. Under that construction, we can see what happened. When Wyatt received the news from Wriothesley, not Cromwell, he panicked at the implication and wrote into the ominous silence, explaining his situation, the contact with Pole, the meeting with Elizabeth Darrell, describing his mental exhaustion and near-ruin. Cromwell read the letter, burned it as potentially incriminating, and then, since 'burning letters was now as dangerous as keeping them',[7] erased its existence from the reply. That there is at least one missing letter is a certainty. Wyatt himself refers to it in his reply to Cromwell: 'Ye know what case I am in. I have written on this unto you,' he writes. Unfortunately, no letter describing what might be called Wyatt's 'case' remains. There is only a reply to the reply to that lost letter, which shows a man in an agony of unrequited sincerity.

Assured I doubt I be not sure.[8]
And should I trust to such surety
That oft hath put the truth in ure [9]
And never hath found it trusty?

Assured I doubt I be not sure. Evidently unreassured by Cromwell's protestations, and sensing himself abandoned, Wyatt presses obliquely for more information, more reassurance. Why does nobody write to him?

I have no letters from no man but from you. I can not

[7] Madeleine H. and Ruth Dodds, *The Pilgrimage of Grace 1536-37 and The Exeter Conspiracy 1538*, (Cambridge University Press, 1915).
[8] Wyatt, LXXXV, in Rebholz, op. cit.
[9] in ure: into use.

tell whether it be that men are more scrupulous in writing news than negligent to do their friends pleasure.

He tries to raise a pleasantry. Courtiers must be merry, no matter what. Castiglione was immovable on the point.

> I have had it told me by some here of reputation that paraventure I was had in suspect both with the King and you, as they said it was told them. But like as I take it light, so I ascribe it to such invention as some of my 'good friends' would be glad to have it.[10]

But fear surges over this feeble breakwater, washing him up at Cromwell's feet:

> But out of game,[11] I beseech your Lordship humbly to help me. I need no long persuasions. Ye know what case I am in. I have written on this unto you. I am at the wall. I am not able to endure to March; and the rest shall all be the King's dishonour and my shame, beside the going to naught of my particular things... I can no more, but remit me wholly to your Lordship.

> *Disdain me not without desert*[12]
> *Ne leave me not so suddenly.*
> *Sith well ye wot that in my heart*
> *I mean it not but honestly,*
> *Refuse me not.*

> *Refuse me not without cause why*
> *Ne think me not to be unjust.*

---

[10] Letter from Wyatt to Cromwell, January 2, 1538, in Muir, op. cit. I have added inverted commas to clarify the sarcasm of Wyatt's reference to his 'good friends'. He means his enemies.

[11] out of game: 'joking apart'.

[12] Wyatt, CXXIV, in Rebholz, op. cit.

Sith that by lot of fantasy
The careful knot needs knit I must,
Mistrust me not.

Mistrust me not though some there be
That fain would spot my steadfastness.
Believe them not sith well ye see
The proof is not as they express.
Forsake me not.

Forsake me not till I deserve
Ne hate me not till I offend.
Destroy me not till that I swerve.
Sith ye well wot what I intend
Disdain me not.

Disdain me not that am your own.
Refuse me not that am so true
Mistrust me not till all be known
Forsake me not now for no new.
Thus leave me not.

✻   ✻   ✻   ✻

Wyatt's game must be obvious by now. Though he wrote religious poetry and political satire,[13] neither the anguish of the
one nor the waspishness of the other let him do what he could
do with the love poetry: protest. Protest was ingratitude. Ingratitude was treason. No voice cried out against Henry's reign
– only here, in these love lyrics designed to take a sliding object. They flash this way and that, changing from poems about
love into poems about something altogether else in the blink of

---

[13] Wyatt's Penitential Psalms and to a great extent his Satires are beyond the ambitions of this study.

an eye. Look at them one way, and they say one thing; look at them in another context, and the meaning bends accordingly. In this way they have, again, common cause with the visual puns beloved of post-revolutionary France (I referred to one in the context of Wyatt's eroticism in Chapter Five). Like them, they go from inscrutability to an almost wanton transparency, so that once you have perceived the image on the oblique plane, it's impossible to return to the former way of looking. But unlike these simple devices with their single surprise in store, the pane of the love lyric gave upon a plurality of latent meanings; nor were these available for general notice, but invisible until activated by the circumstances of the particular reader at the particular moment of reading.

These, then, were occasional poems in a very special sense: not written upon a single occasion but portable, adaptable to any occasion – crucially, to those occasions where the only prudent response was silence. In them, Wyatt found a way to speak about every relationship he had – with his lover, his friends, his enemies, his patron, his God, and with his king – in the forbidden language of complaint.

I am one of them whom plaint doth well content[14]

This is not a pioneering observation. Academics of 40 or so years ago first noticed how the abstractions and courtly generalities of Wyatt's language had translucent properties, and could disclose other concerns than love in a courtier's life. They were not particularly impressed. It was observed that the link between relations of love and relations of power was already inherent in the origins of courtly love lyrics, when a landless knight sued to a lady who was both a love object and, as his social superior, a potential source of preferment, so it was only a step to elide them. It is merely a question of taking things

[14] Wyatt, LXXVI, in Rebholz, op. cit.

literally.[15] George Harding, in the 1950s, remarked how

> The convention of the love-lament offered indirect expression to a range of feelings – depression, protest at bad faith, weariness from unrewarded service – that may have arisen from quite other sources (than love).

The metaphors of courtly plaint stiffen into reality, then dissolve again into harmless romance. By Elizabethan times this was an established device and a subject for study by earnest versifiers of the day;[16] the subject subsequently fell out of fashion. Our current critics of early modern English acknowledge the facility, and move on, the more brilliant ones to the study of Wyatt's satires, his diplomatic letters, and his overlooked psalms, leaving the lyrics with a legacy of under-appreciation.[17] They were entirely unnoticed through the 17th and 18th centuries, criticised in the 19th century for harshness and clumsiness, condescended to in the 20th by critics – who, fearing they may not be art, prefaced their scrutinies with such provisos as 'the study of these poems belongs to sociology rather than literature' – and then, most lately, sidelined as an exhausted topic, about which there was nothing more to say. As was said at the beginning of this book, one seldom finds a word of actual praise for Wyatt, even from his admirers.

Such is the curse of conformity in our age. To call a thing 'conventional', as Wyatt's critics generally have, is to disparage it. It is as though a conventional poem will write itself, and as if convention is the mark of intellectual dullness right from

---

[15] Raymond Southall's excellent study, *The Courtly Maker* (Blackwell, 1964), shows the most interest in this phenomenon.
[16] George Puttenham's *The Arte of English Poesie* (1589) speaks of 'rymes, which might be construed two or three ways', as an aspect of poetic accomplishment.
[17] I don't mean by this that they are ignored in the universities at graduate level. Almost nothing is. I refer to the most influential, most-quoted critical studies of the last 30 years, like those of Mason, Greenblatt, Walker, Powell or Burrow, which have focused on other aspects of Wyatt's work.

its inception, instead of something that occurs when an entire generation vote with their pens for the innovations of one or two geniuses, finding them perfectly adapted to what they want to say. In the case of the transparent lyric in English, this genius is Thomas Wyatt, and we should praise his lyrics for the beautiful, subtle and clever things they are. It seems to the present author that he has not been sufficiently admired for how much he can convey in his slight songs, for the packed compression of his phrasing, for the vocabulary refined to what is most flexible and pertinent, the lines so balanced that the fluctuations of fortune inhere to the syntax itself, for the implications so ambiguous and yet so exact that the poem can pursue the poet into every corner and every psychological crisis of his life. Nor sufficiently admired for his sleight of hand in the use, not just of translations, but of proverbs, common sayings, harmless courtly commonplaces, Chaucerian borrowings to act as baffles for his own utterance and make him not quite responsible for what he wrote. He made the unoriginality of the age into a virtue. He was supremely resourceful. His mind was like a prism in reverse: in went the multivarious experiences of his life and out came a single, continent expression of them all, reading white.

Poetry, being trivial, was already a comparatively safe vehicle for expressions of discontent. Professor Greg Walker has shown that when the Earl of Surrey was tried for acts of *lèse-majesté*, his poetry – teeming with rash ambition – was never brought in evidence.[18] But Wyatt was always conscious of danger. Seditious ballad-makers were not beneath Henry's laws. In 1537 the great Sir Francis Bryan had found himself investigating a riotous assembly of Wolburton shoemakers, to determine whether they were singing critical songs about the

[18] Greg Walker, *Writing Under Tyranny: English Literature and the Henrician Reformation* (OUP 2005).

regime. Such were the uses of poetic skills for the servants of Henry VIII. And consequently, Wyatt found it politic if the subject of his complaint, 'the thing' that it is about and to which it urgently points, remained outside the poem, beyond scrutiny. For instance:

> *Accused though I be without desert*[19]
> *None can it prove, yet ye believe it true.*
> *Nor ever yet, since that ye had my heart*
> *Entended I to be false or untrue.*
> *Sooner I would of death sustain the smart*
> *Than break **one thing of that I promised you.***

What is that thing? Who are you? Who am I? All of this is out of frame, and with it the true intention of the governing verb '*break* one thing of that I promised you', which could also mean 'divulge'.

We appreciate how clever this is when we put it back into the court, where a verse on a folded sheet could be shared, copied, borrowed, circulated, passed from pocket to pocket for a day or two, declaimed with meaningful looks, or quietly muttered into someone's ear with a knowing pull at their sleeve. Stanzas might be excised, lines taken alone, or pronouns adapted to fit to make a point – but ultimately, meaning derived from inside knowledge. *Ye know what case I am in.* A lyric could tell you that a man was in love, or in debt, or in deep trouble: which, depended on whom. The poem turned on such evanescent occurrences as a swivelled eye or a raised eyebrow. Nor would a new development require a new-minted epigram. It was much safer to be economical. For Wyatt, the ability to recirculate a familiar lyric combined with its instability to break the link between cause – what a poem was 'about', and the date of its

---

[19] Wyatt, LXVI, Rebholz, op. cit.

composition. So lines presented as love poems in, say, 1528 might re-circulate in 1538 as critique on a sensitive political matter, but maintain what we call 'deniability'. For example:

Spite asketh spite and changing change[20]
And falsed faith must needs be known.
The faults so great, the case so strange,
Of right it must abroad be blown.
Then since that by thine own desert
My songs do tell how true thou art
Blame not my lute.

These lines had done courtly service, teasing ladies in the pastime. But, as Henry's reign progressed, and his personal, religious and political activities all began to mirror one another in their inconstancies, betrayals and backslidings, it would be more and more possible for shots at faithlessness and inconstancy to pass through ladylike perfidies and hit the king full on. These same lines might do as well to 'blow abroad' Henry's 'falsed faith' and 'great faults' as a monarch. In 1539 they could articulate covert support for the publication of Pole's *De Unitate*, which did indeed ventilate the king's shortcomings. Yet, if they were in circulation before 1536, as is most probable from the context of the whole poem as a pastime piece, they couldn't possibly be 'about' that event. For this reason it is not always fruitful to ask when a Wyatt poem was written. It may not signify its ultimate intention. The lyrics would change with the times and the contingencies of the hour. In this way, they became the unimprovable expression of the courtier's predicament. They gave a voice to what could not be spoken, but they were more than that: they developed along with him, their burden changing from love to politics, from

[20] Wyatt, XCIV, in Rebholz, op. cit.

innocence to experience, from sincerity to cynicism, mutating into the mutability of the times.

Spite asketh spite and changing change

If it is the business of art to express the conditions of its making, these are some of the greatest works of art ever made. Was Wyatt aware of this? Did he mean the poems to function like this? Yes. But the only forum for that discussion is found in the poems themselves. As has already been said, these poems existed in a sealed system where prose need never penetrate. They spoke to one another, in a private conversation where the validation of prose was not required or invited; and they spoke about themselves.

Here is a sonnet talking about its own metamorphic abilities: to see that, we must make a little twist of the mind and read the personal pronoun as we would in a riddle beginning 'My first is in apple but not in pear'.

> *Each man telleth me I change most my device,*[21]
> *And on my faith I think it good reason*
> *To change purpose like after the season.*
> *For in each case to keep still one guise*
> *Is meet for them that would be taken wise;*
> *And I am not of such manner condition*
> *But treated after a diverse fashion*
> *And thereupon my diverseness doth rise.*

Certainly Wyatt knew there was a danger of reading too much into his work. Once a poem was out there, in the court, he couldn't control what people made of it, or what they said. He knew some poems sailed very close to the wind. Such as:

---

[21] Wyatt, sonnet XXX, in Rebholz, op. cit.

Desire, alas, my master and my foe,[22]
So sore altered, thyself how mayst thou see?
Whom I do seek now chaseth me to and fro;
Whom thou didst rule now ruleth thee and me.
Tyrant it is to rule thy subjects so
By forced law and mutability.

Here the seditious sentiment almost breaks the surface: so
nearly that he changed the words (scoring out the specifically
treasonable word 'tyrant') in the 'Egerton MS', his personal
compilation. He was never a risk-taker except, as shall appear,
when risk was politic; but others may have been rasher. We
have already seen how speculation about the meaning of his
poems got sufficiently out of hand for him to issue a warning
poem.

Me list no more to sing[23]
Of love nor of such thing
How sore that it me wring;
For what I sung or spake
Men did my words mistake

My songs were too diffuse
They made folks to muse.
Therefore, me to excuse,
They shall be sung more plain,
Neither of joy nor pain.

The poem is concerned with leakage. It circulated amongst
the Devonshire 'set' as a reprimand, only half-jokey, to silence
speculation that had got beyond safe levels. That speculation
could be of two kinds: there was the matter of *who* the poems
were about – as we have seen – but there was also the ques-

[22] Wyatt, LVIII, notes in Rebholz, op. cit.
[23] Wyatt, CXXXV, in Rebholz, op. cit.

tion of *what* their 'diffuse' intentions might be, both potentially dangerous inquiries. In this lyric, Wyatt starts by saying he will stop writing his too-interesting songs, and then he berates his audience, or readers, for indiscretion. He seems to be trying to embarrass someone – perhaps in public – with a sarcastic rendition of their own reasoning, couched in proverbial doggerel. Whoever flashed the poems about had reasoned thus:

> *What vaileth under key*
> *To keep treasure alway*
> *that never shall see day?*
> *If it be not used*
> *It is but abused.*

> *What vaileth the flower*
> *To stand still and wither?*
> *If no man it savour*
> *It serves only for sight*
> *And fadeth towards night.*

The lyric concludes:

> *... If **this** be under mist*
> *And not well plainly wist*
> *Understand me who list*
> *For I reck not a bean*
> *I wot what I do mean.*

Wyatt was furious. You only needed a few loud-mouths putting in the names, nudging each other in the ribs, for the whole enterprise to become unfeasible. As he says, if this went on the poems would have to change; his suggestive, noncommittal handling of the verse would have to go, if there was to be the slightest chance of his poems being misread by the authorities. We can see this actually happening in the Devonshire MS, where one of the contributors alters Wyatt's pronouns for safety. Wyatt's own manuscript has:

> *Patience withouten blame*
> *Though I offended naught!*
> *I know they know the same*
> *Though they have changed their thought.*

This is all very well without a context, but it is not a sentiment for a book going in and out of a prison cell, as the Devonshire was. Henry's prisoners did not say they were innocent and that their accusers knew it, or anything that could be so construed. Given the opportunity to say a few words at the block, Henry's condemned innocents stood among the ominous straw and proclaimed the king's most merciful justice. Far safer for Thomas Howard and Margaret Douglas, then, to change this poem, so it read unambiguously, as a love lament concerning *she*, who could not be the constituted authority of England. Those readers who had seen Wyatt's version could wot what it did mean.

> *Patience withouten blame*
> *Though I offended naught!*
> *I know **she** knows the same*
> *Though **she** hath changed **her** thought.*

The change of pronoun makes it less like a Wyatt poem. Wyatt always preferred the open possibilities of 'they', or some abstract term that could refer to anything. Sometimes he seems to be reaching for a neuter case, the elegant and useful 'haec' that Latin had. Sometimes, he almost achieves it, as in the famous piece:

They flee from me that sometime did me seek[24]
With naked foot stalking in my chamber.
I have seen them gentle, tame, and meek,
That now are wild, and do not remember
That sometime they put themself in danger
To take bread at my hand; and now they range
Busily seeking with a continual change.

Who, or what, are 'they'? Men, women, or beasts? This greatest
of love poems doesn't mention women at all in the first verse,
or even people, but these mysterious creatures, embodiments of
repealed intimacy. Scholars, themselves stalking the picture in
Wyatt's head, have argued over what sort of animal he meant.
Are 'they' dogs? Are 'they' birds?

And yet no one thinks these lines are about dogs or birds.
With two words – 'naked foot', he conjures humanity. With four
more – 'put themself in danger' – he tells us why their shoes
are off: they have come for some secret purpose. Because men
and women take off their shoes for different private purposes,
we see both men and women. Soft doggy muzzles feeding at
the hand elide in our minds with a lovely woman naked, or the
quiet arrival of a co-conspirator. When 'they' flee, they go as
a composite creature: as his friends at court, his woman, his
good fortune, severally and all together, neither man, woman
or beast but what was vulnerable and trusting in all of them,
leaving the poet alone with his *esprit de l'escalier* ('I would fain
know what she hath deserved'). It is incredibly sad. Most bitter
of all is the revelation that fleeing is not the enemy of seeking,
but its heir. When Wyatt speaks of happiness, in the modern
sense, it is always as something incubating sorrow: the theft of
joy is an inside job. It would be three centuries before England
produced another poet with such a talent for implicating happiness in misery.

[24] Wyatt, LXXX, in Rebholz, op. cit.

John Keats thought:

The feel of not to feel it
When there is none to heal it
Nor numbed sense to steel it
Was never said in rhyme.

But Thomas Wyatt proves him wrong. When he taught 'what might be said in rhyme', he taught this first.

CHAPTER EIGHTEEN

They flee from me that sometime did me seek

In the winter and spring of 1538-9 Wyatt sensed the imminent flight of the friends who once had sought him. Cromwell continued to allege support for the time being, although he ignored the pleas for recall and kept Wyatt on at the imperial court, where he was still of use, as the price of his protection. The minister typically withheld consummation of his favour until the plaintiff was almost mad with anxiety and deprivation; and so he had in Spain with Wyatt. But he also knew when it was necessary to advance a morsel. As Wyatt was most straining for recall and seemed from his state of mind as if he might actually bolt ('I am at the wall. I am not able to endure to March'), there began to materialise in Cromwell's hands the prospect of some abbey lands, the very thing for Wyatt, which would just be coming available – but not, conveniently, until April of 1539. This, by coincidence, was the same month that suited Cromwell for Wyatt's recall. So he had to endure till then.

It was the worst of times to be an English diplomat in Spain. News came through in the autumn of 1538 that Thomas à Becket's tomb, which had stood for centuries as a reproach to interfering kings, was desecrated and his bones burned. Catholic Christendom had seen More as a second Becket, and now Becket's bones seemed like a second More. For orthodox Spain – where imperial ambassadors, returning from England, would soon have to receive absolution from a cardinal before re-entering the imperial court[1] – this was too much. The pope now confirmed Henry's excommunication and let slip Cardinal Pole for a second time, to rally the kings of Spain and France for invasion of England. Full of ideas about trade embargos and offensive action, he headed first for the emperor, at Toledo, and there he was received. Charles and Francis renewed their peace and agreed not to make any other alliance without one another's consent. It began to seem inevitable that England would become, as Wriothesley said, 'a morsel amongst these choppers'. In England, Henry ordered an urgent review of his coastal fortifications.

He was still blaming his emissaries for his misfortunes. He had marked Sir Francis Bryan's homecoming in September by declaring he was 'a drunkard who he could never trust',[2] and removing him from the post of chief gentleman of the chamber – a position Bryan had held since the death of Anne Boleyn. This precipitated him into a near-fatal decline. Wyatt probably had wind of Bryan's downfall: he had lent Bryan the money he lost at cards in June and this, he knew, had become another mark against him. 'If the King's honour, more than [Bryan's] credit had not been before myn eyes, he could have piped in an ivy leaf for aught of me',[3] he told Cromwell. Cromwell replied with a lecture about improvidence. Wyatt had also recently lent 200 ducats to another ambassador, Philip Hoby – 'the which I think had no need of them.'

I think your gentle frank heart doth much impoverish you: when ye have money ye are content to depart with it and lend it... forsee, rather to be provided yourself, than for the provision of other to leave yourself naked. *Politic*

[1] This would have been introduced in 1540. I am grateful to Dr Brigden for this point.
[2] Letter from Castillon to Montmorency, September 5, 1538, in Kaulek, op. cit.
[3] Letter from Wyatt to Cromwell, January 3, 1539, Muir, op.cit. 'he could have piped in an ivy leaf for aught of me' has the sense of 'I would have left him to whistle for it'.

charity proceedeth not this way.[4] [*emphasis mine*]

Wyatt saw that he had better provide for himself. There now was a decision to be made as to how to proceed in the hostility and isolation of his final months in Spain. Up until now, he had conducted his diplomacy according to the old Erasmian ideals, as though Europe were, in Diarmaid MacCulloch's term, a vast *salon*, where civilised men of all nations converted mutual admiration into debate. He had charmed his way into Charles's personal graces, he had done in Spain what the Spanish did, he had parried epigrams with envoys from Mantua, Venice, Naples and France. Now all this was tainted with the whiff of collaboration, he needed a new approach. And so, in the early months of 1539, Wyatt became an English rowdy. He leaned on Charles to send Pole packing. He spoke openly against the pope and went swaggering about telling everyone how rich he was and how he, personally, was going to murder Cardinal Pole. Now no one could doubt where he took his orders.

If the purpose of the exhibition was for everyone to hear of it, it certainly worked in the case of Cardinal Pole, who soon got to hear of it from Grandvela. Writing later that year to his friend, Cardinal Contarini, he related how Wyatt

> had said in public that if the King of England would get (me) publicly proclaimed a traitor, and release [Wyatt] from his embassy, and commit the business to him of [my] murder, with 10,000 pieces of gold, he would pledge his possessions in England – which were great – that he would in six months procure [my] death, and he suggested Rome and its environs as most suitable for the crime.[5]

It seems that no one was as worried about this as Pole, who

<hr>

[4] Letter from Cromwell to Wyatt, Janueary 19 1539, in Merriman, op.cit.
[5] Letter from Pole to Contarini, September 22, 1539, in Haile, op. cit.

had never seen himself as a martyr and tended to take matters of his own security with the utmost seriousness. Contarini thought these were the 'rash and impious words of a furious youth'. Perhaps he, like historians coming later to this story, was unwilling to think that murder sat within the remit of an English diplomat. But Pole's alarm was justified. Now that Wyatt – bald, careful, gracious, 36 – had persuasively reinvented himself as this piratical figure, a 'furious youth', he meant to back it up with action. When Pole left for France, he came after him with everything that he could throw. He sent an assassin ahead of the legate, to waylay him on the route (but Pole went the other way), and despatched urgent letters to Bonner, now in France, to alert him to Pole's approach. In fact, Pole had quietly cancelled the French leg of his mission. To his eternal mystification, his reception in Spain had been decidedly cool, and he decided it would be impolitic to press Francis and cause a rift in the Franco-Spanish entente on which all his plans depended. This was partly Wyatt's doing. Not all his diplomacy was successful but here he must have credit for his role in averting the invasion of England. Pole, he later averred, 'was by my industry dispatched out of Spain, smally to his reputation or contenting'.[6] At the time, he hadn't been so certain.

This rumpus began to try the emperor's patience. He didn't particularly relish Pole's visit, and hadn't wanted to receive him in the first place: as the sovereign responsible for sacking Rome and imprisoning a pope, Charles V could see what it was that Henry disliked in Reginald Pole. Even so, he could hardly connive at plots to murder him brewing in his own court. Wyatt was starting to get on his nerves. In February, just before Pole departed, Charles signalled his annoyance by relaxing his restraining hand on the officers of the Inquisition, who had long desired to prosecute Wyatt for heresy. When Wyatt protested, the usually imperturbable emperor responded with 'a most severe

[6] Wyatt, *Defence*, in Muir, op.cit.

admonition, saying he ought to be careful how he spoke, otherwise he would let the process be made against him'[7] – the process, that is, leading to the English ambassador's being burned at the stake. And so it was that Wyatt found himself in an uncommon position: suspected for papacy at home and heresy abroad, poised between the English axe and the Spanish *autos-da-fe*. A new kind of unhappiness, indeed. But he stuck to his decision, and continued to make his loyalties conspicuous, supplying Cromwell and the king with stratagems for exterminating Pole and undoing the Franco-Spanish entente.

As Dr Jason Powell has demonstrated in his illuminating edition of Wyatt's letters, Wyatt's own fortitude and ingenuity figured large in these accounts.[8] In April, when the simultaneous recall of the French and imperial ambassadors from England had ignited new fears of invasion, he composed a letter designed to get Cromwell's attention. Here, he had the advantage of being England's best poet, and a poet at that of concision, urgency, mystery. In language of tantalising intrigue and shameless self-commendation, he described a mysterious 'practice':

> that is offered to me in Italy, to kindle there a fire, but by mouth only now at my coming home; and then shall be time enough, for about the same time the party [i.e. Pole] doth retire thither. It is of importance... The practice that is offered to me, as I have written before, is more particularly declared unto me, and in mine opinion it is excellent, and will go near, without note of the King's Highness, to set these great friends[9] both in jealousy, and may fortune further... I have given my faith not to write it; but have

---

[7] Letter from Pole to Cardinal Farnese, March 25, 1539.

[8] Dr Jason Powell has written extensively on this aspect of Wyatt's correspondence in his forthcoming edition of the letters: 'The Letters and Original Prose of the Poet Sir Thomas Wyatt: A Critical Edition', doctoral thesis (Oxford University, 2003).

[9] i.e. France and Spain.

me not suspected that I devise this because I would come away, for when I am come I am as ready to go again, but it seemeth me much to the King's service, and I cannot express the things I have by writing. Send therefore my successor hither by post.

The letter, all in cipher, ended on a note of high romance:

Send for me, for it is requisite, and think not that I include that so often without cause; for it is necessary I speak with you. I say, send for me. Spare not my labour for I make no reckoning of rest.[10]

This was irresistible. The king did indeed desire to know 'what is the matter that ye cannot write but declare by mouth'[11] and recalled him instantly. Wyatt left Spain for England on about June 3, as soon as his successor, Richard Tate, could be appointed and despatched. His departure became the subject of an atypical poem:

Tagus, farewell! That westward with thy streams[12]
Turns up the grains of gold already tried,
With spur and sail for I go seek the Thames,
Gainward the sun that shew'th her wealthy pride
And, to the town which Brutus sought by dreams,
Like bended moon doth lend her lusty side.
My king, my country, alone for whom I live,
Of mighty love the wings for this me give.

There was nothing ambiguous about this, a masterpiece of in-gratiation. He meant this one to circulate wide and high. The

---

[10] March ?14, 1539. The original of this part of Wyatt's letter is lost and only exists in this transcription, made for Wriothesley on April 13. LP 14, i, 757.
[11] Letter from Cromwell to Wyatt, April 16, 1539, in Merriman, op. cit.
[12] Wyatt, LX, in Rebholz, op. cit.

headline reads: ambassador quits splendid but decadent Toledo for vital, up-and-coming London. In England (unlike Spain) the principal river flows east, towards God and the dawn. Life in that great ascending city is more prosperous, more manly and sunnier than in tired old Spain. Lines five and six are propaganda for the royal supremacy. Wyatt invokes another right-thinking traveller: Brutus, the Trojan pioneer whose alleged emigration to England formed the heart of Cromwell's rationale for an English 'Empire'.[13] The final couplet concerns itself with what is owed to the king: a good deal. So much in fact that God – every Renaissance Christian's principal creditor – drops out of the picture altogether. No room for Him in this poem. Anxiety sweats from every line. He wants it to be known that he is coming home as fast as he can, 'seeking' London 'with spur and sail' and on 'wings of love'. Why? Because he was going back to make his 'declaration': that is, to account for his behaviour to Cromwell and the king. He was *not running away*. As the events of the next 18 months would show, it was a very important point to make.

[13] Trojan ancestry for the ancient Britons was first claimed by 'Nennius', supposedly a 9th-century Welsh monk. The Nennian account had Brutus, a refugee from the fall of Troy, as the first English settler. This myth was among the 'old authentic histories and chronicles' cited in support of the 1533 Act, which removed the right to refer judicial appeals to Rome.

CHAPTER NINETEEN

Wyatt had two secrets for the king. There were the details of his plan to kill Cardinal Pole in Italy, and of another, to sabotage the friendship of the two Catholic monarchs through interference in northern Italian affairs. Neither was to come to anything, but Cardinal Pole didn't know that, and, as has been said, he had no immortal longings at this point.

Wyatt's whereabouts after leaving Spain had been kept a careful secret, to give the impression that he and his murderous intentions were still on the road in Europe. Pole certainly thought he was. He wrote to his friend, Cardinal Contarini complaining of his (Contarini's) over-casual attitude to reports about Wyatt's plans to murder him. It was all very well for Contarini to say it was bluster, he wrote,

> but – mark the sequel. The ambassador was recalled, he (Pole) was publicly declared a traitor and, at the time of writing, no one knew where Wyatt was.[1]

That was in September. In fact, Wyatt had arrived in England at the beginning of June, and there he stayed, apparently living quietly, and away from the court – although the absence of both Spanish and French ambassadors from the English court imposed a partial news blackout, and made it easier for Wyatt to avoid detection.

He had plenty of business to attend to away from court.

[1] Letter from Pole to Contarini, September 22, 1539. (As transcribed.)

Cromwell had come good on his promises, and throughout the spring and summer of 1540 Wyatt's Kentish estates were swelled (for a rent) with abbey lands. One of these was the monastery of Boxley, site of one of Cromwell's iconoclastic coups upon 'feigned images' – that is, objects with bogus claims to veneration – with respect to its famous 'rood of grace'. This Boxley rood was a cross with an image on it, said to move by miraculous intervention. When Cromwell's agents resorted to Boxley, they pounced on this rood and, discovering it to move by means of 'certain engines and old wire... that did cause the eyes of the same to move and stare in the head.. like unto a lively thing', they exhibited it in triumph before taking it to London to be burned at the stake.

Though the destruction of relics and images caused dismay among the old devout whose familiar comforts they were, few at court put religious scruples above their hunger for land; least of all the most prominent conservative of the reign, Thomas Howard, Duke of Norfolk, who profited egregiously from sales of monastic lands from 1536 onwards. Nor did his religious affinities prevent him from treating with reformers – even with Thomas Cromwell, his loathed enemy – if he could discern a personal benefit.

His relations with the evangelical Wyatt were complicated by Wyatt's friendship with his glorious son, Henry Howard, Earl of Surrey: a young man in whom all the gifts of nature and fortune had combined, with their usual duplicitous effect. We know him now as the second poet of the reign, the progenitor of English blank verse. At the time, he was chiefly known for being fabulous. Wherever he was, was a party. In 1537, when Norfolk was in charge of the awful post-rebellion reprisals in the north of England, Henry asked him to explain the presence of his eldest son at his side. Was he secretly training him up for some position? Norfolk explained it in terms of his son's personal magnetism. Stuck in the north with a large household, constantly on the move, nothing but inquests and gibbets all day and northern amusements at night, he was finding it hard to keep the staff. The boy was a tonic and a draw.

> In truth I love him better than all my children, [he un-truthfully began] and would have gladly had him here to hunt, shoot, play cards and entertain my servants, to the intent that they should have been the less desirous to ask leave to go home to their wives and friends.[2]

On the other hand, the poet Surrey was arrogant, vain and reckless, 'the most foolish proud boy that is in England'.[3] He had been raised as a prince among princes, as the chosen companion of Henry's illegitimate son, the Duke of Richmond; and he had come to believe that he enjoyed these things as the dues of his ancient pedigree, and not because his father was the regime's biggest sycophant: a mistake that would eventually lead to his beheading in 1547. In view of Surrey's exceptional vaingloriousness, which made him insufferable to the highest company, his choice of a mere Kentish gentleman for an object of veneration is strange. For he did revere Wyatt. In an inversion of the expected order – the order, that is, that Surrey himself, 'an unmeet man to live in a commonwealth',[4] would expect – it was Surrey who professed the connection, assuming a starring role in Wyatt's life and a proprietorial attitude to his mind, in the elegiac verses he later wrote.

> *I*, [he wrote] *who know what harboured in that head,*
> *What virtues rare were tempered in that breast,*
> *Honour the place that such a jewel bred*

[2] Letter from Norfolk to Henry, May 9, 1537.
[3] George Constantyne, 'transcript of an original Manuscript, containing a memorial from George Constantyne to Thomas Lord Cromwell', ed. T. Amyor.
[4] At Surrey's trial, Thomas Wriothesley urged the jury to condemn him on these grounds. In Jesse Childs, *Henry VIII's Last Victim* (Jonathan Cape, 2006)

And kiss the ground, whereas thy corse should rest

Not just Wyatt's great qualities, but Surrey's discernment of them are celebrated here. He recognised

A head where wisdom mysteries did frame[5]
Whose hammers beat still in that lively brain...
... A hand that taught what might be said in Rhyme
That reft Chaucer the glory of his wit

That such a man as Surrey should feel himself embellished by the connection is the best piece of evidence there is to show that Wyatt really was the model man of his time; but Surrey was also attracted to the element of intrigue in the practice of poetic ambivalence. He saw what a great game this was for the cleverest of the court's elite; he recognised Wyatt as its inventor and master; and he was an eager but perhaps indiscreet initiate. You could say things in poetry that you couldn't elsewhere. When Wyatt was dead, he alluded to the method: 'A hand that taught *what might be said in rhyme.*'

Surrey was in fact too young to have formed the intimacy he claims. Not only was he closer in age to Wyatt's son than to Wyatt, but the dates don't give much time for close friendship to develop. Surrey made his debut at court (aged 19) in 1536, a year when Wyatt and he were often elsewhere – in the Tower, or at Allington, or on separate campaigns in different places in the north. The following year, Wyatt went to Spain, not returning for two years. In the time remaining to him, there would be only two periods of sustained residence in England. One such stretch was now, in the summer of 1539, when the 21-year-old would be old enough to grasp some of 'what harboured in that head'. Even so, Wyatt was hardly conspicuous at court,

---

[5] Surrey, *Poems*, ed. Emrys Jones (Clarendon Press, Oxford, 1964). Spelling modernised.

where Surrey was. Nor would his stay last long, for very soon Cromwell would recruit him again for a diplomatic mission.

*   *   *   *

In the summer of 1539, all England thought invasion was imminent. The external pressure of war caused English policy, long under pressure from its internal contradictions, to split along the fracture of greatest stress: religion; so that religious and foreign affairs came adrift of one another and began to move in opposite directions. The king, fearful and self-righteous, redirected his own devotions towards traditional piety, and parliament followed with the Act of Six Articles of June 1539, bringing in such retrograde measures as the banning of clerical marriage, and causing reformers to flee for Protestant havens overseas. At the same time, Cromwell pursued his alliance with the Protestant German states, in the form of a fourth wife for his sovereign.

> *Alas, I tread an endless maze*[6]
> *That seek to accord two contraries*

Cromwell did not enter rashly into this union. The little dukedom of Cleves, on which he had his eye, was selected with very special care. Its ruler, Duke William, had close links with powerful German Lutheran princes, but, though anti-papist and anti-Habsburg, the fact that he was not yet avowedly Protestant would make him more palatable to the king than the overtly Protestant Lutherans. Another factor in his favour was his recent election to rule the strategically important and bellicose kingdom of Guelders, despite it having been promised to the empire. As a traditional ally of France right in the middle of Habsburg territories, Guelders had been a headache

---

[6] Wyatt, LXXXV, 2nd stanza, in Rebholz, op. cit.

Henry Howard, Earl of Surrey (*Hans Holbein the Younger*)

for Charles V for years. Now his grievance at the election of William to such a trouble-spot was intensified by the prospect of union between the disobliging and increasingly powerful Duke and the aberrant Henry. For Cromwell, though, this guarantee of imperial irritation was what turned a last-ditch strategy of marriage with a dim little northern princess into a far-reaching and ingenious solution to England's problems. There was only one hitch: the princess herself. Duke William's most likely sister, Anne, was short on allure, and this Cromwell knew from at least the summer of 1539, if not before. How was that to be squared with his other stated objective, for the king to marry 'where that he had his fantasy and love, for that would be most comfort for his grace'?

The story of Cromwell's sending Holbein into Cleves to make a picture of Anne, and the result of it, are well known. Here, only two things need to be said of it. First, to reiterate that Hans Holbein's greatest English patron, and the first begetter of the great majority of his English commissions, was not Henry VIII but Thomas Cromwell. Secondly, if a portraitist was required who could procure the benefit of the doubt while answering the imperative to send back a truthful picture, 'the very image and visage'[7] of the subject, Holbein was the man for the job. Though a sensitive, thorough and clear-eyed recorder of 'physiognomies', Holbein rarely committed himself to limning personality. His work is deceptive in this way. We approach a Holbein portrait thinking its accuracy must be informative, but as we stand in front of it, the features compose and recompose into different expressions of character: humanity turns to severity, pride to imbecility, cruelty to anxiety. We often can't even say with certainty how old a sitter is. In the end, we have no clear idea what these people were like.

The work he now produced was a masterpiece of the noncommittal. Even today, responses to the Cleves portrait vary wildly. Some people find Anne of Cleves exquisite; to others she is a turnip-faced Dutch peasant. Holbein showed her as both. You can see every feature plainly, straight on, but her nose, mouth and eyes sit in their skin oval without expression, like a face retouched for a fashion magazine. The features are regular, the skin clear, the eyes slightly downcast in what might be a show of maidenly modesty. Animation is supplied by the gauze panels of Anne's headdress, wafting upwards to lift the face and give an impression of the lightness lacking from the face itself. It was certainly possible to see the face as pretty, particularly in the light of some encouraging reports that had come though to

---

[7] Instructions to Henry VII's emissaries negotiating a marriage between himself and the widowed Queen of Naples, 1505, *Memorials of King Henry VII*, ed. J. Gairdner (Ross Series 1858).

Anne of Cleves (*Hans Holbein the Younger*)

Henry, of her beauty exceeding even that of the lovely Duchess of Milan, the princess for whom Henry had continued to hope until all prospects of an imperial marriage dissolved in the spring of 1539. She may even have been pleasant-featured. What she wholly lacked were the courtly endowments that Henry admired beyond any cast of feature: charm, accomplishment, grace, musicality, wit. Her upbringing had taught her to abjure these things, as frivolities. One of the English diplomats involved with the negotiations could clearly foresee a mismatch:

> She can read and write [her own language, but of] French, Latin or other language she [has none], nor yet she cannot sing, nor play an instrument, for they take it here in Germany for a rebuke and an occasion of lightness that great ladies should be learned or have any knowledge of music... I could never hear that she is inclined to the good

cheer of this country [our English pastime], and marvel it were if she should, seeing that her brother… doth so well abstain from it.[8]

The king seems not to have absorbed the implications of this until the day he met her. On the contrary, he prepared for her arrival with tremendous orders for courtly requisites, and in polishing those talents most likely to be lost on her: 'going to play every night upon the Thames, with harps, chanmetres, and all kinds of music and pastime', as the French ambassador reported, '[the king] evidently delights now in painting and embroidery, having sent men to France, Flanders, Italy and elsewhere for masters of this art, and also for musicians and other ministers of pastime.'

When they met, it was not a success. Heaving his now considerable person into an exotic disguise, such as he had favoured in the days of his first marriage, he set off for a surprise visit to her lodgings at Rochester, 'to nourish love', as he declared. But there was nothing in her retired upbringing that had taught her how to recognise an ardent king in fancy-dress, so she had no idea who or what he was. He was forced to withdraw and reappear dressed more legibly, as himself. When she did speak to him, it was only about homely things, in German. Nor was she appealing.[9] 'I like her not,' he said to Cromwell. 'She is nothing so fair as she hath been reported.' Trying to make the best of it, Cromwell piped up: 'By my faith you say truth, but me thinketh she hath a queenly manner withal.' But the king was not impressed by this assessment of his requirements. Cromwell, like Wolsey, had misnumbered Henry's priorities. He knew Henry needed a queen, but he forgot that he wanted a lover.

I love true where I did marry

[8] Letter from Nicholas Wotton to Henry VIII, August 11, 1539.
[9] Though Edward Hall reports her as more lovely than any of Henry's wives except the young Catherine of Aragon. Hall, *Chronicle*, op. cit.

Looking around for someone to blame, his eye never settled on Holbein. 'Nothing so fair as she hath been *reported*', he said, not painted, even though the portrait must have furnished the greatest part of his expectations. When he returned in dismay to the picture, did it now seem unattackably, unaccountably accurate? He blamed the courtiers who had flattered Anne's looks (and who now, to the last gallant, asserted their unfitness as judges of feminine beauty); but mainly he blamed Cromwell. 'I am not well-handled,' he snapped at him, as the morning of his marriage drew near. 'If it were not that she is come so far into England, and for fear of making a ruffle in the world, and driving her brother into the Emperor and the French King's hands, *now being together*, I would never have her.'[10]

This 'being together' was the reason why the marriage was intractable. The arrival of Anne of Cleves at Deal coincided with a momentous occasion in French history. At this moment, France's traditional enemy, the emperor Charles V, was travelling through France as the guest and companion of the King of France, in a gorgeous double progress and show of amity. From England, they seemed the picture of unified Catholicism in pursuit of the heretic. This was no time to offend the one ally England had, even if, in the event of a joint attack, Cleves could do little to help her. As one onlooker put it:

> The bishop of Rome, the French King, and the Emperor, be all one, and the King of Scots is the French King's man; and so we be left alone, and nobody with us but these Germans, a sort of beggarly knaves, and they are able to do nothing.[11]

In fact, the danger of invasion was over. Though Cromwell didn't know it, the emperor had neither appetite nor funds for

---

[10] Recalled in a letter from Cromwell to Henry, June 30, 1540.
[11] Lacey Baldwin Smith, *A Tudor Tragedy* (Reprint Society and Jonathan Cape, 1961).

an English war. He was more concerned with making a firm stand against religious dissent and turbulence in the northern reaches of his empire than attacking England, and this is why – paradoxically – the Cleves marriage itself provoked the event that panicked Henry into going through with it: the visit of Charles to France. The map at this point is most eloquent (see overleaf).

As is evident from this, the emperor could only reach his northern territories by sea or by passing through foreign territory. If by sea, then at risk to life on the winter swells; if by land, then through Italy (undesirably expensive in taxes and charges), or through France. Usually the latter would be out of the question, but now Francis had invited him to come as his guest, offering his word of chivalric honour as a safeguard for his passage. Francis had offered, but Charles hesitated to accept the invitation of a long-term enemy whom he had recently imprisoned. He had experienced Francis's word of honour before. Then came violent riots in Ghent, exacerbated by the alienation of Guelders and – the last straw – the prospect of Cleves joined to England, controlling the northern sea traffic. Now his personal intervention in Ghent became imperative. And so, 'betraying signs of ultimate lunacy', as one historian has put it, he put himself in Francis's hands to get there.[12] Francis, meanwhile, was overcome with chivalric impulses and vowed not to mention the settlement of Milan – the only reason for having Charles in the first place – until Charles was off French soil.

The emperor met the king at Bayonne in late November 1539, and was borne off, under the escort of the entire French court, on a tour of French cultural highlights. To mark the occasion, Cromwell swiftly dispatched a special envoy from London with expressions of Henry's joy that his 'two principallist allies and friends [were] come to such reconciliation, friendship, and confidence'; in other words, to stir up trouble between them.

[12] L.B. Smith, op. cit.

This was Sir Thomas Wyatt. Wyatt was to embed himself in the imperial train, find out what he could about the true state of amity between these two, and remain with the emperor when he went into his own territories.

*   *   *   *

Considering the activities of Wyatt on this mission, it is possible to see him as the diplomatic counterpart to Hans Holbein, a subtle promoter of Cromwell's particular schemes. Both were indebted to Cromwell, Holbein for his livelihood and Wyatt for his life – certainly once and probably twice. Cromwell needed men. Even before the Cleves debacle, his position was not unassailable. In the summer of 1539 his enemies had gained ground against him with the conservative reforms of religion, but as the Cleves alliance got underway, he had retaliated decisively with some reformist religious injunctions of his own: in September mandates went out for the English Bible to be set up in every church and for the creed, the Ten Commandments and the Pater Noster to be read in English each Sunday. After that, the conservatives sought his discredit more vigorously than ever. In the winter of 1539-40, therefore, as Cromwell pressed on the king to take the Cleves marriage and his enemies pressed to unseat him, it was wise to send a man with a good supply of fresh loyalty to himself.

There are, of course, no letters to Wyatt from Cromwell with instructions to assert the brilliance of his policies; though it may be significant that all of Cromwell's letters to Wyatt from this time have disappeared. But if the question is asked, what would an envoy in Wyatt's position do if he aimed to promote Cromwell's interests, the answer is probably: emphasise the strategic importance of Guelders, assert the sinister unity of Charles and Francis, and try to create some sort of crisis of Catholic malevolence, preferably involving Cardinal Pole. That

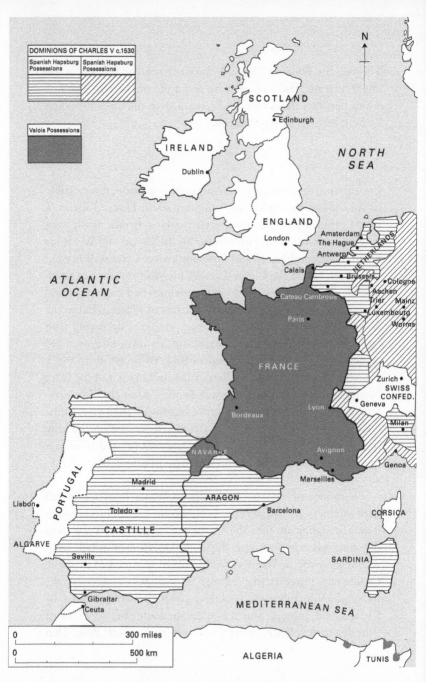

Map of western Europe, showing French and Imperial possessions

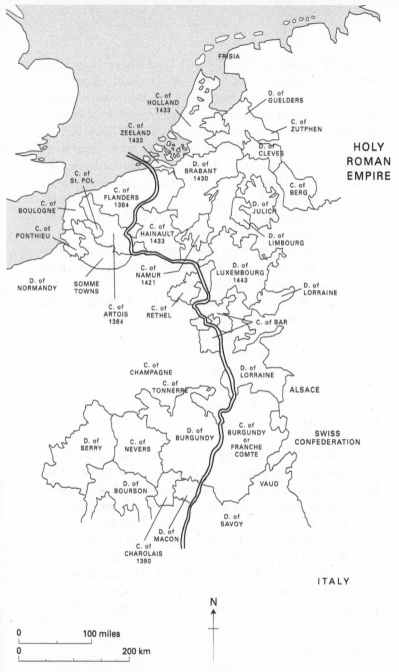

Map of the Low Countries, showing the position of Cleves and
Guelders

is what Wyatt did, and he did it with letters that contain some of the most spirited, dynamic descriptive prose of his age.

Dr. Powell points out that diplomatic dispatches in general began to change in the 1530s, under pressure from Henry's weathervane suspicions and shifting policies.[13] They became noticeably longer, with much more detail of method and strategy, as the diplomats realised that the old system, of leaving the bulk of the explanation to the messenger to deliver by mouth, relinquished too much control over their own role in the narrative. He has also noticed that descriptions of diplomatic heroism rose in inverse relation to diplomatic successes, as Henry's legates, whose missions were often doomed to failure through no fault of their own, pressed for the introduction of an effort grade as well as one for achievement.

In all of this Wyatt, who knew Henry still distrusted him, excelled. His letters from France lift the back off his mission, and show its gears and levers straining to advance Henry's business against the counter-forces of Franco-imperial antagonism. From now on, his letters emphasise the physical hazards, discomforts, inconveniences, humiliations and obstructions encountered in the course of his duties, and the ingenious methods and stratagems he employs – with selfless disregard for his personal comfort or dignity – to prevail. He was not a poet of plaint for nothing. 'In the foyle of this press we are all driven still afore, afore,' he wailed, 'and that we can but in corners lie hidden, where we may hear or see any thing.' Now his letters include those staples of the heroic narrative, the lowly sleeping arrangement – 'this had I written... in evil favoured lodging, and worse bedding' – and the near-insuperable transport difficulty. We learn that posts along the route had been commanded 'on pain of their lives that no man should be horsed unless [he] were from the Emperor, the French King, the Queen of Hungary or [the Constable of France]'. 'Yet,' he continued, 'what by

[13] Powell, J. op. cit.

force, what by means', he managed to get ahead of his quarry. And the next day things were even worse: he was obliged to trail after the kings 'with much ado, upon *plow* horse,' he shuddered, 'in the depe and foul way.'[14] How different this, for Sir Thomas Wyatt, *ordinis equestris*, to those old pre-schismatic days of 1527, when he and John Russell had pranced through Rome on the best horseflesh the pontifical stables could proffer. What, after all, is a knight, but a man on a horse?

The fact that England was held in no estimation at all made it even harder for Wyatt – himself now known by the unhelpful sobriquet of 'that heretic' – to gain audiences and information. But he did manage to get audiences, and his letters have left us a fine account of them. He had been asked to supply the 'words, countenance and gesture' of the two kings, and so he did. When he and Bonner (now resident ambassador with whom he had brokered a temporary semi-peace) met Francis at Blois, he described the whole scene. We learn by whose agency the audience was arranged (the Cardinal of Lorraine's), where they met (at the court, in the queen's outer chamber, at night, following supper and a little musical interlude). Once in the chamber, he reports how many times the king doffed his hat (twice), how he heard Wyatt's words (gently and notingly), exactly what he did with Henry's letters (he read them 'at a cupboard'[15] – flanked by the Cardinal of Lorraine with a candle). We even know what kind of candle it was (a 'quarrier', large and square). Bonner, standing by in the candlelight, interposed an ingratiating remark about Francis' recovered health, duly recorded by Wyatt: 'My Lord of London[16] sayd such was the love and sincere affection of your majestie toward hym that his sickness was your

---

[14] Letter from Wyatt to Henry VIII, December 15, 1539; December 12, 1539, in Muir, op. cit.

[15] cupboard: probably a little private closet, or study, adjoining the main chamber.

[16] Bonner's rise was unstoppable. He was elected bishop of London on 20 October, 1539, before there was time to confirm him in his former see of Hereford.

sickness and his amendment made ye heal again: which word,' adds Wyatt non-committally, 'he seemed to take pleasantly.'

The king then turned to them and 'laying his hand on his breast', in the best chivalric manner, reiterated his vow that there would be no ungentlemanly resorting to business matters, such as concluding over Milan, when the emperor arrived. No, he would not 'move one word of any such thing, for that it were not honest', trusting that when the emperor went into his own territories 'some good thing should ensue'. So Wyatt describes himself taking his leave, pausing only to convey, under cover of a compliment, Bonner's failure to get an interview with Francis before now. [17]

On December 11, Wyatt obtained an audience with the recently arrived emperor, and made his conclusions as follows: first, the emperor was obsessed with Cleves and Guelders: 'he myndeth more Guelders in his heart than he doth Milan and all Italy. And in my conscience, his coming out of Spain in this haste hath been upon the news of your Majestie's alliance with Monsieur de Cleves.' Second, Wyatt found Charles's manner revealing of some fresh compact with France: he had burst out against the Duke of Cleves, and this 'maketh me suspect some farther assurance with France than either of them both declareth'.[18] This he continued to stress, in spite of time passing with no apparent positive outcome for the French. 'We had rather your majesty did yet doubt the worst, that is to say their conclusion, than to conceive uncertain hope of their disagreement', he wrote.[19] Thus Henry received a bracing double confirmation of the rightness of Cromwell's Cleves alliance, as he was waiting for his bride to arrive.

As for the other thing – a crisis to reinvigorate the king's sense of Catholic menace – Wyatt was working on it. The ob-

[17] Letter from Wyatt to Henry, December 2, 1539, in Muir, op. cit.
[18] Letter from Wyatt to Henry, December 12, in Muir, op. cit.
[19] Letter from Wyatt to Henry, Christmas Day 1539, in Muir, op.cit.

vious candidate for such a production, Cardinal Pole, had retired to Rome to nurse his mystification over Charles's failure to come, at Pole's call, to the defence of English Christendom. 'I could not move him to manifest himself openly against the king of England, nor could I clearly understand the reasons which restrain him', he complained. Why would Charles prefer to move against the Turk, when 'there is no doubt that Christians can suffer worse things under this Western Turk... why is the Emperor less ready than other princes in such a cause?'[20] Wyatt's own part in this was an irony that he was disposed to appreciate, now that Pole's presence would have been quite useful.

He had another idea. On December 26 1539, he wrote to Henry on the subject of one Robert Brancetour. The king might remember, he wrote 'that out of Spain I wrote once my opinion for the staying [i.e. the arrest] of Robert Brancetour as he passed through France with Pole. I eftsoones advertise your majesty now of the same... assure your majesty it were for your service greatly to have him'.

This Brancetour was a rich merchant, multilingual and capable, who had travelled widely in Europe and the Middle East. He had been born a Londoner, but had put himself into the service of Charles V many years before. This unusual combination of skills and affiliations meant he was perfectly – perhaps uniquely – well suited to the job as interpreter and guide to Cardinal Pole on his papal legation of 1538. Pole had asked the emperor for his services and been granted them; hence Brancetour's appearance with Pole in France. Wyatt, who seems to have known Brancetour quite well, and detested him, had tried and failed to get him arrested then. Now he was in France again, and Wyatt saw the opportunity to turn him into a kind of manifestation, or avatar, of Pole for Henry to fix on, *faute de mieux*. Everything in Wyatt's presentations was now designed to merge, so far as is possible, the identities of Pole and

[20] Letter from Pole to Cardinal Farnese, March 25, 1539.

Brancetour in Henry's mind. Brancetour is Pole's creature; while in Spain with him he allegedly engaged in Pole-like activities on a small scale, by urging individual Englishmen to turn traitor. Crudely, and not quite likeably, Wyatt invents a connection with Pole's kin, the Exeter 'conspirators': 'And I heard such a word that ere this he was secretly once in England with the Marquess of Exeter, and returned'.[21] Less crudely, he turns his verbal aptitude to the task. Here and there he alludes to Brancetour with language that is usually employed for Pole: 'your rebel', 'your traitor' and (fastidiously) 'the party'. His obsession with catching Brancetour mirrors, in miniature, the king's obsession with catching Pole. Urged on by Cromwell's 'good avyse', it grew into the main issue of Wyatt's correspondence. *L'affaire* Brancetour swelled immensely.

On January 3, 1540, three days before Henry's marriage to Anne of Cleves was solemnised, Wyatt pounced on Brancetour in Paris. The letter he wrote gives the king the full blow-by-blow of this escapade, to show how 'from hour to hour there lacked no applying' in their efforts to apprehend him.[22] The pursuit begins with squeezing permission for the arrest out of the reluctant constable of France, Montmorency. Although at first he 'escaped us by a back door', they corner the constable as he is coming out of Mass, and chivvy him to organise the permissions. That evening, a French provost arrives at Wyatt's chambers to enable the process, and Wyatt's letter moves up a gear, into a racy adventure story that has no parallel in the writings of the time. Suspense, action, pacing, wit – all this from the pen of someone who had once despaired of making English prose accommodate a simple tract. And at the centre of the narrative, the commanding figure of Wyatt himself, in whom a faultless urbanity and presence of mind is shown to combine with physical toughness, not unlike an early modern James Bond. He apolo-

---

[21] Letter from Wyatt to Henry, December 16, 1539, in Muir, op.cit.
[22] Letter from Wyatt to Henry, January 7, 1540, in Muir, op. cit.

gised to the king for writing so 'tediously' of the matter; but this was wholly disingenuous: he sent copies of the letter to half a dozen friends.[23] The drama begins as the provost arrives: '[The provost] was scant arrived but word came that our man was comen. I myself went [to him] with the provost, *without light*.' [Italics mine]. Having crept up on Brancetour in the dark, they burst into his lodgings, and find him writing a letter. Wyatt greets him with sardonic courtesy: 'I told him that since he would not come to visit me, I was come to seek him. And I showed him what pain I had taken, that at the door I had hurt my leg with a fall; that indeed, I fear me, will not be whole this month.' Recognising the voice of his old adversary, Brancetour realises the game is up. 'His colour changed as soon as he heard my voice.' The provost goes to grab him, and Wyatt, without heed to his wounded leg, is into the fray right away: 'I reached to have set hand upon letters that he was writing, but he caught them afore me and flang them back ward in to the fire. Yet I over-threw him and cratched[24] them out, but the provost got them.' Wyatt then has an opportunity to bandy words with the king's rebel. '...After a little dumpe[25] he told me that he had heard me oftimes say that kings have long hands. "But God," quod he, "hath longer." I asked him then, what length thought he that would make, when God's and King's hands were joined together?'

No doubt Henry took note of his ambassadors' ever-present zeal for the royal supremacy; but all was not going to plan. After Wyatt snatched the letters from the fire, Brancetour declared that he was not Henry's subject, but Charles V's. He and his writings should therefore be submitted to the authority of the emperor, who also happened to be in Paris. Wyatt had not foreseen this. Nor had the provost; indeed, the situation had no precedent. The emperor had never been a guest of France

[23] See Powell, op. cit.
[24] cratched: snatched
[25] dumpe: a spell of glum perplexity.

before. Here was a brilliant blocking move on Brancetour's part, striking bureaucratic uncertainty into the heart of the provost, who now scurried off to consult his superiors, returning with the depressing news that 'he must carry the man to his lodgings and not to mine [Wyatt's], nor deliver me the writings'.

Still in full pursuit, Wyatt raced back to HQ for a consultation with Bonner and his other associates. They realised they must act right away. Splitting up, Bonner went to argue with the French authorities, while Wyatt actually forced himself into the presence of the emperor and demanded that this man 'who seemed to hang about his court', as he dismissively put it, be given up to him right away, as stipulated in the existing Anglo-Spanish treaties.

The emperor was superb. He affected not to have been briefed on the matter. What man is this? he asked.

And I told him it was one Brancetour. 'Ah,' quod he. 'Robert.'

'That same, Sir,' quod I.

'I shall tell you,' quod he, 'Monsieur L'Ambassadeur; it is he that hath been in Perse [Persia].'

'As he sayth, Sir,' said Wyatt, determined to give the man no credence for his adventures, and far preferring for him to have been in England, with Exeter. But Charles insists. He tells Wyatt what Brancetour has done for him. It was no small matter: 11 years ago, he had taken on a dying man's mission to persuade Thamasp, the King of Persia, to attack the Turks in concert with Charles. This he had accomplished single-handed.[26] Since then, said the emperor, Brancetour had followed him on all his travels – with no recognition but acceptance as his servant and promise of better to come. Suddenly he finds

[26] See J.J. Scarisbrick's essay on Brancetour: 'The First Englishman round the Cape of Good Hope', Historical Research, Vol 34 (November, 1961).

these arrears on his conscience.

'What!' he said to Wyatt, 'Would ye that I consent to the destruction of a man that followeth me, upon my word, that yet for his service I have not rewarded him but hold him in hope?...
Nay, Monsieur l'embassadeur[sic], I tell you plain, I will speak for his deliverance both to the Constable and the [French] King. And I trust they will not do me so great dishonour as to suffer one that followeth my word to suffer damage. For surely I advise you, that though your master had me in the Tower of London, I would not consent so to change mine honour and my conscience.'

No, no, said Wyatt. The emperor has mistaken the situation. '*I* have not done him to be taken... it is the [French] King and the Constable that hath done it.'

He had his motives for saying that. As we will see, it was part of a wider stratagem. But in the meantime, he lost Brancetour. Charles refused to give him up, saying he would look into the matter when he got into his own territories, and Brancetour took back his letters and slipped off to the Low Countries. Wyatt sent assassins after him, with instructions to befriend him and discreetly cut his throat. But, although Wyatt always showed him in the disparaging light of his faintly disreputable beginnings in England, as a 'man of small quality that had been a merchant's factor and had robbed his master', he was in fact a substantial person. Even before his Persian achievement, he had penetrated the Venetian monopoly on Middle Eastern trade routes, and had somehow won the right to trade on Venetian galleys, usually the prerogative of Venetian citizens. By 1533 Charles had made him 'chief captain' against the Turks and his main man in the Orient; when he talked of the 'reward' he meant to give him, he meant a dukedom. For a man like this, Wyatt's cut-throats were small beer. Pretending to fall in with them, he used what he learned from the acquaintance to get one of them arrested and thrown into a Flemish prison, while he escaped back to Rome and Reginald Pole. The whole escapade was a beautifully presented failure.

After this, Wyatt's energy seemed to fail. He continued in the emperor's train into Brussels and Ghent, as proposed, but his brash intervention over Brancetour had spooked Charles and Francis into a new distrust of him. Wyatt's letters could barely disguise how remote his orbit was from the centre of negotiations, how much he depended on common gossip, and the news he sent back was often hazy, uncertain and late. For instance, it took him until April to find out what promises Charles had made back in November, to secure his passage through France. By then, the information was almost redundant: it was becoming apparent that Charles had never intended to settle Milan on France, and the Franco-imperial accord was now 'as cold as though the things passed had been but dremes'.[27] Despite this, his summings-up of the situation often hit on the truth about the emperor's intentions and methods. He was always extremely intelligent.

One piece of news which got to him still warm was that of Henry's disastrous new marriage. As the duke of Cleves was in town, this soon got around and became the subject of ribald gossip in Brussels. Wyatt offered to silence these 'false rumours and noyses' with a refutation published in German, but there appears to have been no enthusiasm for that, probably because the king was already wondering how to get out of the marriage. Wyatt was keenly aware of his own role in the failed negotiations for the more delicious duchess of Milan the year before. Not that he could have done more, but he knew it would look more annoying if the Franco-Spanish accord dissolved, taking with it the only reason for Henry to be married to Anne of Cleves. Reflecting on this, he wrote to the king with an ingenious construction of his marital predicament, aimed at Henry's weakness for true love:

[27] Letter from Wyatt to Cromwell, April 12, 1540, in Muir, op. cit.

And herein, if I shall be plain with your majestie, I can not but rejoice in manner the eskape that you made there [i.e. from the Duchess of Milan]... [for] there is thought affection between the Prince of Orange and her, and hath beene of long... [*And*] *I have heard it to proceed partly from her own occasion*. [Italics mine][28]

No one but Henry would mind about that.

*   *   *   *

Soon his thoughts turned to revocation. He sent pitiful tales of

Christina of Denmark, Duchess of Milan
(*Hans Holbein the Younger*)

[28] Letter from Wyatt to Henry, March 9, 1540.

expenses to Cromwell: the Flanders posting was costing him a fortune, owing to the unfavourable exchange rate and the high price of staple commodities, like the beer and oats needed to make men and horses go. 'The least fire I make to warm my shirt by standes me in a groat; in my diet money I lose in the value 8 shillings and 4 pence every day... a barrel of beer that in England were worth 20 pence costs me here with the excise 4 shillings.' And these costs were falling where debt already lay deep-piled with the uncleared accumulations of years. He felt his creditors mustering. He owed the king £500 (a vast sum), 'among many other great debts'. He hoped for some latitude with the repayments, so he might 'a little and little to creep out of debt, with selling of little land more; if not, on my faith, I see no remedy. I owe my brother Lee as much, by sides other infinite, that make me weary to think on them.' In this, and in his 'particular things' in England, and in the urgent matter of his revocation, he beseeches Cromwell's intervention 'in whom is mine only trust next the king's majesty'.[29]

> I have sought long with steadfastness[30]
> To have had some ease of my great smart
> But naught availeth faithfulness
> To grave within your stony heart.
>
> ... But of your goodness all your mind
> Is that I should complain in vain.
> This is the favour that I find
> Ye list to hear how I can plain.

By April he began to plead diplomatic redundancy. 'I begin to wax unacceptable here,' he wrote. He was suffering from awful headaches. Even then he would never allow himself a moment

---

[29]Letter from Wyatt to Cromwell, February 10, 1540. Sir Antony Lee – a courtier and Devonshire MS contributor – was married to Wyatt's only sister, Margaret.
[30] Wyatt, CX, in Rebholz, op. cit.

as a deadweight. All his letters find him hectically courting usefulness. He could even turn his homeward journey to the service
of the king. Providentially, the Prince of Salerno – a splendid
individual 'of 30,000 to 40,000 ducats rent, and …greatly esteemed in all Italy, and one of the greatest men of Naples'[31] – had
conceived the notion of travelling to England purely as a tourist
– a request so unusual that it caused a security alert in France
– along with his brother, the Duke of Ferrara. Wyatt proposed
himself as the perfect chaperone for this jaunt. His particular
combination of espionage, *espièglerie* and horsemanship meant
he could 'make him such company as would not prove unhon-
ourable to the King', and keep an eye on him at the same time.

In the end, Salerno delayed his trip, not arriving in England
until the beginning of July, two months after Wyatt's eventual
return. He visited the sights at Windsor and Hampton Court
and left 'eight days after he came', reported the French ambassador, in a tone that suggested he could have predicted as much,
'with one of the Emperor's gentlemen of the chamber'. That
was in the second week of July 1540. If Salerno had stayed a
few more days, he would have been witness to one of the great
events of the decade: the arrest of Thomas Cromwell on charges of high treason.

*   *   *   *

As is well known, Cromwell was executed without a trial, in
a process of 'attainder' that he himself had devised and made
law. After he died, Wyatt is thought to have adapted a sonnet of
Petrarch's for the occasion.

> *The Pillar Perished is whereto I leant,*[32]
> *The strongest stay of mine unquiet mind;*
> *The like of it no man again can find*

---

[31] Letter from Wyatt to Cromwell, April 5, 1540, in Muir, op. cit.
[32] Wyatt, XXIX, in Rebholz, op. cit.

From East to West, still seeking though he went
To mine unhap, for hap away hath rent
Of all my joy the very bark and rind,
And I, alas, by chance am thus assigned
Dearly to mourn till death do it relent.
But since that thus it is by destiny,
What can I more but have a woeful heart,
My pen in plaint, my voice in woeful cry,
My mind in woe, my body full of smart,
And I myself myself always to hate,
Till dreadful death do cease my doleful state?

This is a very clever poem, folding into four lines what will take a paragraph to unpack. Petrarch wrote the sonnet on the deaths of his patron, Giovanni Colonna, and his lover Laura, whose names (Colonna = column, Laura = laurel) support the puns of his first line: 'the tall column is broken and the green laurel'. With a few light touches in the fifth and sixth lines, Wyatt re-casts the poem for his own situation. The classical pillar of the first line undergoes a typically Wyattian metamorphosis, rusticated into an English tree with a trunk, bark and rind, representing what Wyatt would call his 'wealth': his wellbeing and prosperity. Unlike Petrarch's laurel, Wyatt's tree hasn't perished from within. It's been killed from the outside. In a demonstration of practical forestry that we seldom find in Petrarch's sonnets, someone has ripped off its bark, so that the sap – the tree's blood supply, carrying nutrients from the soil – can't reach its limbs and branches. A ringbarked tree will appear healthy for a while, but it can't be saved. Like a marked man, it's a member of the living dead – and if this poem was, as many think, inspired by Cromwell's death, it may be a real death that Wyatt foresees for himself, severed from Cromwell's protection. But it is the penultimate line that puzzles us the most.

What does it mean? Why should Wyatt hate himself over this? His editor, Muir, says, 'We need not suppose... that the last lines of the sonnet, which are original, are an admission that his own diplomatic failures were partly responsible for Cromwell's downfall.'

But they were, and we need. To see exactly where, we have to return to the matter of Robert Brancetour and his non-arrest in France. When Wyatt started to pursue him, he had more than one beast in view. In the summer of 1538, he had seen how issues of precedence between Francis and Charles had almost paralysed the whole Aigues-Mortes conference. It was easy to produce an atmosphere of affronted dignity among them, and particularly in Francis, as the king with the smaller territories. He now saw in Brancetour's unique circumstances – an Englishman following the emperor, on French territory – an opportunity to foment trouble between them. Hence his frequent insistence that the arrest was none of his own doing, but proceeded from 'commandment' of the French authorities. *'It is the [French] King and the Constable that hath done it'*. He reminded Charles that as he was out of his territory, the treaties regarding such extraditions didn't require imperial consent 'of duty'. So, when Charles had then demanded Brancetour's release, he was countermanding French sovereign authority *in France*, most provoking to the French king. The situation, as Wyatt pointed out, was nothing to do with Thomas Wyatt, a mere English ambassador, helpless in a foreign land. It was all the fault of the French: 'Whereby I am blameless.'

> *Perdie I said it not[33]*
> *Nor never thought to do.*
> *As well as I, ye wot*

---

[33] Wyatt, LXXVII, in Rebholz, op. cit.

I have no power thereto.

That was stage one. Stage two came in Brussels, after Brancetour had been released. Wyatt went to Charles for a follow-up conversation over the whole affair, and deliberately antagonised him by accusing him of 'ingratitude' to Henry. This was a gross violation of diplomatic etiquette, so he must have been acting on (now lost) instructions from England to get, by whatever means, some 'matter' from the emperor that the English could put between him and the French king. To obtain it, he must rile him enough to make him drop his guard. Accordingly, Wyatt told him he had been ungrateful to Henry VIII when he ordered Brancetour's release:

> And [the emperor] roundly told me that I abused my words toward him: 'I would that both your master and you wist it well: it is too much to use that term, of "ingrate" unto *me*... I take it so that *I* cannot be toward *him* ingrate. [*Only*] *the inferior may be ingrate to the greater*, and the term is scant sufferable between like.' [Italics mine]

When Wyatt said nothing, Charles suggested – *strongly suggested* may be the phrase we need – that Wyatt's French was at fault. He had surely meant to use another word. 'But peraventure,' he continued, ' because the language is not your natural tongue, ye may mistake the term.' But Wyatt declined the offer, rejected the imputation and proceeded to needle him with an unrequested lecture in philology. Not at all, he remarked. Not only was there nothing wrong with his French, but

> I can not render that term [i.e. ingrate] from my tongue into the French tongue by *any* other term which I

know also to descend out of the Latin. And *in the original* it hath no such relation to lesserness or greaterness of persons. [Italics mine]

This was a low blow, intended to annoy. The emperor's Latin was notably poor.[34] He warned Wyatt he was 'pricking' him with words. But the display of humanistic quibbling over the derivation of the word 'ingrate' wasn't solely for the defence of England's intellectual honour. It gave Wyatt a chance to spell out what Charles had said – to establish what Charles had *meant* – and with this to secure some 'matter' for his masters in England to use against the alliance.

In England they got the point at once. Working the remark up into something more emphatic, with the bit about 'between like' taken out, they sped it to the Duke of Norfolk, then in embassy at the French court, who made much of it to Francis and put it all over the place that the emperor had said he was superior to other kings. 'What, will he have no equal? Will he be God?' said the Queen of Navarre. Naturally, Francis was outraged, and demanded written accounts of the conversation from both English and imperial sources.[35] It was the beginning of the end of the Franco-imperial entente. By the time of Cromwell's arrest, in June, the likelihood of a double attack upon England had receded to nothing, rendering Cromwell's foreign policy redundant and making it possible for Henry to think about offloading his new marriage.

It would be interesting to know what Wyatt thought of his own actions. Could he see that the result of success in Brussels would be to weaken Cromwell and endanger himself, or was it only later that he realised his own contribution to Cromwell's downfall? In March 1540, Cromwell's destruction

---

[34] For a comparative assessment of royal language skills at this time, see Garrett Mattingly, *Renaissance Diplomacy* (Penguin, 1955).
[35] See Powell, op. cit.

was far from certain. As in the case of Anne Boleyn, it came suddenly and its causes are mysterious. Why would a king get rid of his most effective servant?

There is no consensus amongst historians on this point. Was it the result of the Cleves marriage? In May, the Duke of Cleves had become as much of an annoyance as his sister, badgering Henry for aid against Charles just as he was poised to consider a new imperial alliance. Or was it the work of a Catholic faction, led by Norfolk and Gardiner? That was the view of the French ambassador. Or was he pursuing (as was claimed in his attainder) a radical religious policy of his own without the king's knowledge? He had certainly worked on behalf of reform and done Henry the great service of becoming the hate figure, both at home and abroad, for English religious radicalism. Perhaps he had become a diplomatic liability now that a new alliance with Catholic Europe was in prospect. Whichever way, the dissolution of the Franco-Spanish entente weakened him fatally, and the Brancetour affair was the catalyst.

Wyatt had done his best for his master, but it was a retrograde progress he had made for him. The result of all his efforts was to find himself, in spite of himself, working in concert with Cromwell's enemy, the Duke of Norfolk, to the ultimate destruction of his saviour and patron.

To do me good what may prevail?[36]
For I deserve and not desire[37]
And still of cold I me bewail
And raked am in burning fire.
For though I have – such is my lot –
In hand to help that I require
It helpeth not.

[36] Wyatt, LXXXVII, in Rebholz, op. cit.
[37] deserve and not desire: I suggest: 'I render service that I don't want to render'.

It was Norfolk who lunged at Cromwell in the council chamber, on the morning of his arrest, while the Earl of Southampton tore the seal of office from around his neck. It was Norfolk's lovely little niece, Catherine Howard, who danced the king out of the Cleves marriage.

They kept Cromwell alive for long enough for him to devise the necessary proofs for the Cleves divorce, and executed him on the day of the King's fifth wedding: July 27, 1540. Norfolk arranged for an incompetent axeman, 'a ragged and butcherly miser', to be on duty on the day of the execution. Cromwell's neck was not conformed as an apprentice piece for a headsman. His head sat on his shoulders like a cup in a saucer. The executioner 'most ungodly performed the office'. It took a long time.

According to the author of the Spanish chronicle, Wyatt was there to watch Cromwell's last walk:

And amongst all these gentlemen, Cromwell saw Master Wyatt, the knight who had been arrested as the lover of Queen Anne, and called to him, saying: 'Oh Noble Wyatt, God be with Thee, and I pray thee, pray to God for me!' (he had always had a great love for this Master Wyatt). And Wyatt could not answer, so many were the tears that he shed. All those gentlemen marvelled to see how deeply Master Wyatt was moved. And as Cromwell was a very wise man, he reflected on it, and said out loud, 'Oh Wyatt, do not weep; for if I were no more guilty than you were when you were arrested, I should not have come to this!' All the gentlemen loved Wyatt well, so they dissembled; otherwise he might have been arrested to find out if he knew of any treason that Cromwell had plotted.[38]

[38] Hume, op. cit

Though intended to exonerate, this mark of notice did Wyatt no favours. Most of Cromwell's former adherents had forgotten they ever knew him. Southampton's dramatic public gesture probably arose from a sense of needing to publicise his hostility. He had been one of the last to turn. Some of these gentlemen may have dissembled to prevent Wyatt's arrest, but some, like Bishop Bonner and Thomas Wriothesley, had other ideas.

Wriothesley's betrayal of his master, Cromwell, who 'more him loved/than any other',[39] according to a poem on the subject, was remarkable even by the standards of the times and must earn him a special mention in the dispatches of duplicity. From Wriothesley's point of view, however, it was only a promising start: he had to build on it with further proofs of his new affiliation – such as a distracting strike on another of Cromwell's 'minions'. He had stopped liking Wyatt in 1538-9, when Wyatt had distrusted him enough to encipher his letters and leave Wriothesley, on diplomatic business in Brussels, out of the loop of important information. He was an ideal candidate.

Cromwell's death was a new exposure. For a while, though, his former favour still worked in Wyatt above the barked ring. In August of that year, there were extensive and favourable exchanges of lands with the king. He had been thinking about returning to Calais, perhaps in Lord Lisle's post of lord deputy. Conservatives eyed his movements with alarm.[40] But in the meantime, Henry's agents had been sifting through Cromwell's papers and someone found Bishop Bonner's letter from September 1538, accusing Wyatt of contact with Pole and hinting at a wider conspiracy.

In January, he was arrested.

[39] An anonymous poem on the subject alludes to Cromwell's chief betrayer as one who Cromwell 'more him loved/than any other', but who was working with Gardiner to undo him. This person has been identified as Thomas Wriothesley. Brigden, 'The Shadow that You Know,' *Historical Journal*, 39, 1 (1996).
[40] Rumours of this were already circulating. Earlier that year the French ambassador, Sir John Wallop, had written to warn Lord Lisle of this development: 'If [Wyatt] should supply you in your place, that I would much mislike, and soundeth much contrary to those good purposes that you and I and other have travailed in.' Wallop to Lisle, 14 March, 1540.

CHAPTER TWENTY

The news of Wyatt's arrest spread quickly through Europe. The French ambassador wrote the following day, January 18, that an 'unexpected and important event' had just occurred:

> last night two gentlemen of the court, much esteemed here, were led prisoners from Hampton Court hither; and this morning they were, with their hands bound, conducted by 24 archers to the tower. One was Mr Hoyet [Wyatt] whom [King Francis] may have seen last year, ambassador with the Emperor on his passage through France. Although neither Earl nor Baron, he was one of the richest gentlemen in England, with a patrimony of 6,000 or 7,000 ducats yearly; and has always seemed to be more in favour of the king his master than any other great gentleman in this country, and there is none to whom the king shows greater familiarity or appears to love better. Not a month ago, he made him a gift worth 300 crowns rent...
>
> It will be difficult to learn the true cause of their taking, for, by a law made at last parliament, they condemn people without hearing them; and when a man is prisoner in the tower none dare meddle with his affairs, unless to speak ill of him, for fear of being suspected of the same crime.

The other man was probably Ralph Sadler, a recent

ambassador to Scotland and a member of the council; but it is Wyatt who attracts the attention, for he was a known figure in the European courts, and a man who:

> seemed beside to have enjoyed as much favour with the king, his master, as any other lord or nobleman of this kingdom, for there is certainly no one in the whole of England for whom greater esteem and regard have been shown in public, for no one either who has received greater proofs of his master's affection and love. [He was]] more regretted than any man taken in England these last three years, both by English men and strangers, [yet] no man has the boldness to say a word for him.[1]

> *What though each heart that heareth me plain*[2]
> *Pityeth and plaineth for my pain*
> *If I no less in grief remain*
> *What may it avail me?*

The Queen of Hungary was interested, so was the King of France, who remembered him well as the one who had spoken to the emperor 'very audaciously' as Francis recalled, 'pointing his hand to his head as though he took [Wyatt] to be somewhat fantastic'. The letters that shot out from this time are, however, an object lesson in diplomatic Chinese whispers. News leaked accuracy on its journey from the inner court to the ambassadorial lodgings. Marillac thought he was very rich (perhaps a consequence of his liberality, or his boasting in Spain); Chapuys had heard the story of his repudiation of his ex-wife, but thought her father was the Duke of Rutland. On one thing everyone agreed: this was typical of the barbaric goings-on at Henry's court. Henry's error had made of England a chasm

---

[1] Letter from Marillac to Francis, January 18, Kaulek, op. cit.
[2] Wyatt, CVII, in Rebholz, op. cit.

filled with blood and squabbles, into which the right-thinking peoples of Christendom might deliciously peer, with shivers of self-righteous horror.

'No definite charge has been made against Wyatt and nothing proved against him but words, which would not have been noticed elsewhere; but these people are so suspicious they make mortal sins of trifles,' wrote Chapuys. When the news reached the papal nuncio at the diet of Nuremberg, he joked about how easy it was for Englishmen to get themselves beheaded: 'for [how] little the king slaughters his most loved servants!' he marvelled; going on to make the other point that everyone agreed on: 'That ribald[3] ambassador who was in Spain is in prison, and this ambassador says they will cut his head off.'[4]

This arrest was very different from that of 1536, when Cromwell's sheltering wing had folded round him and everything was done on the nod. Now there was no gentlemanly stroll to the Tower, no commodious lodgings, no letters of assurance speeding to Allington Castle. Cromwell was dead, his father was dead, his years abroad had left him disfurnished of 'perfect friends' to mediate for him at court. This time, he was marched to the Tower in chains – one of Wriothesley's signature touches[5] – and shown to a windowless cell. Agents were sent out to Cromwell's house to 'peruse all books, writings, and muniments'[6] there that might pertain to his case; others across Europe to arrest John Mason, now halfway back to Spain to negotiate for Spanish horses, and return him for questioning.

Sir Richard Southwell, the solicitor general, went down to Allington Castle to search 'certain coffers'[7] of Mason's there, remove goods and plate, and interrogate Elizabeth Darrell. The

<hr>

[3] ribald: dissolute, impious. Referring to Wyatt's public disparagement of the pope and Cardinal Pole in Spain the previous spring.
[4] Letter from Cardinal Poggio to Cardinal Sanctae Crucis, February 19, 1541.
[5] He would impose the same humiliation on the Earl of Surrey on his arrest in December 1546.
[6] January 23, 1541, LP 479, 16.
[7] LP 15, no 469.

fact that they used this preliminary sortie as an opportunity to pack up Wyatt's property and, as Chapuys reported, 'place the king's seal on his cupboards', indicates the expected outcome of the affair. Sure enough, a week after the investigation began, Southwell returned to dissolve Wyatt's splendid household: his instructions were to 'send up plate and stuff at Allington castle which appears meet for the king, and also the armoury stuff, guns, jennets, and great horses.' He was to discharge the women of the house – Wyatt's daughter-in-law Jane Hawte and Lady Poynings, the wife of a friend – and dismiss the servants with 'an honest lesson and half a year's wages'.

One further instruction concerned Elizabeth Darrell. Southwell was to 'enquire of Mrs Darrell whether she intended to go to any such place whereas she should be ordered, as *that, wherewithal she appeared to be might be preserved*; and in case she would not declare to him the same, whereby he might conjecture *that might perish which she had conceived*, then to stay her there.'[8](itals mine)

Mrs Darrell had been living openly with Wyatt for some time – probably since Exeter's disgrace had left her with no other protector– and now she was pregnant. To judge from this report, she had not lost her old steel.[9] Her reception of the king's agents, when they arrived at Allington to count the spoons, had left them with no confidence that she would 'go to any such place whereas she should be ordered' when they came back again. She also, it seems, kept up a mulish silence on the subject of her pregnancy, which Southwell now had to negotiate gingerly, on the basis of its appearance. He evidently feared that she was in such a state of distraction that she might miscarry. To cause a miscarriage would be a sin.

The process of attainder had begun. Now there was only one outcome for a suspect.

[8] Acts of the Privy Council, January 20, 1541.
[9] The reader will recall that she refused to sign the Oath of Succession in 1534.

What had happened? The resident ambassadors thought they knew. According to Marillac and Chapuys, Wyatt's fall was factional, the beginning of a general move on the part of Cromwell's enemies to depopulate the court of his associates. Marillac wrote to Francis that Wyatt was Cromwell's 'minion', and, since 'Cromwell virtually subdued and tamed the great lords of England, including the Grand Esquire [Carew], others have sprung up who will not rest until they have done the same with Cromwell's adherents'.

This explanation has served for several centuries and there is truth in it. Wyatt's enemies certainly worked to bring him down by pushing at the Cromwell connection. When the (conservative) ambassador to France, Sir John Wallop – a man with a personal interest in keeping Wyatt out of the post in Calais – heard of his arrest, he tried to finish him off with a malicious embellishment to his next dispatch. When Francis heard the news, wrote Wallop, he didn't just tap his temple with his forefinger: he spoke of the late Privy Seal's 'naughty intentions towards your highness and the Lady Mary, perhaps hinting that Wyatt ... should be of that affinity.'[10]

Faction played a part. But recently, Susan Brigden and Jason Powell have looked into the wider context of the arrest and developed a supplementary theory.[11] This shows that Wyatt was one of a number of Henry's ambassadors – of varying ideological mien and, ironically, including Sir John Wallop – to be arrested at about this time. They shared a common failure: each had been told to catch and deliver an English traitor, and each had failed. In this scenario, Wyatt's arrest was not so much the result of a factional coup as the harvest of suspicions germinating in 1538, nourished by these recent diplomatic failings, and, in Wyatt's case, by the delinquency of his successor as resident in Flanders, Richard Pate, Archdeacon of Lincoln. Like Wyatt,

[10] Letter from Sir John Wallop to Henry VIII, January 26, 1541.
[11] Powell, op.cit.

Pate had found out he was suspected of collusion with Pole. Unlike Wyatt, who had come back to London 'with spur and sail', Pate's response to this news had been to defect with spur and sail to Rome, confirming all Henry's suspicions about his ambassadors. This had happened in December, just as Wyatt was returning to England. Wyatt must have known he could be made the scapegoat for this affair, not least because Thomas Wriothesley – who had let a traitor through his own hands in Brussels, and was thought to be in danger himself at this point – would be happy to deflect the attention onto Wyatt. This was the evil he anticipated.

Wyatt sat in his cell, in darkness. In an epigram he wrote to Sir Francis Bryan, he construed the situation as a black variant of the pastime.

> *Sighs are my food, drink are my tears;*[12]
> *Clinking of fetters such music would crave*

How dainty this seems, for the circumstances. But when we look again, there is something unbalanced here, right in the first line. The expected word order would be 'sighs are my food, tears are my drink.' That would provide the conventional substitutions. But *drink are my tears*? What does that mean? It sounds like he might really be drunk, or losing his mind. That may have been the desired effect. The lines are the ultimate expression of Wyatt's sense that things – good and bad, high and low, friend and foe – were entangled to the point of incoherence. It's as though the 'pleasure' words – drink, music, food – are tossed up together with the 'pain' words – sighs, tears, fetters – like a handful of counters in a game, and left to lie crazily, where they land. He goes on:

[12] Wyatt, LXII, in Rebholz, op. cit.

Stink and close air away my life wears
Innocency is all the hope I have.
Rain, wind, or weather I judge by mine ears.
Malice assaulted that righteousness should save.
Sure I am, Brian, this wound shall heal again,
But yet, alas, the scar shall still remain.

Looked at as a biographical document, the poem tells us one or two things: that he was confined in a cell with no viewable window; that he believed himself the victim of a malicious campaign. Dr Brigden has argued, through biblical references, that the last couplet contained a coded message to Bryan to keep a shared (but lost) secret from their time together as ambassadors.[13] It certainly is a strange declaration: why would a man in Wyatt's position be 'sure' that his wound would heal? Here he was, ignominiously incarcerated, with his goods confiscated, his household shut up, his friends and mistress pulled in for questioning, while he himself underwent interrogation on 38 separate points. Everyone knew he would die, and he must have known it. As Marillac wrote to Francis on January 25:

If a man or woman becomes a prisoner in the said big tower of this city, there is no living creature, however powerful, noble, or distinguished, who dares interfere and mix himself up with the prisoner's affairs. And if he does at all open his mouth, it is for the sake of speaking against the alleged criminal, for fear he himself should be suspected of having shared in his crime.

But he was not going to go silently. He took up his pen and prepared to defend himself.

[13] Brigden, 'The Shadow that You Know', op. cit.

* * * *

The document that comes down to us by the name of 'Wyatt's Defence' is remarkable in many ways. It is both a defence and an indictment of English law. It is 'a unique text' says Powell,[14] 'in that it argues not only against the author's guilt, but also to some degree against the legal and political structure of early Tudor society.' It is therefore a monument of courage; but it's also a display of intellectual ingenuity, a revelation of the complexion of Wyatt's mind and a record of the way he sounded. It was written to be read aloud. It is an exhibition of oratorical genius with a particularly Wyattian twist, of incorporating his own, most distinctive, conversational voice into its passages. Wyatt took a conscious decision to manage his self-presentation. In this document, he would appear as a forthright, honest man whom malicious and devious foes had ensnared in their toils. Not content to bring about his destruction, these enemies aimed to pervert the laws of England and confuse the judges with their twisted interpretations of his deeds and words. Writing in this persona, he produced a witty, subtle and deceptively complex argument, far too long for detailed analysis here; but at the heart of it is a single appeal: *listen to the words*. It is the cry of an evangelical and a poet.

When he wrote it, he didn't know exactly what the charges were. He had had to prepare it without sight of the indictment. Working from the questioning he had undergone and from what he already knew, he must have deduced that Bonner's letter to Cromwell had been found and the charges in it revived. That letter he had seen back in the summer of 1539, when he got back from Spain and had the business out with Cromwell. He knew it contained two substantial allegations, among the general slime. First: that he had had intelligence with the traitor, Reginald Pole, during the conference at Nice in 1538; second,

[14] Powell, op. cit.

[328]

that he had said that the king should be 'left out of the cart's arse, and that by God's blood if he were so, he were well served' – a phrase now construed to mean he wished a traitor's death on the king. Traitors were dragged to the gallows on hurdles hitched to the back of carts. Either of these was enough to kill him, the latter for the crime of 'imagining the king's death' *in speech*: a capital offence since the Treason Act of 1534 had introduced 'the law of words', as Wyatt termed it.

He would address these issues in detail, but before he did, he started with an extraordinary appeal to the judges, requiring them to remember what law was. He reminded them that judges were impartial under English law, that an indictment was not a conviction, that the presence of a man in a court of law was not proof of his guilt, and that it was possible – he even cited an example – for a man to be indicted for treason, and found innocent. So, he rehearsed the principles of the law, allowing the gap between principle and practice to slide open silently. The terms he uses are heavily loaded: You must remember, he said, that:

> Neither [the testimony] of these men which talk here unsworn, nor th'indictment at large is to be regarded as an evidence: for the indicters have found that I have done it. If that be true, what needs your trial? But if inquests fetch [take] their light from indictments at large, then is a man condemned unheard, then had my Lord Dacres been found guilty,[15] for he was indicted at large by three or four inquests; like was his matter[16] avowed, affirmed and aggravated by an help of learned men. But on all this the *honourable and wise nobility* did not once look at: they *looked at the evidence*.[17] [Italics mine]

---

[15] In 1534, cheers had rung from Westminster hall when William, Baron Dacre became the first and only nobleman in Henry's reign to be acquitted on charges of treason. The case had particular relevance to Wyatt's because the evidence of the chief witness had been dismissed as proceeding from malice.

[16] matter: alleged crime.

This is a reformer's argument: Just as Evangelicals elevated Gospel word over the obfuscating commentaries, Wyatt upholds evidence-based law as a light to penetrate the fogs and partialities of an indictment: 'a prepared thing' as Wyatt calls it; 'matter... aggravated by an help of learned men'. With this, the first faint whiff, almost imperceptible, of anti-clerical sentiment is borne to the nostrils of the accusing Bonner, who he knew would be present. At the same time, it bands Wyatt and the judges, 'the honourable and wise nobility', together on the side of the law, and makes his accusers, the 'men who talk here unsworn', look like enemies of justice.

He continues to move against his accusers. Scathingly identifying the two central charges – 'the two marks whereunto mine accusers direct all their shot of eloquence' – as 'a deed and a saying', he turns to the jurors and, again, urges them to consult the law. Was he a traitor to contact Pole, at Nice?

'*Rehearse the law*. Declare, my lords, I beseek you, the meaning thereof. Am I a traitor because I spake with the king's traitor?' No, not by law, not unless that traitor is 'helpen, counselled, advertised by my word. There lyeth the treason, there lyeth the treason!' And was this his own case? No. He had no communication with Pole. He did send Mason, but as a spy. And besides, if this was treason, he was not alone in it, for who was there with him when the decision was taken? None other than Bonner and Heynes. Well, well. 'My accusers themselves are accused, if this be treason.' And not only that: while Wyatt never thought it other than a legitimate means to 'suck out' information from Pole, Bonner and Heynes had evidently thought it treasonable enough to denounce Wyatt for it. Why then did they collude in it?

While the interesting implications settle, he inquires into his putative motives for treason:

---

[17] Wyatt, 'Defence', in Muir, op cit. Because the argument is quite dense in places, I have made some small alterations to Muir's punctuation for the sake of clarity.

Ye bring in now that I should have intelligence with
Pole because of our opinions are like, and that I am
papist. I think I should have more ado with a great sort
in England to purge my self of suspect of [being] a
Lutheran, than... a papist.

This is masterful in its evasions. Wyatt knew better than to
disclose his religion in a law court, when three religious conservatives and three reformers had recently been executed, in
a display of Henrician even-handedness, on the same day. He
seems to have answered the charge, but all he has really done is
block it with an equal and opposing charge and vanish, with a
faint smoke of grievance left behind: a trick he perfected over
years of handling Petrarchan contraries, in the hard school of
lyric poetry. Nor is this the only place where Wyatt the orator
takes strength from Wyatt the sonneteer. He does it again at the
next serious point, his alleged crime against Henry under 'the
law of words'. Again he invokes the law itself; not to question
its excellence, but to examine how this law might be abused by
the *slipperiness of words themselves*. What *exactly* is he supposed to have said?

If [those who depose against me] misagree in words and
not in substance, let us hear the words they vary in. *For
in some little thing may appear the truth*, which I dare say
you seek for your conscience' sake. And besides ...*altering of one syllable, either with pen or word*... may make
in the conceiving of the truth much matter or error. For
[although] this change: '*I fear*', or '*I trust*', seemeth but
one small syllable changed... yet it maketh a great difference, and may be of an hearer wrong conceived and worse
reported, and yet worst, altered by an examiner. Again,
'*caste out*' or '*left out*' maketh the difference, yea, *and the
settings of words, one in an other's place, may make great*

difference, though the words were all one.[18] [Italics mine]

Here speaks the carefully correcting mind of the Egerton MS. Who knew more about the altering of one 'syllable' to change sense? Who knew more about setting words in one another's place to change their meaning? Words were never more 'all one' than the courtly poet's limited lexicon. But he, who had spent thousands of hours placing, discarding, exchanging and rearranging his little pouchful into ever more equivocal juxtapositions, understood their potential. 'I beseech you therefore,' he concluded, 'examine the matter under *this* sort.'

The Wyatt of the poems is still more evident when he comes to the circumstantial evidence. In addition to some slighting remarks about Wyatt's morals, Bonner had bulked out his principal charge with fragments of Wyatt's conversation, taken out of context, to adduce his generally treacherous attitude. They relied for their incriminating force entirely on the way they were interpreted. It was really a matter of tone; but, as Wyatt knew, it was no small matter to let the prosecution control the tone. Anne Boleyn had died for as much. Fortunately, he understood very well how this was done: he had played the conjuror's scarves – see! Now red, now green! now earnest, now joke! Now literal, now metaphor! Now me, now him! – in his own poems for years. He was on home ground here. He took control of the tone, and he did it in a very ingenious manner: though the remarks brought in evidence against him had been bleakly ironic, he now urged the jury to take his words literally. *Listen to the words.*

So: he was accused of 'grudging' his former imprisonment and complaining about it, and desiring to 'revenge' himself upon the king. He had said he 'wished the king had sent me to Newgate' rather than as an ambassador. Well? What of it? How

---

[18] all one: the same.

does that prove a malicious desire for revenge?

'Would he, that would revenge, wish him self in *Newgate*?...
A man would think rather [that] he, being an *Ambassador*,
might do more despite towards the king.' This was a dig at
Wriothesley, Bonner and Gardiner, all the king's eager ambassadors, as well as an irrefutable remark.

What else? It was alleged against him that he had said:

> God's blood! the king set me in the tower and afterward
> sent me for his ambassador. Was not this, I pray you, a
> pretty way to get me credit?

'As though,' said Wyatt with a wounded air, 'to say, I should
think, nay.' But of course it was an excellent way to get him
credit. What else would it be? 'Trowe ye that I should think it
was *not* a way to get me credit? It got me so much credit that
I am in debt, yet in debt for it,' he concluded with a graceful
joke.

What else? Bonner accused him of consorting with 'nuns' – a
sly insult, nicely combining papistry with whoring. Well? So he
had, he said, as though oblivious to the secondary meaning of
the word. The nuns in Barcelona were very nice gentlewomen,
thank you very much, and all the elegant people of the court
resorted to them. They rode out with them and went afterwards
to 'sit company together with them, talking in their chambers:
gentlemen of the Emperor's chamber – earls, lords, dukes, and
I among them. I used not the pastime in company of ruffians,
but with such [as they] or with the Ambassadors of Ferrara,
of Mantua, of Venice – a man of 60 years old – and such [like]
vicious company!'

With this, Bonner's accusations begin to look like spiteful
misrepresentations of a plain man's words, and a gentleman at
that. But Wyatt was saving the best till last. With this picture
of himself as decorum's *beau ideal* firmly fixed in the jurors'

minds, he turned his attentions to the contrasting case of 'the Right Reverend father in God, the Bishop of London', as he introduced him with sarcastic deference. Edmund Bonner's morals, manners, his vanity, his embarrassing and inappropriate courtly pretension now came under Wyatt's scrutiny. He would have been there, in the courtroom.

> I pray you now let me turn my tale to Bonner... for his crafty malice abuseth the other's simpleness. Come on now, my Lord, what is my abominable and vicious living? Do ye know it or have ye heard it? I graunte *I* do not profess chastity, but yet I use not abomination.

This last sentence must, I think, be read with a strong sardonic emphasis on the second of the three 'I's: *I* do not profess chastity. Wyatt is a gentleman, not a priest under (recently revived) laws of priestly celibacy. But Bonner, he's a priest. The court has already heard about Bonner's exorbitant requirements in the way of fine horses and fancy harness. Turning to address him in person, Wyatt recalls their evenings together in Nice:

> Did you ever see a woman so much as dine or sup at my table? None, but for *your* pleasure that woman that was in the galley, which I assure you may well be seen, because before you came neither she, nor any other came above the mast. But because the gentlemen took pleasure to see you entertain her, therefore they made her dine and sup with you, and they liked well your looks, your carving to the Madonna, your drinking to her, and your playing under the table. Ask Mason!... Ask Wolf, that was my steward. They can tell how the gentlemen marked it and talked of it. It was a play[19] to them, the keeping of your bottles that no man might drink of them but your self, and

---

[19] play: big joke

that the '*little fat priest was a jolly morsel for the signora*'.
This was their talk. It is not my devise. Ask other whether
I do lie. [Italics mine]

That would have brought the house down. Bonner could never
have recovered from it. Fortunately for him, he never had to
hear himself described like that in a courtroom. Nor did Wyatt
ever stand up in Westminster Hall and test the strength of his
arguments against the foregone conclusions of Tudor justice.
In the first place, there was no opportunity: as Powell observes,
'prepared speeches were [not] allowed in defence until the moment of contrition after conviction'. And in the second place,
there was no trial. For reasons we will come to in a moment,
Wyatt was suddenly released.

At once, his 'Defence' ceased to be a tool to save his life and
became an ornament of his reputation, something for admirers to keep copies of and, centuries later, for scholars to find
and puzzle over as one of the many mysteries that occlude the
historical Wyatt. When was it written? How could it name
people who were in the courtroom, if there had never been a
courtroom? How could it be a response to an indictment he had
never heard? And anyway, why did he bother if no one would
hear it? Powell has three suggestions: that he wanted it to be
'smuggled to individual jurors'; that he wrote it after his release, on a wave of indignation; or, that he really did compose it
in his dark prison, 'intending it for the trial and never realising
or forgetting the facts of the courtroom'.[20] To our frustration,
we will never know: the only record that might relate to it is
principally concerned with another imprisoned diplomat, the
erstwhile French ambassador, Sir John Wallop.

'He [Wallop] wrote a book of all these follies and offences
to be presented to the king and refused all trial, only yielding to
the king's mercy…Wyatt acted in the same way.'

[20] Powell, op.cit.

Wallop's and Wyatt's books of 'follies and offences' have never surfaced. This may be a reference to Wyatt's 'Defence' after a thorough churning in the diplomatic news channels, but it is not an obvious progression. In any case, the 'Defence' didn't save Wyatt's life. Poetry did.

CHAPTER TWENTY ONE

In this also see you be not idle: [1]
Thy niece, thy cousin, thy sister, or thy daughter,
If she be fair, if handsome be her middle,
If thy better hath her love besought her,
Advance his cause and he shall help thy need.

L ove returned to the English court in July 1541. As befits
history's most famous serial monogamist, the king had
chosen his fifth wife as a man seeking an antidote to his fourth.
Anne of Cleves had possessed 'a queenly manner withal', but
there was nothing queenly about Catherine Howard. She was the
daughter of Lord Edmund Howard, a dim and 'smally friended'
younger brother of the Duke of Norfolk, who had long failed
to prosper in the competitive arena of Henrician public life and
was miserably conscious of himself as a drag on the family trajectory. Now, just as fortune was about to amaze him by making
him the father of the Queen of England, he died, leaving his
brother *in loco parentis* of the perks.

Catherine had acquired her education in her grandmother's
household, variously established at Horsham in Sussex and
Lambeth on the south bank of the Thames in London. It was
not exactly the Burgundian Court. Along with linament and
jelly-making, the Dowager Duchess of Norfolk offered a little
music and handwriting, just enough for Catherine to snog the
music teacher, Manox, and master the notes of assignation

---

[1] Wyatt, CLI, in Rebholz, op. cit.

that led her to bed with a young gentleman of the household, Francis Dereham. Everyone in the maiden's chamber, where the girls slept, could hear the to-do behind Catherine's bed-curtains. 'Hark at Dereham, broken-winded,' joked the young people.

Catherine Howard (*Hans Holbein the Younger*)

Catherine came to court during Anne of Cleves' brief queen-hood. Her uncle Norfolk had seized the opportunity of there being, at last, a queen of sorts with vacancies for ladies, and found this very pretty niece a place in the queen's chamber. Soon after this, he took her to Stephen Gardiner's house when he knew the king was about to pay a visit, with his marrying mood unquenched.

Henry was by now very fat, very lame and very smelly from the suppurations issuing from his ulcerated leg. But he 'took an immediate fantaise' to Catherine; whereupon the family machine swung into action: Norfolk to press the imprisoned

Cromwell for a case against the Cleves marriage; the dowager duchess to install Catherine within easy reach of the king at her house in Lambeth and instruct her 'in what sort to entertain his highness, and how often'; and the entire Howard clan to chorus praise for her 'pure and honest condition'. If anyone thought to mention the business with Manox and Dereham (which was certainly known to the dowager) at this delicate early stage, they decided against.

The Howards had it in mind for Catherine to be a more biddable version of Anne Boleyn, and give them all a second go at the benefits rightfully accruing to the relatives of the queen. The evidence suggests that they got them. The king, indulging his manhood for the last time, adored his new little wife. He kissed her in public and covered her miniature person with gold and precious stones, while a crew of Howard relatives, operating her mouth from behind, made sure she worked more miracles for them than any of the jewelled effigies that awaited destruction at Cromwell's house in Chelsea. Lands and titles flowed out upon them. The court and the chamber duly filled up with religious conservatives and Howard allies. Even Lady Rochford, the banished widow of George Boleyn, was restored and installed as Catherine's intimate.

The queen begged Henry for favours, and also for clemency: she interceded for her cousin John Leigh, an ambassador suspected of treason, and for the hand of another cousin, Edmund Knyvet, just as the palace cook appointed to hack it off – as a punishment for brawling – was steadying his cleaver. All was granted.

This brings us back to Wyatt. In March 1541, just at the time he was in the Tower, there occurred a temporary suspension of these delights at court. The king was suffering, said the French ambassador, from a *'mal d'esprit'*, and he shut himself away and saw no one, not even Catherine. But as March wore on, he brightened enough to arrange for the new queen to be shown *'en*

Royne', for the first time, among pageantry and cannon-fire in a grand progress up the Thames. There was a tradition of this, which everyone by now was getting quite used to, and one of its customs offered a great opportunity to well-placed petitioners. Before the royal boat passed beneath the first bridge, the new queen was permitted to sue for favours, and let the king show her how love inclined him to clemency and 'steered him still towards gentleness', as Wyatt's *canzone* had it.[2] The pageant took place on March 19, 1541. Chapuys described the occasion:

> The king lately took his queen to Greenwich, and as it was the first time after her marriage that she had to pass through London by the Thames, the people of this city honoured her with a most pleasing reception, the Tower saluting her with salvoes of artillery. From this triumphal march the queen took occasion and courage to beg and entreat the king for the release of Maistre Huyet [Wyatt], a prisoner in the said tower, which petition the king granted.[3]

She pled for the conservative Wallop, and for Wyatt, listening to those salvoes from uncomfortably close quarters.

Henry did genuinely like Wyatt, in so far as he liked anyone, and was probably predisposed to listen to such a plea. All the same, it was Catherine's intercession that saved him. But why him? And who prompted her? Was she just being politically even-handed? It is sometimes thought that the idea of the courtier-poet caught her romantic fancy, but it is highly unlikely that the impulse came from Catherine herself. Apart from anything else, she could hardly have known him. Nor was he an obvious candidate for Howard sponsorship on account of his religious sentiments or birth: Howard blood circulated to him only

[2] Wyatt, LXXIII, in Rebholz, op. cit.
[3] Spanish Calendar, March 27, 1541, letter from Chapuys to the Queen of Hungary.

through his estranged wife, Elizabeth Brooke, who was any-way positioned in the calcified extremities of that system. The composition of the council who met on January 22 to review Bonner's letter included at least one ally – John Russell, the Lord Admiral, and at least one enemy – Wriothesley. We know there were others besides Wallop who wanted Wyatt dead, because Surrey refers to them in his epitaph. Indeed, to read Surrey on the subject you would think Wyatt had no friends beside himself.

'Divers thy death do diversely bemoan,' he begins; but goes on to reveal this supposed diversity of grief as merely a diversity of resentment:

> *Some, that in presence of thy livelyhead*[4]
> *Lurked, whose breasts envy with hate had sown,*
> *Yield Caesar's tears upon Pompeius head*
> *Some, that watchèd with the murderer's knife*
> *With eager thirst to drink thy guiltless blood,*
> *Whose practise brake by happy end of life,*
> *Weep envious tears to hear thy fame so good.*
> *But I, that know what harboured in that head*
> *What virtues rare were tempered in that breast,*
> *Honour the place that such a jewel bred*
> *And kiss the ground, whereas thy corse doth rest,*
> *With vapoured eyes…*

Surrey seems to have known a lot about Wyatt's adversity. Could he, the great admirer and promoter of Wyatt's poetry, have interceded with his father on Wyatt's behalf? He did intercede routinely in that quarter, and had a record of success. His excellent credit during these months of 1541 culminated with his receiving the garter in April; so it is fair to suppose that a favour placed through him with his cousin, Catherine, was

---

[4] Sonnet 29, *Surrey*, *Poems*, ed. Emrys Jones, 1964. (spelling modernised).

doubly acceptable to the king; and Wyatt doubly redeemed by poetry. First, through the king's weakness for the glow of courtly love, second, through his value to Surrey, as the originator of an English poetic achievement to which he, Surrey, was heir.

In support of this suggestion, we might look at the conversation that occurs between the lines above and some other lines of Wyatt's. Wyatt only wrote three lyrics about good fortune – it wasn't really his subject. One of them, which we have already seen in the context of Anne Boleyn, allows the source of redemption to hover between divine and human agency. It could now adapt gracefully to show gratitude to a kinsman of Anne's:

> *Whereto despaired ye, my friends?*
> *My trust alway in **him did lie***
> ***That knoweth what my thought intends,***
> *Whereby I live the most happy.*

In view of this, Surrey's claim to know what Wyatt's thought intended ('I, that know what harboured in that head'), set in a sonnet about Wyatt's thwarted enemies, may well be a way of alluding to his part in Wyatt's escape.

The timing was lucky for Wyatt. Eight months later, there would be no Queen Catherine Howard to plead for him. Her obliging way with the family promotions made enemies among individual refusés, and also with the evangelicals, who could see her only as a bridgehead for religious conservatism. These two elements fatally combined when she refused a request for placement to one of the Dowager Duchess of Norfolk's chamberers, Mary Lascelles. It may have influenced her decision that this Mary had often stolen the key to the (locked) Maidens' chamber, where Catherine had slept, and let in Dereham and his friends to 'banquet and be merry there till two or three o'clock in the morning'. If so, she took the wrong inference, because

Mary had a brother at court, one John Lascelles, a friend both of Cromwell and God's word. He was already looking for purchase against the Howards when the resentful Mary came to him with stories of high jinks in the dorm with Dereham and Manox.

It fell to Cranmer to tell the king and he, with customary boldness, put it in a letter and gave it to someone else to thrust at Henry during Mass. But Henry's 'affection was so marvellously set upon' Catherine that he dismissed it as a malicious rumour. Instead of prosecuting Catherine, he ordered an investigation into the perpetrators; and in the ensuing frantic scramble to prove her guilt, something much worse came out: she had been having a liaison with a young gentleman of the court, Thomas Culpeper, *since her marriage*. Even on the recent royal progress to the north, when the queen came back from her programme of fetes and pageants, she had secretly met Culpeper 'in the queen's stool chamber and other suspect places' by the contrivance, so the multitude of informers said, of the reinstated Lady Rochford. Now the king found himself playing poetry's least gratifying role: the old fool.

Henry wept and roared and blamed the council. Catherine blamed Lady Rochford and Culpeper; Culpeper blamed Lady Rochford and Catherine; Lady Rochford blamed Catherine and Culpeper. The Duke of Norfolk was beside himself with grievance, and urged Henry to burn his niece alive. He wrote to the king at length, deploring how

the most abominable deeds done by two of my nieces against your highness hath brought me into the greatest perplexity that ever poor wretch was in; fearing that your majesty, having so often, and by so many of my kin, been thus falsely and traitorously handled, might not only conceive a displeasure in your heart against me and all other of that kin, but also, in manner, abhor to hear speak of any the same.

Wherefore, most gracious sovereign lord, prostrate at your feet, most humbly I beseech Your majesty to call to your remembrance that a great part of this matter is come to light by my declaration to your majesty, according to my bounden duty, of the words spoken to me by my mother-in-law[5] when your highness sent me to Lambeth to search Dereham's coffers; without the which I think she had not been further examined, nor consequently her ungracious children.[6]

To spare the king the pain of listening to the charges, he was allowed to give assent *in absentia* to the bill condemning Manox, Dereham, Culpeper, Catherine and Lady Rochford to death, for high treason; the first two in what Catherine's biographer has called 'a total... disregard for the most basic... principles of justice',[7] for by no stretch of ingenuity could it be treasonable to have fumbled with Catherine before her marriage. Nor can it be certain that Catherine and Culpeper had committed any actual crime, except against basic intelligence. But all five were executed in February 1542 under the terms of a hasty new statute that made a royal wife's conduct the responsibility of her handlers. From now on, it would be a treasonable offence to conceal from the king the knowledge of any past or present 'will, act or condition of lightness of body in her which for the time being shall be queen of this realm', with the same penalties for withholders as for perpetrators.

The repercussions of this were swiftly acknowledged by all: as much by Norfolk's energetic assistance at his niece's inquisition, as by the actions of Jane Rochford's father, Lord Morley, who expressed his approval of Henry's justice by a more ingenious method, putting his famous humanist scholarship at

[5] mother-in-law: stepmother. Norfolk is referring to the dowager duchess.
[6] Letter from Norfolk to Henry, December 15, 1541.
[7] L.B. Smith, op. cit.

the service of his daughter's attainder. He translated a selection from Boccaccio's compendium of exemplary females, *De Claris Mulieribus*, with those stories left out in which fathers were found to blame for a daughter's misconduct, or disparaged for allowing their child to be sacrificed, or admired for showing sympathy for condemned offspring – and presented it to Henry in a splendid volume.[8] But perhaps the most eloquent demonstration of the statute's dampening effects on court life came in the belt-and-braces proposal of Catherine Parr as the king's next, and final, wife. The king would be her third husband.

But for Wyatt, the miracle had happened. Fate reversed and, as chiefly happens in dreams condemned men wake from, she retraced all the events that had sewn him into his doom, un-picking every stitch but one. The lock on his cell turned the other way, and the door opened on the white dazzle of a March morning. The king's seal flew off his cupboards. His confiscated goods, horses and valuables, already packaged, warehoused and assigned to deserving petitioners, slipped from the grasp of whomever was expecting them, back onto the carts, back down the river to Allington. His servants followed, then he, with his fugitive lands and offices restored, reappeared at his own fireside in his silvery castle in Kent.

There is a picture of him at home in Allington. It comes to us in an epistolary satire he adapted from the exiled Italian poet, Alamanni, and addressed to his friend, John Poyntz. After some 80 lines of invective directed at the hypocrisy and tyranny of court life (but sheltered by the undeniable fact that the satire was extant and written in very choice Italian), it ends with an invitation to stay. Wyatt's significant additions to the last passage are in bold:

This maketh me at home to hunt and to hawk[9]

[8] See James Simpson, 'The Sacrifice of Lady Rochford' in *Triumphs of English: Henry Parker, Lord Morley*. ed. Axton and Carley. (British Library, 2000).
[9] Wyatt, 1st Satire, CXLIX, in Rebholz, op. cit.

And in foul weather at my book to sit;
In frost and snow then with my bow to stalk.
No man doth mark whereso I ride or go;
In lusty leas in liberty I walk.
And of these news I feel nor weal nor woe,
Save that a clog doth hang yet at my heel.
No force for that, for it is ordered so
That I may leap both hedge and dike full well.
I am not now in France to judge the wine,
With savoury sauce the delicates to feel;
Nor yet in Spain where one must him incline,
Rather than to be, outwardly to seem.
I meddle not with wits that be so fine.
*Nor **Flanders'** cheer letteth not my sight to deem*
Of black and white nor taketh my wit away
With beastliness they, beasts, do so esteem.
Nor I am not where Christ is given in prey
For money, poison, and treason at Rome -
A common practice used night and day.
But here I am in Kent and Christendom
Among the muses where I read and rhyme,
Where if thou list, my Poyntz, for to come,
Thou shalt be judge how I do spend my time.

Wyatt's first editor, Nott, thought he wrote this in 1541, but everyone since has dated it to the months after his first imprisonment in May 1536, when he was supposedly rusticated to Allington Castle and told to mend his ways. It is thought that the 'clog at my heel' – a term for a gaoler's block on the leg – alludes to some kind of imposed restriction on his movements. Recent analysis of the ink, paper and scribal hands used in the poem's various transcriptions has corroborated the 1536 date. If this is now indisputable – and to ink analysis, reader, who says nay? – it shows that Wyatt achieved in this

quite specific utterance the same flexuous capacity to accommodate, or even predict, events in his future that we see in his
most slyly generalising lyrics. Like a sitter 'growing into' the
face on his portrait, Wyatt's life and circumstances grew into
the First Satire, as this poem is known, so that by the closing
months of 1541, it was a perfect fit. Henry was more tyrannical
then, his courtiers more acquiescent. In 1541 England had been
an 'empire' for nine years, not three, enough for England's religious and cultural isolation to grow a skin, and its inhabitants
to distil the beginnings of emancipated self-reliance, as reflected
here in Wyatt's formulation of country life: one that looks, not
just back to classical precedents, but forward, to the high water
of the Anglican gentry. Kent and Christendom, proverbially inimical, have reconciled under the supremacy. Abroad is bloody;

John Poyntz (*Hans Holbein the Younger*)

and an English gentleman living on his rents, with books in his library, livings in his pocket and game in his coverts is the pinnacle of God's creation. Through the grassy gloaming comes the shadow of Mr Knightley, strolling home to Donwell Abbey.

Even the details of this poem fit better with Wyatt's life in 1541. If the letter was written in the summer of 1536, why has Wyatt put 'frost and snow' outside? That autumn Wyatt was back in the king's good graces with a brand new sheriffdom of Kent and with no 'clog' at his heel, then or thereafter. Then there are Wyatt's alterations to Alamanni's catalogue of vicious foreign countries. He changed the source so that the list mirrored his own diplomatic postings up to 1541 (including those *after* 1536). Alamanni's 'Germania' (Germany, where he had not been) is changed to 'Flanders' (where he had been, but not until 1540). There is no discernible reason for the change except the personal significance that was lacking in 1536.[10] As for the clog, the terms of his freedom were far more onerous in 1541 than in 1536. When Wyatt walked out of the Tower in March, one thing was not restored to him. He received his pardon upon what the foreign ambassadors thought 'rather hard conditions': namely:

> that the said Wyatt should confess the guilt for which he had been arrested; and secondly that he was to resume conjugal relations with his wife, from whom he had been separated for upwards of 15 years. Wyatt had cast her away on account of adultery, and had not seen her for many years; he will now be obliged to receive her, and should he not do so, and not lead a conjugal life with her, or should he be found to keep up criminal relations, even with the two other ladies that he has since loved, he is to

[10] A note on the translation of place names from the Italian: 'Germany' and 'Flanders' were sometimes used interchangeably in both English and Italian. However, 'Germania' was most commonly rendered as 'Germany'. Likewise, the usual Italian word for 'Flanders' was 'Fiandra'. I am grateful to Professor David Ekserdjian for clarification on this point.

suffer pain of death and confiscation of property.[11]

No one knows who the other lady – if she is not an example of diplomatic misinformation, perhaps deriving from the presence of Lady Poynings, his friend's wife, at Allington Castle– might be. It could refer to some attachment of 15 years before. In any case, she now became a clause in one of the most extraordinary stipulations in Tudor legal history. The shires were full of men living in open adultery, and whereas there were occasional drives to shoo out the concubines and put the discarded wives back in, there was nothing amounting to a capital threat.[12] Wyatt's condition is the only example of its kind in his time.

> *Such hap as I am happed in*
> *Hath never man of truth, I ween.*
> *In me fortune list to begin*
> *To shew that never hath been seen*
> *A new kind of unhappiness.*

The genesis of this extraordinary verdict is impossible to discover. It may have originated with the Howards, enlisting the king – momentarily flush with priggish uxoriousness – in a scheme to get their client and kinswoman back onto Wyatt's balance sheet. Whatever the cause, when viewed in the context of Wyatt's life and work, it has an aptness bordering on the sublime. Here is a penalty that seems to have escaped from the world of romance into the practical penal code of Tudor England. That Wyatt alone – a man whose whole creative life was spent in the intertidal strand where *realpolitik* and poetry mingle – should be the one to incur it, is an instance of poetic justice that takes

[11] Spanish Calendar, March 27, 1541, letter from Chapuys to the Queen of Hungary.
[12] For instance: August 22, 1536: a commissioner for the dissolution of the monasteries reports to Cromwell that knights and gentleman in Cheshire, Coventry, Stafford and Derby were 'living openly with their concubines'. He has 'sent commandment to them...to put from them immediately such concubines as they have hitherto notoriously and manifestly kept, and take again their wives'.

some beating. These terms condemned him to live out the conundrums of his own riddles:

> Like as the bird in the cage enclosed[13]
> The door unsparred[14] and the hawk without,
> 'Twixt death and prison piteously oppressed,
> Whether for to choose standeth in doubt -
> Certes, so do I, which do seek to bring about
> Which should be best by determination,
> By loss of life liberty, or life by prison.

The question for his own case would now be: is it better to live 'imprisoned in liberties' or to be done with it altogether?

The thought of Wyatt in this intolerable predicament, forced to live with a woman he hated and apart from the one he loved, has led some readers to speculate that he faked his own death, after making a will bequeathing lands around Montacute, in the West Country, to Elizabeth Darrell. But there is nothing in Wyatt's story to suggest he would so disgust his father's ghost, as to undo 50 years of Wyatt graft for the sake of a submerged life in Somerset with a woman of modest means. Besides, Besse married after his death. The bequest was intended to look after her, to make her a marriageable prospect without him, and to leave something for their son, Henry (aka Francis) who was born in the spring or early summer of 1541.

Aside from the business with his wife, everything was going well for him.

> In faith I not well what to say[15]
> The chances been so wondrous,
> Thou fortune, with thy diverse play
> That causeth joy full dolourous

---

[13] Wyatt, XC, in Rebholz, op. cit.
[14] unsparred: unlocked.
[15] Wyatt, LXXXVI, in Rebholz, op. cit.

And eke the same right joyous.
Yet though thy chain hath me enwrapped,
Spite of thy hap, hap hath well happed.

Once again, his disgrace was a springboard for promotion. Catherine's life had given him life, her death brought him lands from her attainted lover, the unhappy Thomas Culpeper. The following year, when the king went back to warring with France, Wyatt was lined up for vice-admiralty of the English fleet, under Russell, with captaincy of a dozen vessels. He became a subject for encomia:

Renowned commander of the nereids[16]
Renowned commander of the Peirids
The Darling of Mars and our age.

and a useful person for entertaining Spanish dignitaries, as negotations for Spanish cooperation were now once more afoot. At the end of September, an unexpectedly prompt Spanish envoy landed at Falmouth, needing an escort to London. Wyatt was sent to collect him. His friend, John Mason, later reported that he had ridden hard for Falmouth, changing horses frequently, 'having more regard for the royal mandate than his health'. Mason omitted to mention the other incentive for speed, though he must have known it: the road to Falmouth ran near the Somerset-Dorset border, almost directly through the little town of Montacute, where Besse Darrell and her baby son were now quietly installed.

According to Mason, this immense exertion, combined with 'extreme heat of the sun' (an uncommon feature of an English October) made Wyatt fall sick on the journey. He was 39 and his health had been on the slide for some time. His headaches in France had sometimes been so bad he could

---

[16] Leland, *Cygnea Cantio,* in Muir, op. cit.

hardly hold his pen, and in prison he had succumbed to the now-extinct febrile disorder which struck Tudor Englishmen on alternate days: a 'secondary ague'. Now, on the road to Falmouth, 'black pestilence on him took hold'. He was 'seized with a most violent fever' and collapsed at Clifton Maubank, the house of his friend, Sir John Horsey, at Sherborne – just a few miles east of Montacute and Besse Darrell.

He lay at Sherborne for three days, dying. Perhaps they sent for Besse and she came to him, to comfort him as he died. We must hope so.

*   *   *   *

Wyatt did not return to Allington. He is thought to have become the first tenant of a family vault which Horsey was preparing for himself at the great church in Sherborne. As for his reputation, Henry Howard, Earl of Surrey, came forward to claim it the moment he died. He wrote several elegiac poems hinting broadly at foul play during Wyatt's lifetime, and positioning himself as Wyatt's artistic heir. Others enlisted behind him to produce memorials in prose and verse. Wyatt's old friend John Leland composed extensive Latin verses, remarkable for providing the least information about their subject over the longest possible stretch, and dedicated them to Surrey with words designed to please:

> Accept, Illustrious Earl, this mournful song
> Wherein I praised your Wyatt, whom in brief space
> Death brought beneath the earth. He greatly loved
> Your name. You revered him while he was alive,
> And since his death have given him due praise
> In such a song as Chaucer had approved
> As sweet, and worthy of his mother-tongue.

Their names have been linked ever since, as the joint fathers of English lyric verse.

When the first printed anthology of lyric verse appeared in 1557, the illustrious earl had eclipsed 'depe-witted' Wyatt and received top billing, but the two of them were the only authors with a substantial body of ascribed work. The collection was Tottel's *Songs and Sonnetts*, a famous book,[17] many times reprinted in Elizabeth's reign and popular as a courtship manual among members of the growing 'middle' class – the mercantile families and minor gentry who were the ultimate inheritors of the broken-up monastic lands. For the profit of these, the 'studious of English eloquence', the printer Richard Tottel wrestled Wyatt's lyrics from the 'ungentle hoarders of such treasures' and nailed their slypper riches with a sixpenny nail. They were read by people for whom they were never intended. They went back to being inert.

Tottel trimmed their errant metres and arranged them under explanatory headings: 'The Lover complaineth himself forsaken'. 'The Lover hopeth of better chance.' Now a novice in the field of love could advance his selection with confidence, bucked by editorial authority. Now a poem like 'Accused though I be without desert', with its manifold allusive possibilities, was fixed forever as 'The Lover suspected of change prayeth that it be not believed against him'.

It was a conscious act of populism on Tottel's part, and its appearance marked a sea-change in lyric poetry, into something open-facing, excursive, accessible and gregarious. Print culture took lyric poetry into the provinces and small towns, where it was eagerly received. Merchants' wives served fruit on plates with little verses on the undersides. At the end of the meal you turned the plate over and read off the lines to your neighbour. Music-masters were a growing sector, as quite modest domestic establishments felt the sudden lack of them. The epigram went

[17] Sometimes known as *Tottel's Miscellany*.

public. Now it was a thing written

> upon the wall or mantel of a chimney in some place of
> common resort, *where it was allowed that every man*
> *might come*, or be fitting to chat and prate, as now in our
> tavernes and common tabling houses, where many merry
> heads meet, and scribble with ink and chalk, or with a
> coal such *matters as they would every man should know,*
> *and descant upon.*

With a woman on the throne, the correspondence between the courtly lady and the sovereign – ultimate source of all benefaction and all deprivations – turned explicit and overt. The smart courtier saw that this was something to emphasise, not conceal. The queen's red hair and black eyes called Petrarch's Laura to mind. All Elizabethan courtly lyrics doffed their caps to the queen.

Inevitably, the elite decamped. Wyatt and Surrey got honourable mentions as 'first reformers of our English metre and style', in Puttenham's overview of English poetry, *The Arte of English Poesie* of 1589, but they were by then of largely antiquarian interest. By the last decades of the 16th century, the new world and everything in it was pouring into the language. Wyatt's lexicon seemed porridge-plain, its sentiments bathetic, its metaphors quaint. Worse than this, it had ceased to be prestigious. Wyatt's lyrics had always measured their depth in the intelligence – in every sense – of their reader; now they would be read by the inerudite and clueless. At the further reaches of Tottel's poetic diaspora were dim squires and puffed-up functionaries, whose courtship practices – Tottel firmly in hand – were hilarious to a new generation of bright young sophisticates. The *Songs and Sonnetts* became an iconographic attribute for Squire Slackwit. Malvolio, Shakespeare's most ludicrous lover, has a poem of Wyatt's about him. In *The Merry Wives of Windsor*,

Abraham Slender need only declare 'I would rather than forty shillings I had my Book of Songs and Sonnets here' to establish his credentials as a dullard.

Wyatt's genius was incompatible with print culture. The manuscripts went their separate ways, the connections went dead, and the lights that had winked a private semaphore from poem to poem went out. Within a generation, what once had been safe conduct for secret thoughts became a byword for the simple-minded and declamatory. For a long, long time, no one could see what earthly thing Sir Thomas Wyatt had done to be called 'depe-witted'. We are only beginning to see it now.

Whoso list to hunt, I know where is an hind,
But as for me, helas, I may no more.
The vain travail hath wearied me so sore,
I am of them that farthest cometh behind.
Yet may I by no means my wearied mind
Draw from the deer, but as she fleeth afore
Fainting I follow. I leave off therefore
Sithens in a net I seek to hold the wind.
Who list her hunt, I put him out of doubt,
As well as I may spend his time in vain.
And GRAVEN WITH DIAMONDS in letters plain
There is written her fair neck round about:
Noli me tangere for Caesar's I am
And wild for to hold though I seem tame.

Picture credits:

ACKNOWLEDGEMENTS

I would like to thank the many kind people who have helped me with this book. I have been very fortunate in my agent, Peter Straus, who encouraged the project, and in my perceptive and diligent editor, Aurea Carpenter. The York Herald, Mr Henry Bedingfield; Dr. Susan Foister, Dr. Jason Powell, Dr. Chris Stamatakis, Professor David Ekserdjian, Dr Lesley Miller, Dr Geoffrey Parnell, Mr Matthew Connolly, Mr Tommaso Corvi-Mora, and Sir John Guinness, have all been very generous with their help and advice. Katherine Sanderson was a most helpful and efficient picture researcher. Thank you to the tireless and ingenious staff at the Bodleian Library, The British Library and, especially, those at the London Library who often had to walk me to my request. Thanks also to Field Marshall The Lord Inge and Major-General Keith Cima for enabling me to visit the Bell Tower, and to Sir Robert and Lady Worcester for their warm hospitality at Allington Castle.

I would like to acknowledge the great debt I owe to Dr Susan Brigden for her friendship, grace and tact as well as for her inestimable assistance.

I am most grateful to Dr Colin Burrow and Dr Suzannah Lipscomb for reading the manuscript for blunders and inaccuracies, and for offering advice. All the remaining errors are my own, as are the readings of the poems.

Thank you to my husband, Con, for putting up with a lot of plaining; and to Pandora, Sibylla, John and Tom, Alex, Jason and Drusilla for the same.

I owe my interest in early modern poetry to Miss Janet Gough, to whom this book is dedicated as a way of saying - thank you.

BIBLIOGRAPHY: SECONDARY SOURCES

Ackroyd, Peter, *The Life of Thomas More*. Chatto and Windus, 1998.

Anglo, Sydney, The Court Festivals of Henry VII: A study based on the account books of John Heron, Treasurer of the Chamber. Manchester University Press, 1960.

Anglo, Sydney, *The London Pageants for the reception of Catherine of Aragon*, Journal of the Warburg and Courtauld Institutes, 26.

Aston, Margaret. *England's Iconoclasts*. Clarendon, Oxford 1988

ed. Medcalf, S., *The Later Middle ages*, (Methuen 1981)

Axton, Marie, and Carley, James P. (eds.), *'Triumphs of English': Henry Parker, Lord Morley, Translator to the Tudor Court*. British Library, 2000.

Baldi, Sergio, *Thomas Wyatt: Writers and Their Work*. Longman, Green & Co., 1971.

Baron, Helen, 'The "Blage" Manuscript: the Original Compiler Identified', *Review of English Studies, new series*, 45 (1994).

Baron, Helen, 'Mary (Howard) Fitzroy's Hand in the Devonshire MS', *Review of English Studies*, new series, 45 (1994).

Bellewes , G.O., Archeologica Cantiana; Rev. S.W. Wheatley, Vol XLI, 1929, p 132.

Bellewes, G.O., Archeeologica Cantiana; The Cobhams and Moresbys of Rundale and Allington, Vol XXIX.

Bennett, H.S., *Chaucer and Fifteenth Century Verse and Prose*, Clarendon Press, 1990.

Bennett, H.S., *English Books and Readers 1475-1557*. Cambridge University Press, 1952.

Bennett, H.S., *English Books and Readers 1475-1557*: Being a Study in the History of the Book Trade from Caxton to the incorporation of the Stationers' company. Cambridge University Press, 1952.

Bernard, G., *Anne Boleyn, Fatal Attractions*. Yale, 2010.

Bernard, G., *The King's Reformation: Henry VIII and the Making of the English Church*. Yale, 2005.

Blockmans, Wim: *Emperor Charles V 1500-1558*. Hodder Arnold, 2001.

Boffey, Julia, *Manuscripts of English Courtly Love Lyrics in the Later Middle Ages*. D.S. Brewer, 1985.

Bohn H.G., Plan and Details of the Architecture of Allington Castle and Church with ten etchings: *Carter's Ancient Architecture*, 1845.

Bradford, William, M.A, ed. *'Correspondence of the Emperor Charles V and his ambassadors at the Courts of England and France*, from the original letters in the Imperial family Archive at Vienna; with a connecting narrative and biographical notices of the Emperor... together with the Emperor's Itinerary from 1519-1551'. Bentley, 1850.

Brigden, S, Thomas Wyatt in Italy, *Renaissance Quarterly* 58 (2005) p 464-511.

Brigden, S., 'The Shadow that You Know. Sir Thomas Wyatt and Sir Francis Bryan at Court and in Embassy'. *The Historical Journal*, Cambridge University Press, 1996.

Brigden, S., *New Worlds, Lost Worlds: The Rule of The Tudors 1485-1603*. Allen Lane, The Penguin Press, 2000.

Brigden, S., *London and The Reformation*. Clarendon, 1989.

Buck, Stephanie and Sander, Jochen. *Hans Holbein the Younger, Painter at the court of Henry VIII*. Essays to accompany the exhibition at the Hague in 2003. Thames and Hudson, 2003.

Burke, P., *The Renaissance Sense of the Past*. E. Arnold, 1969.

Burnet, Gilbert, *History of the Reformation of the Church of England*. Ed. Pocock, 1865.

Burrow, Colin, 'Horace at Home', in Charles Martindale and David Hopkins (eds.), *Horace Made New: Horatian Influences on British Writing from the Renaissance to the Twentieth Century* (Cambridge: Cambridge University Press, 2009).

Burrow, Colin, 'The Experience of Exclusion: Literature and Politics in the Reigns of Henry VII and Henry VIII', in David Wallace (ed.), *The Cambridge History of Medieval English Literature*. Cambridge University Press, 1999.

Burrow, Colin, 'The Reformation of the Household', in James Simpson and Brian Cummings (eds.), *Cultural Reformations: Medieval and Renaissance in Literary History*. Oxford University Press, 2010.

Byles, Alfred T.P., ed., The Book of the Ordre of Chyualry, translated and printed by William Caxton. Early English Text Soc., London 1926.

Campbell, Thomas P., *Henry VIII and the Art of Majesty*. Yale, 2007

Carley, James P., *The Books of King Henry VIII and His Wives* British Library, 2004.

Carlson, D., King Arthur and Court Poems for the Birth of Arthur Tudor in 1486. Humanistica Lovaniensia, 36, 1987.

Chambers, Edmund Kerchever, *Sir Thomas Wyatt and Some Collected Studies* (London: Sidgwick & Jackson, 1933).

Ed. Chambers and Pullan, *Documentary History of Venice 1450-1630*. Oxford, Blackwell.

Chappell, Willliam, 'Some account of an unpublished collection of songs and ballads by king Henry VIII and his contemporaries', *Archaeologia*, 41, (1867).

Childs, Jessie, *Henry VIII's Last Victim. The Life and Times of Henry Howard, Earl of Surrey*. Jonathan Cape, 2006.

Coleman, Christopher & Starkey, David (editors), *Revolution Reassessed: Revisions in the History of Tudor Government & Administration*, Oxford University Press, 1986.

Coss, Peter, *The Lady in Medieval England, 1000- 1500*, Stroud, 1998.

Court Festivals of Henry VII: A study based on the account books of John Heron, Treasurer of the Chamber. John Rylands Library, Manchester University Press, 1960.

Cressy, David, *Literature and the Social Order: Reading and Writing in Tudor and Stuart England*. Cambridge University Press, 1980.

Cummings, Brian, *The Literary Culture of the Reformation: Grammar and Grace* Oxford: Oxford University Press, 2002.

Daalder, Joost, 'Are Wyatt's poems in Egerton 2711 in Chronological Order?' *English Studies*, 69, ii June 1988.

De Cossart, Michael, *This Little World: Renaissance Italians' View of English Society*. Liverpool, Janus, 1984.

De Cossart, Michael, *This Sceptred Isle: Renaissance Italians' View of English Society*. Liverpool, Janus, 1984.

Deitz, F.C. *English Government finance 1485-1558*. University of Illinois, Studies in Social Science, Vol 9, No. 3.

A.G. Dickens, ed., *The Courts of Europe: Politics, Patronage and Betrayal 1440-1800*. Thames and Hudson, 1977.

Dodds, M.H. and R., *The Pilgrimage of Grace and the Exeter Conspiracy*. Cambridge, 1915.

Duffy, Eamon, *The Stripping of The Altars: Traditional Religion in England 1400-1580*. Yale University Press, 1992.

Elton, GR. *England Under the Tudors*. Methuen, London, 1955.

Elton, G. R. *The Tudor Revolution in Government: Administrative changes in the reign of Henry VIII*. Cambridge University Press, 1953.

Elton G.R., Thomas Cromwell's Decline and Fall, Cambridge Hist. Journal x (1951).

Fehrenbach, Robert J., and Leedham-Green, Elisabeth S. (eds.), *Private Libraries in Renaissance England: A Collection and Catalogue of Tudor and Early Stuart Book-Lists*, 6 vols to date (Binghamton, NY and Tempe, AZ: Medieval and Renaissance Texts and Studies; Arizona Center for Medieval and Renaissance Studies, 1992–2004).

Ferguson, A., *The Indian Summer of English Chivalry*. Durham, N. Carolina, 1960.

Finlay, Robert, *Politics in Renaissance Venice 1450-1630*. E. Benn, 1980.

Fisher, H.A.L, *The History of England, 1485-1547*, Vol V of The Political History of England in 12 volumes, ed. William Hunt and Reginald L. Poole, 1910.

Fisher, T., Account of Allington Castle, and its Successive Owners, by, with a plate. *Gentleman's magazine*. March 1811.

Fletcher, A and MacCulloch, D., *Tudor Rebellions*. Longman, 2008.

Foister, Susan, *Holbein and England*, Published for Paul Mellon Centre for Studies in Art, Yale, 2004.

Forster, Leonard Wilson, *The Icy Fire: Five Studies in European Petrarchism* Cambridge University Press, 1969.

Fraser, Antonia, *The Six Wives of Henry VIII*. Weidenfeld and Nicholson, 1992.

Freeman, Arthur, 'To guard his words, the ... nature of a bible designed by Henry VIII', *Times Literary Supplement*, December 14, 2007.

Friedmann, P., *Anne Boleyn*. Macmillan, 1884.

Froude, James Anthony, *Henry VIII*. London 1913.

Furley, L.P., *A History of the Weald of Kent*. Ashford, 1874.

Greenblatt, Stephen, *Renaissance Self-Fashioning from More to Shakespeare*. University of Chicago Press, 1980.

Grammitt, David Ian, *Calais 1485-1547*.

Gransden, Antonia, *Historical Writing in England from 1300 to the Early 16th Century*, in 2 vols. Routledge Kegan & Paul, 1982.

Griffin, Emma, *Blood Sport: Hunting in Britain since 1066*. Yale, 2007.

Grosvenor, B. ed. *Lost Faces, Identity and Discovery in Tudor Royal Portraiture*. Philip Mould, 2007.

Guy, John, ed., *The Tudor Monarchy*. Arnold, 1997.

Guy, John. *Kent Castles*. Meresborough Books, 1980.

Gunn, S. J. Charles Brandon, Duke of Suffolk, 1484-1545. Oxford, Blackwell, 1988.

Gwyn, Peter, *The Kings' Cardinal: The Rise and Fall of Thomas Wolsey*. Barrie and Jenkins, 1990.

Haile, Martin, *Life of Reginald Pole*, Sir Isaac Pitman &Sons, 1911.

Harris, Barbara J., The View from my Lady's Chamber: New Perspectives on the Early Tudor Monarchy. *Huntingdon Library Quarterly*, Vol 60, No. 3, 1997.

Harris, Nicholas, ed., *Privy Purse Expenses of Henry VIII, 1529-30, MDCCCXXVII*. London, 1827.

Hawes, Stephen, *The Pastime of Pleasure: an Allegorical Poem*, ed. William Edward Mead (Oxford: Early English Text Society, 1927).

Hayward, Maria, *Dress at The Court of King Henry VIII: The Wardrobe Book of the Wardrobe of the Robes*. Leeds, Maney, 2007.

Heale, Elizabeth, 'Women and the Courtly Love Lyric: The Devonshire MS (BL additional 17492)', *Modern Language Review*, 90, ii (April 1995).

Heale, Elizabeth, *Wyatt, Surrey and Early Tudor Poetry*. Longman, 1997.

Henry VIII's Library and Humanist Donors. *In Reassessing Tudor Humanism*, ed. Jonathan Woolfson. Palgrave Macmillan, 2002.

Hutchinson, R., *The Last Days of Henry VIII: Conspiracy, Treason and Heresy at the court of Henry VIII*. Weidenfeld and Nicholson, Robert Hutchinson, 2005.

Ives, Eric, *The Queen and the Painters. Anne Boleyn, Holbein and Tudor Royal Portraits*, Apollo Magazine CXL, 1994.

Ives, Eric, *The Life and Death of Anne Boleyn*, Oxford, Blackwell, 2004.

Keay, Anna. The Elizabethan Tower of London. The Haiward and Gascoyne plan of 1597. London topographical Society, 2001.

Knecht, R.J., *Renaissance Warrior and Patron: the Reign of Francis I*. Cambridge, 1994.

Knowles, David, *The Religious Orders of England*, Vol 3: Cambridge University Press, 1948-1959.

Lerer, Seth, *Courtly Letters in the Age of Henry VIII: Literary Culture and the Arts of Deceit*. Cambridge: Cambridge University Press, 1997.

Lewis, Clive Staples, *The Allegory of Love: a Study in Medieval Tradition*. Oxford, Clarendon Press, 1936.

Lewis, Clive Staples, *The Discarded Image: an Introduction to Medieval and Renaissance Literature*. Cambridge University Press, 1964.

Lewis, Clive Staples, *Poetry and Prose in the Sixteenth Century*, new ed. Oxford: Clarendon Press, 1990.

Lipscomb, Suzannah, *1536: The Year that changed Henry VIII*. Lion Hudson, 2009.

Loades, D.M., *John Dudley, Duke of Northumberland*. Clarendon Press, 1996.

Loades, D.M., *Mary Tudor, A Life*. Oxford, Blackwell, 1989.

MacCulloch, Diarmaid. *Reformation: Europe's House Divided. 1400-1700*. Allen Lane, 2003.

Maltby, William, *The Reign of Charles V*. Palgrave, New York, 2002.

Marotti, Arthur F., *Manuscript, Print and the English Renaissance Lyric*. Ithaca, NY: Cornell University Press, 1995.

Marshall, P., 'The Rood of Boxley, the blood of Hailes and the defence of the Henrician church.' Journal of Ecclesiastical History, xlvi, 1995.

Mason, Harold Andrew, 'Editing Wyatt: an Examination of the Collected Poems of Sir Thomas Wyatt', *Cambridge Quarterly*, 5, iv, 1971.

Mason, Harold Andrew, *Humanism and Poetry in the Early Tudor Period: an Essay*,. Routledge & Kegan Paul, 1959.

Mattingly, G., *Catherine of Aragon*. Jonathan Cape, 1950.

Mattingly, G., *Renaissance Diplomacy*. Jonathan Cape, 1955.

Mayer, Thomas, *Reginald Pole: Prince and Prophet*. Cambridge University Press, 2000.

Merriman, Roger Bigelow, *Life and Letters of Thomas Cromwell*. Oxford University Press, 1902.

Partridge, Eric, *Shakespeare's Bawdy*. London: Routledge, 2001.

A Perambulation of Kent, conteining the description, Hystorie, and Customes of that Shyre, collected and written (for the most part) in the year 1570, by William Lambard of Lincoln's Inn, Gent. Imprinted at London, for Ralph Newberie, Anno 1576.

Richardson, Glenn, *Renaissance Monarchy: the Reigns of Henry VIII, Francis I and Charles V*. Arnold, 2002.

Russell, Jocelyne G., *The Field of Cloth of Gold*. Routledge & Kegan Paul, 1969.

Ridley, Jasper, *The Tudor Age*. Constable, 1988.

Saintsbury, George, *The Earlier Renaissance*. Blackwood & Sons, 1901.

Saintsbury, George, *History of English Prosody from the Twelfth Century to the Present Day*, London: Macmillan, 1923.

Scarisbrick J.J. 'The First Englishman Round the Cape of Good Hope?' *Bulletin of the Institute of Historical Research*.(BIHR) xxxiv, 1961.

Scarisbrick, J.J., *Henry VIII*. Yale, 1997.

Scott-Warren, Jason, *Sir John Harington and the Book as Gift*. Oxford University Press, 2001.

Sessions, William A., 'Surrey's Wyatt: Autumn 1542 and the New Poet', in Peter C. Herman (ed.), *Rethinking the Henrician Era: Essays on Early Tudor Texts and Contexts*, ed. (Champaign, Ill.: University of Illinois Press, 1994).

Siemens, R.G., 'New Evidence on Wyatt's "A Robyn"' in British Library Additional MS 31, 992. Notes and Queries no. 46, XLVI.

Simonds, William Edward, *Sir Thomas Wyatt and His Poems*. Boston, Mass.: Heath & Co., 1889.

Sir Thomas Wyatt and 'Sephame" Notes and Queries CXCVII, June 1952 .

Skelton, John, *The Complete Poems of John Skelton*, Laureate ed. Philip Henderson. London: Dent, 1931.

Smith L.B., *A Tudor tragedy. The Life and Times of Catherine Howard*.
Jonathan Cape, 1961.

Somerset, Anne, *Elizabeth I*. Weidenfeld and Nicholson, 1991.

Southall, Raymond, *The Courtly Maker: An Essay on the Poetry of Wyatt and His Contemporaries*. Oxford: Blackwell, 1964.

Southall, Raymond, 'The Devonshire Manuscript Collection of Early Tudor Poetry, 1532–41', *Review of English Studies*, 15 (1964).

Southall, Raymond, 'Ye Olde Mule', in *English Language Notes* (September 1967).

Stamatakis, Chris, 'Turning the Word: Sir Thomas Wyatt and Early Tudor Literary Practice', D.Phil thesis (Oxford University, 2008).

Stanford E. Lehmberg, *Sir Thomas Elyot, Tudor Humanist*. Austin, Texas, 1960.

Starkey, David, The Court: Castiglione's Ideal and Tudor Reality: Being a discussion of Sir Thomas Wyatt's 'Satire addressed to Sir Francis Bryan'.
Journal of the Warburg and Courtauld Institutes, 45, (1982).

Starkey, David. *The Reign of Henry VIII: Personalities and Politics*, Vintage, 2002.

Starkey, David, ed: *Henry VIII: A European Court in England*, Exhibition catalogue, National Maritime Museum, London 1991

Starkey, David, ed., *The Inventory of King Henry VIII*, I: The Transcript, London, 1998

Starkey, David, *Henry, Virtuous Prince*. HarperPress, 2008

Starkey, David, *Six Wives: The Queens of Henry VIII*. Chatto and Windus, 2003.

Starkey, David & Doran, Susan, ed., *Henry VIII, Man and Monarch*.
London, British Library, 2009.

Stevens, John E., *Music and Poetry in the Early Tudor Court*. Methuen, 1961.

Strong, Roy, *The Cult of Elizabeth: Elizabethan Portraiture and Pageantry*.
Thames and Hudson, 1977.

Thirsk, Joan. *Food in Early Modern England: phases, fads and fashions*.
Hambledon Continuum, 2007.

Thirsk, Joan, *Horses in Early Modern England: For pleasure, for Service, for Power*. Reading, 1978.

Thomas, Keith, 'The Place of Laughter in Tudor and Stuart England', *Times Literary Supplement*, 21 January, 1977.

Thompson, F.M.L., ed., *Horses in European History*. British Agricultural History Society, 1983.

Thomson, Patricia, *Sir Thomas Wyatt and His Background*. Palo Alto,

Calif.: Stanford University Press, 1962.

Thomson, Patricia (ed.), *Thomas Wyatt, the Critical Heritage*. Routledge & Kegan Paul, 1974.

Thornton, Dora, *The Scholar in His Study: Ownership and experience in Renaissance Italy*. Yale, 1997.

Tillemans, *T.H. King and Courtier: A Cultural Reconnaissance into an Age of Transition*. Folcroft Library Editions, 1977.

Thurley, Simon, *The Royal Palaces of Tudor England*, Yale University Press, 1993.

Veale, Elspeth M., *The English Fur Trade in the Later Middle Ages*. London Record Society, 2003.

Walker, Greg, 'The Fall of Anne Boleyn reconsidered', *The Historical Journal* (2003)

Walker, Greg, *Writing Under Tyranny: English Literature and the Henrician Reformation*. Oxford University Press, 2005.

Ward, Adolphus William, and Waller, Alfred Rayney (eds.), *The Cambridge History of English and American Literature,* vol. 3: *Renascence and Reformation* Cambridge: Cambridge University Press, 1909.

Wiatt, William H., On the Date of Sir Thomas Wyatt's Knighthood, JEPG, LXIII (1964) p 770-772.

Wiatt, William H., Book review of Thomson, Sir T. W and his Background, JEPG, LXV (1966) 164-167.

Wiatt, William H. Sir Thomas Wyatt's astrologer, *English Language*, Vol IV, no. 2, December, 1966.

Wiatt, William H. Sir Thomas Wyatt and Anne Boleyn, *English Language*, Vol VI, No 2, December, 1968.

Wilson, Derek. *The Lion's Court. Power, Ambition and Sudden Death in the Reign of Henry VIII*. Hutchinson, 2001.

Wilson, Derek, *Holbein, Portrait of an Unknown Man*. Weidenfeld & Nicholson, 1996.

Wyatt, M., *The Italian Encounter with Tudor England: a cultural politics of transition*. M. Wyatt, Cambridge, 2005.

Yates, Frances. A., *Renaissance and Reform: the Italian Contribution*. Collected Essays Vol II. Routledge, 1983.

BIBLIOGRAPHY: PRIMARY SOURCES

Manuscripts:
British Library, Egertọn MS 2711
British Library, Devonshire MS. Add. 17492
Sir Henry Wyatt's Will: PRO PROB 11/26 (London, Public Record Office)
Printed:
Anonymous, *Crónica del Rey Enrico Octavo de Inglaterra*, trans. Martin
A. Sharp Hume, *Chronicle of King Henry VIII of England* (London: Bell
& Sons, 1889).
Anonymous, *The Kalendar of Shepherdes, being Devices for the Twelve
Months* (London: Sidgwick & Jackson, 1908).
Alamanni, Luigi, *Opere Toscane* (Florence, 1532 and Lyon, 1532–3).
Ascham, Roger, *English Works:Toxophilus; Report of the Affaires and
State of Germany; the Scholemaster*, ed. William Aldis Wright
(Cambridge: Cambridge University Press, 1904).
Barclay, Alexander, *The Introductory to Wryte and Pronounce French*
(London: Early English Text Society, 1521).
Blundeville, Thomas, *The Four Chiefest Offices Belonging to
Horsemanship*, part II : *the Art of Riding* (London, 1565).
Bourchier, John, Lord Berners, *The Boke of Duke Huon de Burdeux*,
(1534), ed. S.L. Lee (London: Early English Text Society, 1888).
Bradford, William (ed.), *Correspondence of the Emperor Charles
V and His Ambassadors at the Courts of England and France*
(London: Richard Bentley, 1850).
Brewer, John Sherren, Gairdner, James, and Brodie, Robert Henry (eds.),
Letters and Papers, Foreign and Domestic, of the Reign of Henry VIII, 21
vols (London: Longman, Green, Longman & Roberts, 1862–1932).
Bruce, John, 'Recovery of the lost accusation of Sir Thomas Wyatt, the
poet, by Bishop Bonner', *Gentleman's Magazine*, 33 (1850).
Bruce, John, 'Unpublished anecdotes of the poet, Sir Thomas Wyatt',
Gentleman's Magazine (September 1850).
Burne, Gilbert, *The History of the Reformation of the Church of England*,
ed. Nicholas Pocock (Oxford: Clarendon Press, 1865).
Byrne, Muriel St Clare (ed.), *The Lisle Letters* (Chicago: University of
Chicago Press, 1981).
Byrne, Muriel St Clare (ed.), *The Lisle Letters, an Abridgement*,
selected and arranged by Bridget Boland (London: Secker &
Warburg, 1983).
Calendar of State Papers, Spanish, ed. Gustav Adolph Bergenroth, P. de

Gayangos and Martin A.S. Hume.

Calendar of State Papers, Venetian, ed. Rawdon Brown, Cavendish Bentink, et al.

Carles, Lancelot de, 'Anne Boullant, Epistre ... De La Royne D'Angleterre' (1545) in Georges Ascoli, *La Grand-Bretagne devant L'opinion française depuis la guerre de cent ans jusqu'à la fin du XVIè siècle* (Paris, 1927).

Castiglione, Baldesar, *The Book of the Courtier* (New York: W.W. Norton & Co., 2002).

Caxton, William, *The Book of the Ordre of Chivalry*, ed. A.T.P. Blyes, London 1926

Cavendish, George, *The Life of Cardinal Wolsey*, ed. Samuel Weller Singer (London: Harding, Triphook & Lepard, 1825).

Craig, Hardin (ed.), *Machiavelli's The Prince, an Elizabethan Translation* (Chapel Hill, NC: University of North Carolina Press, 1944).

Ellis, Henry (ed.), *Original Letters, Illustrative of English History*, 3 series in 11 vols. (London, 1824, 1827, 1846).

Elyot, Thomas, *The Boke Named the Gouernor* (1531) (Menston: Scolar Press, 1970 facsimile edition).

Elyot, Thomas, *The Dictionary of Sir Thomas Elyot, Knight* (London: Berthelet, 1538).

Erasmus, *The Epistles of Erasmus*, ed. and trans. Francis Morgan Nichols (London: Longmans, Green & Co., 1901).

Fehrenbach, Robert J., and Leedham-Green, Elisabeth S. (eds.), *Private Libraries in Renaissance England: A Collection and Catalogue of Tudor and Early Stuart Book-Lists*, 6 vols to date (Binghamton, NY and Tempe, AZ: Medieval and Renaissance Texts and Studies; Arizona Center for Medieval and Renaissance Studies, 1992–2004).

Fish, Simon, *A Supplicacyon for the Beggers* (1529), ed. Frederick James Furnivall (London: Early English Text Society, extra series 13, 1871).

Foxe, John, *Acts and Monuments*, ed. Josiah Pratt (London: Religious Tract Society, 1877).

Gairdner, James (ed.), The Paston Letters 1422–1509 (Edinburgh: John Grant, 1910).

Giustinian, Sebastian, *Four years at the court of Henry VIII; selection from dispatches written by the Venetian Ambassador Sebastian Giustinian and addressed to the Signory of Venice, January 12, 1515 to July 26, 1519*, 2 vols., trans. and ed. Rawdon Brown (London, 1854).

Hall, Edward, *Chronicle: The Triumphant Reign of King Henry VIII*, ed. Charles Whibley (London: T.C. and E.C. Jack, 1904).

Harpsfield, Nicholas, *A Treatise on the Pretended Divorce between Henry VIII and Catherine of Aragon*, ed. Nicholas Pocock (Camden Society, 2nd series, 21, 1878)

Harrison, William, *A Description of England in Shakespeare's Youth*, ed. Frederick James Furnivall (London: New Shakspere Society, 1877).

Hawes, Stephen, *Minor Poems*, ed. Florence W. Gluck and Alice B. Morgan (Oxford University Press, 1974).

Henry VII, *Memorials of King Henry VII*, ed. James Gairdner (London: Rolls Series, 1858).

Henry VIII, *Songs, Ballads and Instrumental Pieces Composed by Henry VIII*, collected and arranged by Lady Mary Trefusis (Oxford: Roxburghe Club, 1912).

Henry VIII, *The Love Letters of Henry VIII*, ed. Jasper Ridley (Weidenfeld & Nicolson, 1988).

Henry VIII, *The Love Letters of Henry VIII*, ed. Henry Savage (Allan Wingate, 1949).

Heywood, John, *A Dialogue Containing All the Proverbes in the English Tongue* (1546) (Manchester: Spenser Society, 1867).

Heywood, John, *A Dialogue of Proverbs Concerning Two Maner of Marriages* (London, 1546).

Heywood, John, *Proverbs, Epigrams and Miscellanies*, ed. J.S. Farmer (London, 1906).

Jansen, Sharon L., and Jordan, Kathleen H. (eds.), *The Welles Anthology: MS Rawlinson C. 813, a Critical Study*, Medieval and Renaissance Texts and Studies, 75 (Binghampton: State University of New York, 1991).

Jerdan, William (ed.), *Rutland Papers* (London: Camden Society, old series, 21, 1842).

Kaulek, Jean Baptiste Louis (ed.), *Correspondance politique de mm. de Castillon et de Marillac, ambassadeurs de France en Angleterre 1537–1542* (Paris: F. Alcan, 1885).

Leland, John, *Assertio Inclytissimi Arturii Regis Brittaniae, in The Famous Historie of Chinon of England*, ed. William Edward Mead (London: Early English Text Society, original series, 165, 1925).

More, Thomas, *Utopia*, trans. and ed. Robert Adams. New York and London: W.W. Norton & Co., 1975. Queen Marguerite of Navarre, *Heptameron*, ed. and trans. Paul Chilton (London: Penguin, 2004).

Muir, Kenneth, *Life and Letters of Sir Thomas Wyatt*. (Liverpool University Press, 1963).

Muir, Kenneth, *Sir Thomas Wyatt and His Circle: Unpublished Poems Edited from the Blage Manuscript*. (Liverpool University Press, 1961).

Muir, Kenneth, *Unpublished Poems in the Devonshire Manuscript*, Proceedings of Leeds Philosophical Society, Literary and Historical Section, 6, 1947.

Nichols, John Gough (ed.), *The Chronicles of Calais in the Reigns of Henry VII and Henry VIII to the Year 1540*, (London: Camden Society, old series, 35, 1846).

Nichols, John Gough (ed.), *Collection of Ordinances and Regulations for the Government of the Royal Household, made in Divers reigns from King Edward III to King William and Queen Mary* (London: Society of Antiquaries of London, 1790).

Norbrook, David (selection), and Woudhuysen, H.R. (ed.), *The Penguin Book of Renaissance Verse*. (London: Penguin, 2005).

Nott, George Frederick (ed.), *The Works of Henry Howard, Earl of Surrey, and of Sir Thomas Wyatt the Elder*, 2 vols. (London, 1815–16).

Palsgrave, John, *L'esclarcissement de la langue francoyse* (1530) (Menston: Scolar Press, 1969 facsimile edition).

Pocock, Nicholas (ed.), *Records of the Reformation* (Oxford: Clarendon Press, 1870).

Pollard, Alfred W., and Redgrave, Gilbert R., *A Short Title Catalogue of Books Printed in England, Scotland and Ireland, and of the English Books Printed Abroad, 1475-1640*, revised by W.A. Jackson and F.S. Ferguson (London : Bibliographical Society, 1976).

Powell, Jason, 'The Letters and Original Prose of Sir Thomas Wyatt: A Study and Critical Edition', D.Phil thesis (Oxford University, 2003).

Roper, William, *The Life of Sir Thomas More*, ed. E.V. Hitchcock (London: Early English Text Society, 1935).

Nicholas Sanders, *De Origine ac Progressu Schismatis Anglicani* (1585), trans. and ed. David Lewis as *The Rise and Growth of the Anglican Schism* (London: Burns and Oates, 1877).

State papers of Henry VIII, 11 vols. (London 1830–52).

Statutes of the Realm, 12 vols. (London, 1810–52).

Stow, John, *Annales* (London, 1615).

Strype, John, Ecclesiastical Memorials (Oxford: Oxford University Press, 1822).

Tottel, Richard, *Tottel's Miscellany*, 1557–1587, 2 vols., ed. Hyder Edward. Rollins (Cambridge, Mass.: Harvard University Press, 1965).

Turberville, George, *The Booke of Falconrie or Hauking* (1575) (New York: Da Capo Press, 1969 facsimile edition).

Turberville, George, *The Noble Art of Venerie or Hunting* (London: Purfoot, 1611).

Tyndale, William, *The Obedience of a Christian Man*, ed. David Daniel (London: Penguin, 2000).

Wiffen, Jeremiah Holmes, *Historical Memoirs of the House of Russell* (London: Longman, 1833).

Wilson, Thomas, *Art of Rhetorique*, (London, 1553).

Wynkyn de Worde, *The Noble Tryumphaunt Coronacyon of Quene Anne, 1533*, in *An English Garner*, vol. 2, ed. Edward Arber (London: Constable, 1879).

Wriothesley, Charles, *A Chronicle of England During the Reigns of the Tudors AD 1485–1559*, ed. William Douglas Hamilton (London: Camden Society, new series, 11, 1875).

Wyatt, Sir Thomas, *The Papers of George Wyatt*, ed. D.M Loades (London: Camden Society, 4th series, 5, 1968).

Wyatt, Sir Thomas, *The Poems of Sir Thomas Wyatt*, 2 vols., ed. Agnes Kate Foxwell. University of London Press, 1913.

Wyatt, Sir Thomas, *Collected Poems of Sir Thomas Wyatt*, ed. Kenneth Muir and Patricia Thompson. (Liverpool University Press, 1969).

Wyatt, Sir Thomas, *Poems*, selected by Alice Oswald. (Faber & Faber, 2008).

Wyatt, Sir Thomas, *Sir Thomas Wyatt: The Complete Poems*, ed. Ronald Alexander Rebholz. (Penguin, 1978).

Wythorne, Thomas, *The Autobiography of Thomas Wythorne*, ed. James M. Osborn (Oxford: Oxford University Press, 1962).

Zall, P.M., ed., *A Hundred Merry Tales and Other English Jest Books of the Fifteenth and Sixteenth Centuries*. (University of Nebraska Press, 1977).

INDEX

Illustrations are indexed as, for example, 45ill. and appear at the end of the sequence of references. Notes are referenced as, for example, 59n. The index includes entries for poems under their first lines; entries for poems that are NOT by Thomas Wyatt include the author's name in brackets after the line, e.g. 'Time that is intolerant' (Auden). Entries for members of Wyatt's family are given as, for example, Wyatt, Henry (father of TW).